A Perfect Mistake

Laura Brown

A Perfect Mistake

ISBN-13: 978-0-6484825-8-1

To Heather:

We met because you agreed to read this novel—even though it was a bit outside of your normal read—and I'm so glad you did! What started as critique partners quickly grew into a close friendship. I can't imagine going through this writerly journey without you by my side.

Chapter 1

Nica

I needed to get laid. At least, that's what my amber cocktail made me think—correction, my *third* amber cocktail. If the first two hadn't murdered my inhibition, the third managed to land the final blow.

Minus my usual filter, my eyes wandered around the room, hunting for a man to prey on. The bar was packed for a Tuesday night. Waves of chatter encompassed me, creating a low hum in my ears. But I didn't care about the noise, not when a particular delicious specimen held me captivated, with hair the hue of rich caramel sticking out in different directions. He sat at the bar, hunched over his drink. A brunette with boobs practically spilling out of her top tried to speak to him, but he shook his head and tapped in front of his ear twice, before turning back to his drink.

She may have slinked back to her friend, but I bit my lip, taming down the grin threatening to split my face. Perfect. My fingers itched to communicate, or smooth down his messy hair.

Perhaps both.

Before I could make up my mind, his broad shoulders stiffened and he turned. My alcohol-induced bravado vanished, and I tried to wrench my gaze away. Except, I didn't move. Not an inch. Total disconnect from cranial activity to body movement. Damn fruity drinks. A pair of brown eyes locked with mine. Crap. I knew better than to be rude and stare.

Quick, sign something, I willed my hands, *anything.*

About to attempt a feeble fingerspelled "*Hi*," I was rendered incapacitated when he sent me a nipple-hardening, throw-out-the-vibrator kind of grin.

"Nica, what have you found?" my friend Lexie Edwards squealed, then let out a soft growl. "Yummy! Veronica, go get him."

At the sound of my full name, I found the will to tear my eyes away from the man. I turned to Lexie, with every intention of telling her no and finding a cab home but "I need to get laid" popped out. And my inhibitions really were toast, because instead of warmth spreading over my cheeks, it spread in a decidedly lower area. Not able to look at Lexie, possibly ever again, I clunked my head down on the table.

"I've been telling you that for years. Does your body even know what to do anymore?" Lexie brushed my wild mass of hair off the table, probably littered with crumbs. Crumbs I could handle. Words, not so much.

I raised my head, wobbling like a bobble head. Lexie didn't have the same problem—we'd had the same amount to drink and she didn't appear affected at all. Her silky hair flowed to her shoulders like a hot fudge waterfall, not a strand out of place, unlike my unruly curls. It wasn't fair, perfect hair and a tolerance for alcohol that resembled a frat brother.

"I didn't mean to say that."

"Yeah, you did." Lexie glanced in the direction of Sexy Caramel Hair. "I think you should go for it."

"You always think that."

"Yeah, but this guy agrees with me." I followed Lexie's pointer finger. His back to the bar, he rested on his elbows, watching me. "Want me to screen him?" Lexie asked.

"You could try, but I'm pretty sure he's Deaf, and you haven't picked up many signs." I managed an ounce of sobriety and faced my friend. "And please don't use any of the ones you know right now."

Lexie grinned. "What? You don't want me swearing in front of a guy ready to do you on the bar?"

"Do me on the…?"

I turned to face him, only to come eyelevel with a hard chest. I sucked in a breath, filling my lungs with an island oasis that was not part of the bar. I shifted my eyes up his chest, over the Adam's apple speckled in five o'clock shadow, up to his face. The dim overhead light illuminated his eyes, green specks swirling into my vision. Hazel, not brown, the softer color hidden by long eyelashes.

And I really hoped he couldn't lip-read.

Wish not granted. "*What's your name?*" he signed. The noise level doubled, care of a heavy bass song.

"*N-I-C-A*," I fingerspelled to the beat of the music. Dammit, get a grip.

"*C-A-M.*" He traveled a searing gaze over my body and back up to my face, waking up every part of me in the process. "*Deaf?*"

I shook my head. "*Hearing. You?*"

"*Deaf.*"

"What's he saying?"

I jumped at Lexie's voice, the silent trance he'd created broken into millions of scattered confetti. My heart threatened to break out of my chest, and I placed a hand there, in hopes of keeping at least one part of me contained. "His name's Cam and he's Deaf."

"Works for me." Then, seeming content with my wellbeing, she headed to the bar. Stranger danger wasn't exactly on Lexi's radar.

I reminded myself to breathe, no easy task with a hunk standing in front of me, and my chest constricted tighter than an eighteenth-century corset.

Cam spun a wooden chair around, straddled it, and leaned against the backing. "*Are you having as rough a day as I am?*"

I let out a laugh and nodded. "*Hell yeah. One of those days that can only be cured by several drinks.*" My head swayed a bit too much to the side, and my entire body followed, until Cam's strong hand landed on my shoulder. I contemplated getting up and walking away, anything to save my dwindling dignity. I might have, too, if he wasn't still holding onto me. "*Sorry, I don't normally drink to this degree.*"

"*Me neither.*"

He placed his hand over mine, fingers stroking the backs of my knuckles. Each touch lit a fuse deep inside. The type of fuse I'd never extinguish on my own.

"*Want to get out of here?*" I wasn't anticipating that coming from my hands. *What are you doing, Nica?* He could be an axe murderer, married, a hobo…or an animal in bed. My eyes traveled between the slats of the chair, down the buttons of his gray shirt. He appeared fit and trim, and I bet there were muscles underneath that shirt.

I dragged my gaze off his belt buckle and picked up my drink, fully intending to drown out my humiliation. Only he stopped me, placing his hand over the glass. My lips grazed his skin, salty and smooth. My eyes shot to his.

"*I think you've had enough for tonight,*" Cam said with one hand while he leaned back and set the glass at the opposite end of the table. He glanced around, halting when he found Lexie laughing and flirting with two guys. "*I'd better accept your offer to make sure you get home safe.*"

I gaped at his words, glad he couldn't hear the squeak I released.

"*I don't normally do this either. I'm barely handling my own liquor.*" He smirked. "*And no, that's not a line.*"

I laughed, maybe from the alcohol or the whole so-not-Nica situation. I didn't pick up strangers, not like Lexie. I wanted companionship. My parents' divorce taught me that only friendship could survive, amazing chemistry would leave me heart broken. But, for one night, I'd allow myself the pleasure of this stranger. There was something familiar about him, something safe. I couldn't put a finger on it.

After getting two thumbs up from an overly-excited Lexie, I headed out to find a taxi with Cam. I planned on going home, nothing more, but when Cam placed a warm hand low on my back to keep me steady, my breath caught. His fingers pressed against the hem of my silky shirt and I craved more. This situation spelled trouble.

The houses blurred past on the ride to my apartment, all the while making me very aware of the body next to me. He oozed a sort of strength at near intoxicating levels, and it required everything in me to keep my hands off. Sadness threatened to worm its way back in and kill the mood, the same sadness that had me drinking in the first place. I didn't let it win. I needed this, an escape for a single night. Tomorrow would come whether I wanted it to or not, but tonight I wouldn't have to be alone.

By the time the taxi slowed, a sense of reality had seeped in. I knew nothing about this guy, only that he knew ASL, and damned, I still wanted him. I'd thought him handsome in the bar, but with the street light casting shadows across his face, he resembled an out-of-reach fantasy.

"That's where I live," I signed as the taxi came to a stop in front of the old brick factory building I called home. *"You coming to make sure I don't get lost?"* Not giving him a chance to respond, I climbed out of the car, knees wobbling in relief when he joined me.

We entered the stale, off-white hallway that lead to the musty elevator. A neighbor had once left an air freshener in here, but it somehow made things worse. I stared at the numbers, fighting the anticipation with every inch we climbed. I swore his gaze lingered on my face, and I feared if I turned to him we'd never make it out of this elevator in one piece.

My foot threatened to snag on the worn maroon carpet when we exited, and Cam steadied me with a hand on my shoulder for the second time that evening. Like the first, his touch a pleasure burn. And it hit me, this was the first time he touched me since we left the bar. Not normal male behavior. Key in place at my door, I glanced up at him. *"Thank you for bringing me home. Another guy would have been all over me in the cab."*

He stepped forward, an unmistakable hunger present in his eyes. The air grew warmer the closer he came. *"Don't thank me yet. I can still change my behavior."*

"I'm still inviting you in, not my normal behavior and all but a flashing green light." I searched his eyes, trying to decode him before I took this last step. And he continued to keep space between us, letting me call the shots. *"I'm just grateful I found a nice guy."*

My pulse raced as I entered the narrow walkway into my apartment, eyes on Cam. I couldn't believe I had a stranger in my home for a booty call.

The door clicked shut behind him, and for a moment we studied each other, guided by the moonlight. I prepared to take matters into my own hands when the nice guy behavior cracked. Cam backed me up against my refrigerator. Two fingers tilted my chin up, my frequent breaths making sure both of us were very aware of my aching breasts. He leaned in until our mouths were inches apart, then paused. Questions dominated his gaze, questions I didn't want to contemplate. Not now. Now was for action. I closed the gap for him, tugging on his neck until he relented, colliding his smooth lips against mine. A sense of comfort washed over me, surprising the hell out of me. What was comforting about a sexy man holding me close? A sexy man with what felt like a fine set of muscles pressed against my flat belly. Other things were pressed against me as well.

Thank you, God.

He ended the kiss but didn't move away. Those muscles taunted me, teasing me to get a better look. With hands that only shook a little, I found the top of his dress shirt and unbuttoned the first button. There was nothing flabby about the pectoral muscles revealed. A small patch of soft brown hair sat in-between, calling my name. I leaned forward and kissed the smattering of fine hairs.

A growl rumbled from his throat before yanking my head towards his. He found my lips in a hard, bone-melting kiss. This, this was what I needed, hundreds of times better than drinking with Lexie. Cam's hands drifted under the hem of my shirt, his skin the best kind of fire. Until he tugged my shirt over my head, sending me into a mini panic. Why had I put on my basic, boring, white cotton bra? Way to kill the mood. Only he didn't appear fazed. He trailed his tongue down my neck and along the outline of the bra until my toes curled. Oh yeah, white cotton was fine.

Only I didn't want to be fine, I wanted to be naked. With him. I backed up, keeping my hands on him, until we made it into the bedroom, unbuttoning the rest of his shirt along the way. Six pack abs, damn. I trailed my fingers over his tight stomach muscles, tempted to bite them. My legs hit the edge of my bed, and I fell backwards and dragged him with me.

He stroked my hair away from my eyes, his eyes dark. Desire lived there, of that much I was certain. With his body on top of mine, I felt it. A compassion shone, hinting at emotions I didn't dare contemplate.

I kissed his lips briefly before sliding my tongue inside his mouth. When he sucked I almost lost it, the last remaining tension in my body going on a paid vacation. I moaned. Didn't matter he couldn't hear—I couldn't stop the sounds. And for once I didn't need to worry about making too much, or too little, noise. My head rose off the bed, needing more of him. Craving more. After all, I only had him for one night and needed everything I could get.

He broke the kiss. I opened my eyes, seeing questions, seeing concern. I didn't want to talk.

"*It's OK*," I signed.

His lips quirked into a grin. "*You sure?*" We were so close the end of his sign touched my chin, and he stroked a lazy finger down my throat. "*Because as much as I'm enjoying myself, I make it a point not to take advantage.*"

My body was on board for being taken advantage of. And I nearly let those words tumble free. "*I'm sure*," I managed instead, letting my finger drift down his neck. His shoulders relaxed as he melted into me. Everything else faded away, all thoughts forgotten except how good he felt.

He slipped his fingers beneath my bra strap, sliding it down my arm, before tugging the material to uncover my breast. The cool air hit my sensitized peak before his warm palm pressed against my nipple, and I nearly purred. He kissed my neck, making a trail down my body, over my breasts, and down to my belly button. Without communicating I helped him take off my bra. The rest of our clothes soon followed.

Flesh to flesh, every inch of him drove me to crave more. I started to think he was some God-like creature who happened to grace me with his presence at the bar. Would be fitting, too, since I'd never see him again. My eyes traveled over him. His legs were as defined as his upper body. Between his legs he was ready for me, waiting. God-like or not, some precautions needed to be taken. I rolled over and reached into my nightstand, shoving aside random items until I found a package of condoms. *Please don't be expired.*

He moved up my body until his hard length settled at the top of my legs. I stumbled upon opening the box, feeling him at exactly the right spot, wanting him more than I'd wanted anything for quite some time. Condom in hand, I turned and found us face to face, our bodies aligned a little too perfectly. Some of his hair was now plastered to his forehead, sexy as hell. He grinned and collected the package from me.

I settled onto my back, the tiny voice I'd been ignoring so well speaking up. I let out a shaky laugh; even if the voice grew louder, I would drown it out. I hadn't come this far not to know what he felt like inside me.

Cam kissed me from my ankle up. I squirmed as his lips moved slow, so slow. More, I wanted more. I contemplated flipping him over and straddling him, putting myself out of my misery, when he found my breasts. *Oh dear God this man's mouth is heaven.*

He held my eyes prisoner as he positioned himself. Eye contact, ASL depended on it for communication. Silent words passed between us, and I hoped all he read was *"hell yes."* For added encouragement I wrapped my legs around him, tugged until he got the hint, a devious smile crossing his face when he pushed inside, filling me so completely I gasped. I waited for fear to creep in, for the reality of having sex with a stranger to whack me in the head. It didn't. He felt…right. Maybe it was the alcohol, but no one had ever felt this good before. For strangers we were well matched.

He continued watching me as he moved in and out. I moaned in encouragement before catching myself. Instead I arched into him, desperate to push him faster. Harder. More. The twinkle in his eyes showed he enjoyed the torture. The popping veins of his corded arms told me he struggled to restrain himself. I continued to move with him, the deliciously slow strides eradicating thought processes. All-consuming need pulsated within me, from head to toe and all the glorious spots between.

When he bent to suck my nipple, I lost my tenuous grip on control. Without warning, my climax hit. I shuddered over and over as he continued moving against my sensitized skin. Cam leaned down, kissing me hard on the lips, before building up speed, building me up again until I followed his own release.

I woke up several hours later, my cheek resting on his chest. His arms were around me, holding me tight, our skin still warm in the cool night air. He was fast asleep, his caramel hair even messier than at the bar. I searched myself for the regret, but all I found was sorrow at the thought of never seeing him again. Convinced he would be gone in the morning, I tried to stay awake to watch him sleep. Exhaustion won out. I snuggled in and decided to let the morning bring what it would.

Chapter 2

Nica

The pressure behind my eyes did not appreciate how bright the sun shined on my hungover self. I squinted through my sunglasses as I made my way into Independent Senior Services. I handled the neutral tones of the small reception area, but the eye-popping colors of the fundraiser event table made my head spin. I focused instead on the diluted colors in the thank you cards from clients and family members. Somber was the right shade for a hangover. Too bad Mother Nature hadn't gotten the hint.

I mumbled a hello to the receptionist, entered the door to the client services department, and walked two rows down to my pod. One hand held my steaming cup of coffee, the other was plastered to my throbbing head, damn pain meds were taking forever to work. I didn't dare remove my sunglasses; the sunlight leaking through already had me squinting. It was so much easier to not feel hungover when I was in bed, gazing at Cam.

For the two minutes before he left, at least.

He gave me his number, and in a silly orgasm-meets-hangover state I responded. I wasn't fooling myself, nothing more would happen. The chemistry we had, it wouldn't last. I wanted someone I could grow old with and be compatible enough that we'd survive the odds. Intense attraction would only crash and burn.

Shame.

I sat at my desk, three desks in, closest to the window. I put down my coffee and placed my head on my desk, needing five more minutes of dark and quiet and comfort, only to come in contact with one of the many smooth folders that ruled my life: the obituary of a favorite client, Vinny.

Death. It was part of the day-to-day existence of being a case manager for elder services. I'd lost quite a few clients over the years—that's how most of them stopped using my services—but every once in a while one came along that hurt more than the others. Vinny hurt more.

His obituary had torn at my heart and reminded me of how alone I was. If I didn't change things soon I'd be more alone than Vinny. I pushed his folder aside. *Get to work, Veronica.*

"Well, well, well, what have we here? Nica's late for work?" Rebecca Wilder, my friend and coworker, teased as she hung up her phone.

I rolled my head to the side. "Vinny died yesterday, and Lexie made me celebrate his life with a drink." *Or three. And God-like sex.*

"Veronica Anders got drunk? On a work night? I love it," exclaimed Rebecca, her jet-black wavy hair bouncing against her shoulders. I forced myself into a sitting position and glanced around. The rest of our pod remained empty, but there was probably someone listening from one of the neighboring pods. Even at eight in the morning. *Or ten past eight*, I reminded myself.

"You should've picked up a guy like Lexie does, that would've put you in a good mood. I know it would put me in a good mood," Rebecca said.

I cringed. "Sex isn't the answer to everything."

"It should be." Rebecca eyed me over her travel coffee mug. "I wonder, are you speaking from experience?"

I froze with a hand on my mouse. The shards of pain ignored, I opened my eyes wide and threw my friend a fierce glare.

"Whoa, I'm right. Who was he?"

I opened my mouth to protest, but words died in the back of my throat. I couldn't believe I was that transparent and darted my eyes to the ceiling.

"Yikes, woo-hoo, way to go Veronica," shouted Rebecca.

"Shut up," I mumbled. I stared at my phone. *Ring please*, I begged, anything to get out of this conversation.

"Was he at least good?"

No escape, not with yummy thoughts of Cam now infiltrating my brain. "Better than chocolate."

Rebecca gasped. "Damn. Please tell me you're seeing him again?"

I sighed. "I have his number, he has mine. I don't think so." And I really didn't want to get into the why, no sense being viewed as jaded by my friend. My phone rang and I lunged for it, ready to kiss whoever called. "Good Morning, Independent Senior Services, Veronica Anders speaking."

Rebecca returned to her desk.

"Hi Veronica, this is Sally Stone from Hospice House. I wanted to let you know one of your clients was transferred here last night."

I grabbed my yellow pad of paper and began writing: *Sally Stone, Hospice House.*

"Cassandra Thompson."

My pen froze for a second, then I scribbled: *Cassie transferred.* "How's Cassie doing?"

"She's doing well."

"What communication access have you been able to provide?" Cassie was one of my culturally Deaf clients.

"We have an interpreter scheduled for tomorrow and Cassandra's grandson stopped by."

Not good enough. Cassie thought the world of her grandson, to the point of playing matchmaker as often as possible, but I had no clue what his communication skills were. I'd never met him, though we talked often through e-mail. He worked long hours, and I considered him a concerned but detached caregiver. Detached wasn't going to work for someone at Hospice House.

I feared Cassie wasn't getting what she needed. Family members always had nice things to say about the treatment my clients received while at the end of life. But Cassie communicated in ASL. It was scary enough to be moved to Hospice, to be dealing with end-of-life issues, without having communication ones as well.

"I'll be by to check on her. I'm fluent in ASL and can help with any questions Cassie might have."

"Oh, she's doing fine here."

I bit my tongue. Too often I'd been told my Deaf clients could communicate fine. Later, when I met with them, I found out how little they really understood. I checked my schedule, relieved to see my morning was open. "I would feel better seeing Cassie. I'll be there shortly."

I set my phone to Do Not Disturb and marked myself out in the computer system. I grabbed Cassie's file and stuffed it in my workbag. I pulled out my picture ID and attached it to the lapel on my dress shirt. Sunglasses forgotten, I collected my coffee and headed out to rescue my client.

*****

Cam

The mound of paperwork on my desk called to me from miles away. All marked "urgent" in the recesses of my mind, though only one or two percent warranted that label. Worse since I dropped everything the day before after what would henceforth be known as The Call. The only call that could get me to leave work unattended.

The Call started the clock ticking down the final moments of my grandmother's life. So even though the piles of work continued to stack high and demand my attention, I couldn't blame myself.

Not after The Call also lead to The Night.

I swerved around a Camry, the driver hunched forward, hands at ten and two, behaving like they had no destination to get to; meanwhile, I had about twenty places I needed to be right this second. Good for them if their lives were stable enough to drive below the speed limit. Mine might never be that way again.

No, focus on The Night, not The Call or the drivers destined to make my blood pressure soar. The Night, the woman, the amazing sex. I wasn't looking for more than that, not wanting to turn into my father who handed his balls over to my mother before I'd been born. I'd take things one fun night at a time. The only good thing to come out of this shittastic storm of events.

Of course, if I had gone home like I damn well should have, then I wouldn't be stuck behind a student trailer driver who hadn't figured out how to stay in one lane.

The universe hated me today.

Bad enough I had to drive from Peabody to my Boston condo, only to shower, change, and head back to the North Shore. I used ten minutes at home to answer a few emails, trying to ease the growing inbox. An inbox I could delegate, but my job, my business, my responsibility.

I swore in two different languages as a car cut in front of me, only to reduce speed. Even thoughts of Nica and her hot bod didn't help. Not when I saw the Florida license plate with the perpetual left blinker flashing; a gut-wrenching reminder I still needed to notify my parents about Grandma.

My stomach lurched when I parked at the Hospice location, and my workaholic brain shut the hell up. One thought rolled through my mind: my grandmother was going to die here. Soon. No other shit mattered. Not work, not the extra travel, not my evening activities. The latter had been an escape. A needed one. But that escape had ended, and real life had my number and demanded hell.

After a deep, centering breath I forced myself to go in.

The bubbly receptionist waved awkwardly. She blinked at me, smile planted on her face, and I raised my eyebrows. The last time I checked my ears didn't bite. Nor were they contagious. I moved to sign in while she held up a finger and scribbled on a piece of paper before thrusting it under my nose.

I accepted it from her, vacant smile back on her face.

Grandma's awake, she's meeting with her social worker now.

I nodded and headed down the hall.

As I approached the room, my grandmother's door inched open. I waited a minute, but no one emerged. I stepped to the side, letting the social worker finish up, trying not to tap my foot in impatience and envision how many digits my inbox had soared to.

I wondered if this was the social worker Grandma always talked about. The thought alone caused me to laugh and my foot to still. For years Grandma had matchmaking aspirations between me and the social worker. Then again, Grandma always had matchmaking aspirations, really bad matchmaking, take one look and run the other way kind. We'd never met but had e-mailed many times. I contemplated taking another step to the side to avoid any additional matchmaking attempts when the door opened further. A female with familiar blond curly hair backed out of the room. She waved to my grandmother and closed the door. Before I could chastise my dick on the urges the hair created, I found myself face to face with Nica.

She froze, an expression of pure bewilderment that I surely mirrored. Eyes wide enough that white surrounded her irises. On the lapel of her pink button-down shirt she had an ID badge. Her picture was on the badge, under the logo for Independent Senior Services, with her name: Veronica Anders.

Nica. Veronica. Shit.

I let out a slight laugh and ran my hand through my hair. *What are the odds?* "*N-I-C-A is short for Veronica?*" I used the sign name Grandma always used, a *V* mimicking curls. Curls I had run my hands through.

She nodded, her cheeks flushed, still clueless.

I placed one hand on my chest and fingerspelled with the other hand. "*C-A-M-E-R-O-N T-H-O-M-P-S-O-N.*"

Her eyes widened even further. The hand holding her coffee cup went to her mouth, shaking enough that liquid risked escaping. She signed with the other, also not steady. "*Oh no, I…*" We both glanced around the empty hall. Not that anyone else would understand us. Nica verified my grandmother's door was closed.

"*I guess we only used our full names in our e-mails?*" I asked.

"*I believe that's correct. You work long hours, I didn't expect you to be here.*" Shaking hands aside, she communicated like Grandma said she did: not quite fluent, but at ease.

My smile faded. *"I took the morning off. I'm going into work later. I've got plenty of time saved up, so I'm here for whatever she needs."* Didn't matter I didn't use said time, The Call was reason enough to break that system. I'd find a way to stomach it.

Nica stepped towards me, hand poised to place on my shoulder. Before she made contact she paced back and I didn't miss it was a big one. *"Normally a client here is out of my control. I'll help as needed…"* Her hands fumbled and she broke eye contact. *"Though this is really a mess right now."*

"I planned to contact you later today."

Her eyebrows rose, and I got the distinct impression for someone who'd replied to my text from this morning she really didn't want further contact. Fair enough, it wasn't my usual motto either. Made things easier all around. At least neither one of us was expecting anything more.

"You, Veronica, the case manager, to discuss Grandma. I'm hoping I still can?" E-mailing Veronica was one of the many items on my overloaded to-do list for the day. Having her be Nica made it all the more enticing and moved it up a few levels. Maybe she had a videophone, and I could see her while we talked? As long as she didn't want more we could have a little fun. Anything to add fun to my current situation became an immediate plus.

"Yes, of course. We'll…figure something out." This wasn't the relaxed woman I met last night, or left this morning. This person carried herself in professional mode. Did Grandma get the standoffish behavior, or was it reserved for the likes of me?

If I thought waking up in her bed was awkward, I was mistaken. *"How is she?"*

Nica relaxed an inch, turned to the closed door. *"Good, really good. You can't knock your grandmother's spirits. I was worried about communication access. They said you had been here, but I didn't know if they meant the Deaf grandson, or how well you could communicate with them…"* Her hands stilled. She bit her lip and looked at me.

I shoved my hands into my pockets. "I manage," I spoke. After years of speech therapy, and a mother who demanded I speak at

16

home, I could function in the hearing world. When I chose to.

She smiled, a reserved smile, but at least those tempting lips turned up. "*Make sure they get an interpreter, for both of you.*" She glanced at the closed door. "*She'll be happy to see you.*"

I watched Nica walk away, admiring the way her black dress pants outlined her rear end. She really did have a spectacular ass. Memories of her flesh had my blood boiling. But one glance at my grandmother's door shook me back to reality. The warmth faded to a frigid degree. I sucked in a deep breath and entered.

"*Good morning,*" I signed as Grandma looked up. She was in a hospital bed, set to a sitting position. A crocheted blanket of pastel colors covered her lap. Not one of her blankets; I'd never seen her use quite that many colors at once. A bit of life sparked in her blue eyes. Compared to the half asleep woman I'd seen yesterday, she was vibrant.

"*Did you meet Veronica?*" her shaky hands signed. She shifted upwards, glancing behind me. No doubt that extra spark in her was due to the timing.

"*Yes.*" I didn't mention I met her last night.

"*Isn't she cute?*"

"*I thought she was older than that.*" Whenever Grandma talked about Veronica I always envisioned a woman in her forties, wearing beige frumpy clothes. Would fit with her previous matchmaking attempts.

"*I said she was young.*"

"*You're ninety, young is a relative term.*"

"*Young enough for you.*"

I shook my head and laughed. Only my grandmother would play matchmaker on her deathbed…with the woman I just slept with.

*****

Nica

I sat in my car with my head on the steering wheel, trying to breathe deeply. *Fuck.* I slept with my client's grandson. A caregiver. A caregiver I'd had e-mail conversations with for the past six years. *Fuck. Cam. Cameron.* I should have figured it out. I knew he looked familiar.

I could lose my job over this. I *should* lose my job. I'd crossed professional lines.

I slipped out my phone and noticed a text from Lexie. Good, exactly the person I was going to call.

Lexie: *How did the hot date go?*

I was now living in my own personal hell, very hot. Not trusting myself to type, I dialed Lexie's cell. Voicemail. *Crap.* Lexie was a fellow social worker, so she would understand the full extent of the shit I walked into. On the other hand, Lexie wasn't exactly the voice of reason. She'd be singing praise for my one-night stand.

Me: *Date good. Morning after…interesting.*

I calmed my shaking nerves by reminding myself I hadn't known who Cam was. It was one night. As long as nothing else happened I could brush this occurrence under a rug. Or fifty. But even with a hundred rugs I wasn't so sure I could get out of this mess.

My phone rang, Lexie's name flashing across my screen. I accepted the call, Lexie's voice in my ear before I could speak. "Define interesting. You left with him, has your libido returned to the land of the living?"

In contrast to the chill of the quandary I'd landed in, my good parts warmed in reverence. And then some. "Yes."

Lexie squealed on the other end of the line. "Are you going to see him again?"

I glanced at the building, where the topic of the conversation hung out with his grandmother. "Already have."

Lexie gasped. "Nica?"

"It's complicated."

"Of course it is. You *always* make it complicated."

I stopped scoping out the front door, preparing to duck if he emerged. "I don't *always* make it complicated."

"Yes, yes you do. You search for the complicated right away, and that's your reason to not get invested. Because complicated makes the leaving easy. You, my dear, are always searching for the exit sign."

There may have been some truth in Lexie's assessment, but I wasn't getting into it. Not now, not ever if I had my way. "No, this time it really is complicated."

"Prove it."

The trees continued to sway, a reminder of exactly where I was and how that related to Lexie's question. "He's the grandson of one of my clients."

Silence greeted me. As I contemplated checking my signal, Lexie gasped again. "You're shitting me."

"I wish I was."

"So, like detached never involved grandson or…"

"Primary caregiver."

"Well, shit, Nica. This is bad. And that's coming from me."

I whimpered.

"Wait, you said you saw him again already?"

"Yes. How do you think I came to this realization? I went to visit a client at Hospice, and there he is outside the door." I clamped my mouth shut, more words bubbling up inside, like how good he looked in the daylight. And smoothly shaven was just as delectable as stubble. Bad thoughts, very bad thoughts.

A leaf flittered across my windshield. "Oh my God, you really like him." Lexie's voice rose to a shrill level.

"Doesn't exactly matter with this situation now, does it?"

"Oh, hush. This is good. Just don't pull a Nica until after the grandmother is gone."

I shook my head. "What are you talking about?"

Lexie sighed. "A Nica: to mess up a relationship before it becomes too serious. If it does become serious, then you pull a Veronica: to sabotage said relationship."

I felt the distinct pressure of a headache building. "Are you really using my names as verbs?"

"Yup."

"Where are you coming up with this?"

"You have a commitment problem."

My grip tightened on my phone. "I don't have a commitment problem. Can we focus on the ethical quandary?" I was ready to yank my hair out.

"I could hit on a grandson in front of my supervisor with only a sideways glance."

"We really need to get you over to my agency."

"I like dabbling in the dark side of social work. Join me, Nica, join me in your lust for family members."

"I hate you."

"You love me and you know it."

I focused my attention on the time. "As fun as this conversation is, I have to get back to work."

"Where you can hunt for more grandsons?"

My stomach lurched. "Okay, now I really hate you, Alexandra."

Lexie made a kissing noise. "Good bye, Veronica."

I disconnected the call and steadied my breathing. The front door to Hospice opened, and I ducked, only to see a stranger leave. Calming my racing heart, I shifted into reverse, before I made more of a fool out of myself—though not even the changing leaves of fall could offer comfort.

Back at work I ignored the receptionist, slinked back to my desk, threw my bag on the floor, and plopped down in my chair. I inhaled deep as I stared at my black computer screen. I needed to open the system and remove myself from Cassie's case. Maybe, just maybe, that would be my saving grace. Transfer her case, don't tell anyone the reason why.

I had to keep her. As the only case manager with Deaf Culture knowledge, wasn't it my duty to pretend last night never happened?

I woke up my computer and accessed her file. I updated her move to Hospice House and left out everything related to Cam.

Chapter 3

Cam

The rubber steering wheel stretched beneath my death grip as I held a heated debate with myself, rivaled only by the real life debates I had with my mother. To say we butted heads took it far too lightly. We lived on different planets, heck, galaxies. I inherited her ambition, so we could, and did, argue for hours.

I needed to update Dad on Grandma and hoped to elicit a response from him that wasn't predetermined by Mom. Didn't matter that Grandma was his mother, he turned his back on family and hearing loss when he married. Some sick joke I must have been.

Several options would get the required information across. I could text them and hope they paid attention. I could e-mail them, though it may take a day for them to notice. I could call the video relay and have an interpreter do my dirty work—because heaven forbid Mom acknowledge ASL as a language. Or I could call one of my brothers and let them deliver the news.

Dan or Ben's help was tempting—so fucking tempting—but caring for Grandma was my burden. One I willingly, and not so willingly, accepted. Grandma raised me. The two of us, plus Grandpa when he was alive, were the only Deaf members of our family, so we naturally came together, especially when my father forgot his upbringing and let Mom reject me. Caring for Grandma now was the least I could do.

I pulled over and parked at a coffee shop. I could always grab a drink after the call to thank them for letting me use their parking space, but after talking to my mother I'd need something a lot stronger than caffeine.

I set up my phone on the dashboard, angled so my signs would be visible from my camera—ignoring the ever-growing number in my inbox. I needed a surge of willpower to not get lost down this rabbit hole and forget about my parents completely. Confident the phone wouldn't topple over, I connected to the video relay and waited for an available interpreter to appear on screen. Once she did—and I always got a kick out of a female voicing for me to my own parents—I signed the number and told her who I was calling.

"*C-A-M-E-R-O-N?*" was the first thing Mom said when the call connected.

"*Any other Deaf people care enough to call you?*"

The interpreter signed that pots and pans clanked in the background.

I breathed deep to center myself. "*Grandma's been moved to Hospice.*"

"*She's been receiving Hospice services for a while now. Why is this suddenly so important?*"

It was just like Mom to not care about anything that wasn't related to her. "*No. Grandma was moved to Hospice House last night. They expect she only has a week or two left to live.*"

"*Oh,*" the interpreter elongated the sign, face indicating a lack of compassion on Mom's part. Not that I needed the explanation. Thirty years of existence meant I expected this reaction. Would it be rude to put Dad on the line? I might have, if the man hadn't lost his balls a long time ago. I doubted even his mother's death would make a difference.

"*You and Dad need to come up.*"

The interpreter, a frown on her face she couldn't disguise, explained my mother was laughing. "*She just moved. She'll be fine for a while longer. We'll fly up when the end gets close.*"

"*Hospice House is the end. If you don't fly up soon you might be scrambling to get here in time for the funeral.*" The bitterness of my words hit me hard. Funeral. Death. The loss of the maternal support in my life.

"*Testy much? Calm down, kiddo. I'll talk with your father, and we'll see what we can do. We can't fly up for an undetermined amount of time. Call S-A-R-A-H, have her help out.*"

The pressure between my eyes grew. "*Then tell Dad he may never see his mother again. And enough with S-A-R-A-H.*"

"*S-A-R-A-H is a perfectly nice young woman that you've been brushing off.*"

Grandma was dying and Mom was more interested in setting me up on a date that surely even Sarah was sick of by now. "*Because I'm not interested.*" Not then, not now.

"*You need someone to take care of you.*"

I blinked at the interpreter, but, nope, saw the signs right. "*Because of my grandmother or because I'm some invalid?*"

"*C-A-M-E-R-O-N.*"

Kudos to the interpreter, she managed to convey the distaste Mom usually linked into my full name.

"*Drop the S-A-R-A-H thing, I'm calling Aunt K-A-T.*"

I disconnected from the relay and rammed one tight fist into the side of my door and cursed with the string of profanities I wanted to unleash on my mother. Thanks to my brothers I did this in both languages. It didn't help my mood.

Another deep breath and I loaded FaceTime and clicked on my aunt's name.

Her white hair stuck up in all sorts of wild directions when she appeared. "*What's wrong?*"

"*Grandma's been moved to Hospice House.*"

"*Oh no, so soon?*" She glanced around, blue eyes bulging and completing the bag lady look. "*We have a bit of a crisis here at the store. I've been working eighteen-hour days. Do you think she'll make it to the weekend?*"

I contemplated hitting my head on the steering wheel. "*She's holding on for now.*"

Aunt Kat's eyes watered. "*Call me if anything changes. I can drop all this if I have to, but I'd rather get this settled first so I have more time for Mom.*"

I opted to text the rest of the family. No way could I handle another phone call like this. If I was honest, I couldn't fathom this being the end. The whole Hospice concept was scary, but Grandma still acted like her vibrant self. I couldn't wrap my head around the end looming so close.

Family sucks.

The digital overhead clock flashed 11:50am when I finally made it to work. I walked into 409 Marketing, the firm I started with Matt Chang when too many doors were closed. The exposed brick welcomed me back to the real world. I settled into my seat at my workstation, happy to see most staff busy at work—the exception being Matt, flirting with his girlfriend, Ashley Hucks, both my good friends. Otherwise I would give them shit for not picking up the slack from my absence. Granted, they knew better: I didn't like anyone touching my projects.

Matt turned as I switched on my computer, his designer haircut and designer shirt understated by the open collar. *"How's Grandma?"*

"Good spirits, hard to imagine the end is near."

"Maybe it isn't," Ashley signed, making her way around to my desk wearing another of her pencil skirts she loved so much.

"That's the point of the move." My two friends avoided eye contact with me. They didn't understand it either. I switched conversations. *"She's still trying to play matchmaker."* Not that she had a good track record—barely a blip of a track record. After setting herself up with my grandfather she crashed and burned every single time. Still, I couldn't explain why this time felt different.

Matt rolled his eyes. *"At least she can't get any worse than the last time. Right?"* Yeah, Grandma's suggestions had become notorious. A reason why Nica was surprising, to say the least. Not what I had expected.

Ashley nudged him. *"Maybe it's time to humor her."*

"I already did," I signed before I caught myself. I didn't even look at my friends. Instead I grabbed my mouse to check my messages. Matt knocked it out of my hand and across the desk.

"How?" Matt's other hand blocked my access to the mouse.

I leaned back. *"It's complicated."*

"Ooohh, a story! I'll get the popcorn." Ashley scurried off to her desk,

her long hair swaying behind her, and returned seconds later with a bag of popcorn. I collected our bowl from the window, and Ashley dumped the popcorn in, hopped up on my desk, and grabbed a handful. *"Start at the beginning."*

"Make sure you describe this woman." Matt held his cell phone to his ear. I focused on Matt's lips, even though I knew exactly who was being called. "Grant... break. Now. Cam finally got some."

I groaned, hoping Matt heard it. *"Why not text Grant? He has a hearing loss, too."*

"And he still calls me and then says 'what' a million times. At least you don't try and hear."

We dug into the popcorn, and I started organizing my inbox while we waited for Grant Peterson to arrive, the fourth member of our hodgepodge group that started in college.

Grant sauntered into the office in a blue shirt with the words "Grant's Peak" over one peck. The way it stretched across his fit frame meant only one thing: the shirt was a size too small—on purpose. He owned a rock-climbing gym next door.

"Is it story time? Does Ashley have the popcorn out?" His mouth moved as he signed. Grant was a sim-com user: simultaneously communicating in ASL and English. Made his ASL grammar funky at times. I had no clue how it affected his English.

Ashley raised the bowl as she munched. Grant sat down next to her and grabbed a handful.

"Cam was about to tell the story of how he got laid," Matt signed.

I groaned but knew there was no way out of sharing, not with this group. *"I met a woman at a bar last night. I was drinking after everything with my grandma. She was drinking for reasons I still don't know. We went back to her place and…"*

"All right, now we're talking." Matt held up a hand for a high-five. I hesitated, but accepted. If I didn't they'd never let me work.

Ashley stopped eating. *"Is nice Cam turning into prick male?"*

"You can't take that title away from me." Grant stole the popcorn bowl as if that were his precious title.

Ashley shook her head, wrenched the bowl back, and turned her attention back to me.

"I'm not done. I left this morning." At Ashley's narrowed eyebrows I held up both hands. *"After leaving my number. Ran home to get ready for work. Went back to visit Grandma and discovered she's V-E-R-O-N-I-C-A A-N-D-E-R-S. Remember my grandmother's social worker? That's her."*

"This chick you've been lamenting to about your grandmother's stool sizes?"

I glared at Matt. *"I've never had a conversation about my grandmother's stools."*

Grant cupped his ear. *"I'm not hearing a problem."*

I smoothed down my pants. *"It's not a problem, just shocked. What are the odds that my one-night stand turns out to be my grandmother's case manager?"*

"Yes," Grant shouted, or at least I assumed he shouted based on the sudden turning of heads from the other hearing staff. *"Confirmation that you haven't castrated yourself with long hours."*

I contemplated slugging Grant the next chance I found.

"Was she hot?" Matt asked.

Ashley shoved Matt's shoulder.

Thoughts of Nica made my pants tight. *"Yes."*

"Prove it."

I proceeded to describe Nica's hair and figure as only one intimately acquainted would, in a visual language that lent itself best for physical descriptions.

"Nice," Matt and Grant said at the same time.

Ashley shook her head. *"Did she know who you were?"*

"Not a clue."

"Are you going to see her again?"

"I need to talk with her about Grandma."

"That's work, what about pleasure?" Ashley threw a piece of popcorn at my face. I caught it in my mouth.

"Yes, now you're talking, Ashley," Grant said. *"When will you dump Matt and take a walk on the wild side?"*

"Can it! I need to know that Cam is getting personal with the social worker."

I shook my head. It was always a three-ring circus when the four of us came together. *"I think personal is off the table."* I wasn't looking for a committed relationship, not after Dad gave up everything important to him when Mom lured him in. I didn't want someone changing me.

"*You don't want her again?*" Matt asked.

I paused. The thought of Nica still made my blood hot, even sober. Especially after seeing her in the daylight.

"*He's got it bad—finally!*" Ashley raised her hands. "*Cameron Thompson's heart grew.*" She lowered her hands and eyed me evilly. "*Though not as fast as other parts, apparently.*"

Grant laughed and slapped his knee.

"*If she's hot and can help with Grandma, she's a keeper,*" Matt said.

I started to smile and wiped the expression clean. "*Grandma's been trying to set us up for years, this will only end badly.*" Reason two not to get involved: even a short fling would blow up in my face.

"*Screw Grandma's track record, you need more personal in your life.*"

I opened the email of highest importance, ignoring Ashley. Grant bid his farewells and headed back to his gym, but not before requesting to visit Grandma. Ashley reached for the mug filled with wooden lettered tiles. She spilled them out on Matt's desk, her back to me. Matt helped her shuffle them around. I continued responding to messages, only to be interrupted when the tiles tumbled to my desk.

Hands frozen over the keyboard, I eyed my conniving friends. I picked up the letters, turning a few over to see the gibberish word they spelled: RAHLCLE.

I went back to my screen, using it as a decoy as I rearranged the letters in my head. I could spell HEAR but that left CLL. I could spell CLEAR but that left HL. Finally I found the right combination.

I moved the tiles until they were facing my friends, spelling CALL HER. I raised my eyebrows. Ashley grinned and left for her seat, and Matt cleaned up the letters. I returned to my e-mail and struggled to keep thoughts of Nica out of my mind.

*****

Nica

I glanced at my supervisor's closed door, tapping a finger on my mouse. I had to talk to her; I was ethically bound to disclose the situation with Cam. But I also knew exactly what would happen: I'd be back here, packing up my stuff. I'd lose my job, and my licensing. Heck, not my job, my career. All because of one night with a stranger. Surely in the history of social work I couldn't be the only one to stumble into an ethical landmine like this. Yet it felt like I was the only one.

The door opened, and I retrieved a file to enter in notes, going through the motions while my brain continued to stumble around the situation with Cam. In layman's terms, I was chickenshit. Though wouldn't anyone be? This entire situation akin to turning oneself in for a crime, like walking out of a shop with an item after forgetting to pay.

At least my crime had been a lot more pleasurable. Still, was it enough to dissolve my entire career? Of all the things that could go wrong from a one-night stand, I never fathomed this, and I decided then and there to never pick up a stranger again. At least without a background check. A thorough one.

How did one really have this conversation? "Hi, wanted to let you know I have carnal knowledge of one of our caregivers." No, my sex life had nothing to do with my work. Or rather, it shouldn't have. One night with Cam had disintegrated the line.

I continued working, mind off sexy forbidden men. When the door opened again I froze. Heart hammering, I sat like a foolish lump until my cell phone chirped, giving me a much needed distraction. I rummaged around my desk, finally finding the phone tucked into my purse in a drawer. Two new text messages awaited me.

Cam: Can we talk about Grandma?
Cam: Or e-mail?

My pulse picked up a beat, or twenty. I had no clue how to handle the situation. I glanced again at Tess's office, only to find it empty. Too late. I had to figure out how to handle this on my own.

I thumbed my phone, trying to figure out how to respond to Cam. *Never contact me again* worked, but he deserved more than that. And if I was honest with myself, so did I. My lure to him had to do with more than Cassie, it also had to do with the man himself.

Nica: Sorry, I didn't see your text. I'm not sure it's appropriate for me to talk to you at work given the circumstances.

Understatement of the year.

Cam: Then can we meet? I'm coming back up after work to check on Grandma. I know it's complicated, but let me treat you to dinner.

My hands stilled. I needed to say no: it wasn't appropriate. To say yes all but sold my career up the river. Yet a silly grin grew on my face, because like it or not, Cam tempted me worse than apples tempted Eve.

Cam: It's the least I can do after everything you've done for Grandma.

Nica: I usually get a card, maybe flowers or an edible arrangement. Never dinner.

My cheeks burned, and I scrunched down in my seat. *Get a grip on yourself.*

Cam: First time for everything. What do you say?

I glanced at my computer screen, scrolled through my client list, and brought up Cassie's file. In the caregiver section I opened up Cam's name. No cell phone listed—he couldn't hear a voice call. This wasn't business as usual. Then again, usual didn't involve knowing what each other looked like, never mind naked.

Nica: I have a late meeting tonight, maybe tomorrow?

Goodness, I was going to hell. Straight to hell. And the unemployment line.

Cam: Thanks. No one else gets what's going on, not even my family. I really need to talk with you. And in person makes it even better.

Nica: You're welcome.

I had no idea what I was doing. I shouldn't have agreed to dinner. I should walk away, avoid the ethical landmine, save my dignity. Instead I was stepping right on the landmine. I'd find out soon whether it was a dud or not.

On the screen I had Cam's work and videophone number as well as his address visible. He had an apartment or condo in Boston, and his e-mail address showed where he worked. My computer system was better than Facebook stalking, which now that I thought about I'd have to do. I opened up Cam's text and made a new contact. I ignored the pang of guilt as I copied down his information. I'd lump it together with the rest of my behaviors that were just south of kosher.

Just south? Who was I kidding? It *was* south, deep south.

On instinct I opened up a note to write in my interaction with a caregiver. And froze. What was I going to write? *Going out for dinner with grandson who looks damn good naked and was amazing in bed?* The Office of Elder Affairs would love to read that one. I wouldn't be the only one in trouble; my supervisors would be dragged down with my sinking ship.

My eyes wandered through the listing of notes. A third of them were titled: *e-mail with family member.* That meant Cam. He was the only one involved with Cassie, at least the only one who communicated with elder services. I continued scrolling down the list back six years to when Cassie first started services. Even back then a third of the notes were related to him.

Six years. We had known each other for six years. Never meeting—he was never able to take time off from work. But there was a history; the notes staring me in the face were proof.

I searched for my supervisor again, but she hadn't returned. I needed to get the hell off this case before I made things any worse. A part of me knew it was already too late. But I had one last idea, a stab in the dark to salvage the situation.

I grabbed my phone and switched to Lexie's thread.

Nica: I need a favor.

Chapter 4

Nica

I walked through the double doors of the subsidized apartment building where Cassie and my other Deaf clients lived. The lobby resembled a living room, with chairs and couches encouraging socialization. I paused at a bulletin board, catching a hand-written paper tacked up:

Cassie Thompson is now at Hospice House, room 3

I skimmed over the other announcements: a sign up for repair work, information about my presentation tonight about elder services, and a flier for a trip down to one of the casinos. Good stuff—and then Cassie. The paper would soon be replaced with her funeral arrangements.

June, one of my clients, waited by the meeting room, leaning on her cane. Her short white hair was set in tight curls, her jeans and long-sleeved peach top appropriate for the weather.

Before I entered the room, June signed. *"You know that Cassie moved to Hospice House?"*

I held in a breath. The elders in the building loved to gossip and were close with one another. I should have known this was coming. *"I know."*

"Terrible thing. Her grandson's been by to collect some of her stuff."

I wanted to ask when, wondering if I avoided another awkward path-crossing, but knew better. I never fed into the gossip. I forced myself not to react and kept the conversation focused on June. *"How are you doing?"*

"Good."

"How's your cleaning person?"

"Fine. Cassie really wanted her grandson to settle down before she died." June and Cassie were partners in crime. Except for a brief period two years ago, when they were feuding over a supposed stolen pan, they were inseparable. Anything important to Cassie was important to June.

I pushed forward into the room, getting stuck into three more conversations about Cassie before the presentation finally began. Hands clasped behind my back, I waited as the office manager, Amanda, introduced me. Presentations weren't exactly part of my job, but I did this one every few years for my Deaf elders. Sometimes there were new residents, or changing needs, and a presentation made sure they were aware of the resources available to them.

My phone vibrated in my back pocket, probably Lexie trying to convince me not to pawn Cam off onto her. I couldn't risk my job, not when there wasn't a single other case manager who could do this presentation and ensure the needs of this population were met.

I forced all those thoughts aside and went into discussing elder services and all that we provided. From money management to personal care, and all the spots in between. Interruptions happened frequently and I went with the flow, used to this group by now.

At one point a figure entered the room, hovering just inside the door. This new gaze all but burned, and I couldn't resist checking on my new attendee, only to freeze and end up sputtering out my sentence.

Cam stood by the wall, a bag I recognized from Cassie's apartment at his feet. Shit. June hadn't meant he'd come and left, she'd meant he was here, had been here this whole time in his grandmother's apartment. He crossed his arms and gave me a slight nod, but there was a look in his eyes, a hint of a curve to his lips, that I didn't know what to do with.

For six years we never met, and now we'd bumped into each other three times in less than twenty-four hours.

June waved Cam over to the empty seat beside her. Front row, of course. He pushed off the wall, and I did my best to return to the presentation and not notice each slow stride that brought him closer to me. Coincidence, that's all.

Too many coincidences for my liking.

*****

Cam

I leaned back in my seat, watching Nica in her element. Her love for her job, for her clients, shined through in the animated way she signed. She went over everything elder services could provide—some points I knew, others I didn't, taking the time to explain things thoroughly. Not all of these elders had the access to education I had. Heck, like me, they were probably forced to speak at home. Unlike me, at school as well. While I could crack open a text book or email and understand the information fluently, my Grandmother's peers didn't always have the same knowledge.

Heck, I read most of Grandma's mail for her.

I rubbed at the ache in my chest then crossed my arms. Grandma should be here, not wasting away at Hospice House. I sure as hell didn't need to stick around, but once I saw Nica I had to stop by. If for no other reason than to make sure I did everything I could for my grandmother.

June nudged my shoulder, eyes flicking back and forth between Nica and me. *"I think Cassie had a good idea about you two."*

I resisted the urge to roll my head back. *"Funny, I remember a story you told me, about a certain gentleman you didn't appreciate being set up with last year."*

June laughed. *"True. But throw enough Jell-O at the wall and something's bound to stick."* She glanced again at Nica. *"I like this one. Yes. Go for it."*

I couldn't hide my laugh. *"Wait till I tell Grandma you now agree."*

June's smile shifted to one filled with sorrow. *"It's the least I can do for my dear friend."*

Grief clawed at my gut, and I had to glance away, discovering the presentation had finished. The crowd at the front had dispersed, and Nica placed the remaining papers with her agency information into her bag. I pushed myself up and covered the few feet between us. *"I was hoping to chat with you."*

Her cheeks pinked, and it reminded me of last night, in her bed. I had to shake the thoughts aside.

Her hands rose. *"I'm not sure that's—"*

"Appropriate? Who cares?" I gestured into the room where desserts had now been brought out. *"We chat here. No foul play."*

She nodded and set her bag down. *"Fine."*

We settled in at the end of one of the rectangular tables and for whatever reason were left alone. *"Nice of you to do this."*

One side of her mouth quirked, like a laser through me. Why did this woman still get to me? *"How do you think your grandmother discovered elder services in the first place?"*

Come to think of it, Grandma hadn't explained much. Or she was already on her matchmaking kick so I didn't pay enough attention. *"Still, you don't have to."*

Nica nodded. *"Actually I feel like I do. I knew this building was here, with mostly deaf elders who could benefit from my services. If I don't make sure they know what's available to them am I really doing my job?"*

"Good point." I leaned forward on my elbows, catching that while we might be left alone, June had her laser eyes on us. *"They're watching."*

Nica sat up a little straighter. *"Of course they are."* She gestured toward the wall where I had left my bag. *"That for your grandmother?"*

"Yup. A few clothes, one of her candles, yarn, playing cards and pictures. I'll drop them off before heading home."

Nica's gaze shifted over my shoulder and her eyebrows creased. *"Something's wrong in the kitchen."* She jumped up, heading straight to the little meeting room kitchen and stopped abruptly. *"Where's Amanda? There's water everywhere."*

I pushed past her and sure enough, water covered the floor. I fiddled with the sink handles but the water wasn't coming from here. By now a crowd had gathered at the opening. *"Contact maintenance."* Then I shoved up my sleeves and opened the sink cabinet. More water gushed out. I knelt in the puddle, trying to figure out where the problem started, but needed more light. Before I had a chance to ask, a light shined in the area. I glanced over to see Nica with her phone flashlight on, angling into the area.

"Thanks."

"I think the problem's by the cold water."

I checked and noticed she was right. Water seeped from the connection. I tried to wrap my hands around the coupling nut to tighten, but my fingers kept slipping. I lifted my head. *"Anyone know how to shut the water off?"*

Amanda shoved her way through. *"In basement. Repair guy come."* She bent next to Nica, surveying the mess, then rushed out.

I tried to grasp the pipe again, but couldn't get a grip. I scooted back. *"I need a towel."*

June handed me one, and I wrapped it around the nut. I wrenched down, turning the nut a few rotations. The water flow seemed to diminish, so I twisted it again, hands slipping as the towel became saturated. A few more turns and I managed to reduce the water to a trickle. Someone handed me a bowl and I placed it underneath. It sat in a puddle, but at least it would catch anything new.

I stood up, shaking off my wet hands. My pants were soaked, as was my shirt up my back.

"I think it's possible you collected more of the water than the floor," Nica signed, not even trying to hide a laugh.

My feet felt squishy, but that could be my socks more than the floor. Water still covered the area, and Nica's beige pants were wet from the knees down. *"You're wet, too."* The double meaning slipped out unintended, but thoughts of Nica and wet went straight to my head, and not the one on my shoulders.

Her eyebrows rose, but her eyes heated as a silent and seductive joke brewed between us. She glanced down at her own damp pants. *"Seems that way."*

I may have had too much to drink our one night together, but I remembered the touch and feel of her, and even though it shouldn't, it pulsed within me, a fire refusing to go out.

We were handed towels to dry off, and I used the distraction to get my head on straight. Ten minutes later the repair guy had arrived, and Nica and I stood outside. My clothes were still wet, but at least the night air wasn't too bad. "*Interesting night,*" I signed.

"*Agreed. Sorry you got delayed heading to your grandmother.*"

I shouldered the bag. "*I can always leave it with the staff if she's asleep.*" The outside lighting hit Nica's cheekbones, and I had the urge to lean in. Last night I did. Tonight, off the table. Yet this irresistible pull remained; one that even the reminder of my grandmother couldn't distinguish. "*I'll see you tomorrow? When I can talk more freely?*" And not be cut short by a burst pipe.

Nica hesitated, but eventually nodded. "*Have a good night.*"

"*You too.*"

My clothes stuck to me on all sides, so I cranked the heat in my car. Funny how everyone had gathered when Nica heard the water, but it was she who knew exactly what I needed with the flashlight.

*****

At half past six the following evening, I walked back into Hospice House, Grant trailing behind me, his hands deep in his pockets. "*Thanks for joining,*" I signed.

Grant shrugged. "*I'm here for Cassie, not your ass.*"

Before we made it to my grandmother's room, a hand on my shoulder stopped me. I turned to a tall woman in her late fifties with short copper-red hair.

"… Cameron?" she asked. Her eyes flittered back and forth between the two of us. Grant stepped back, even though he probably understood more of what was said than I had.

I studied her lips and debated how I wanted to play my cards. While I had ample experience in identifying my own name, I wasn't sure how much I'd be able to understand from her. All I wanted was to see my grandmother, not be stuck in a five-minute conversation destined to take a half hour. I searched for an ID badge, something, anything, to let me know the importance of this interaction.

The reminder of where I was hit me upside the head. All interactions at this point did matter. Which meant I needed to understand what was said. I gestured for a paper and pen.

The woman said something, grabbed a paper from the reception desk, and felt her pockets before plucking a pen from behind her ear and writing.

Cameron?

I nodded.

I'm Sally Stone, one of the social workers here. We've noticed you're the only family contact for Cassandra, and no one else has visited.

Again, her eyes flittered to Grant, standing silent like my personal bodyguard. He wouldn't say shit unless I asked him to.

Decision number two, did I speak or write back? I opted to go with the easiest choice and shoved my hands into my pockets. "That's right. I've been the one caring for her. This is my friend. The rest of the family has been notified—" I clenched my jaw, then forced it to relax, I had no idea how understandable I'd be with it clenched "—but will probably not make it here before the weekend."

Sally's face softened.

I'm sorry. We can talk with them if you feel it would help.

She stepped closer and placed a hand on my shoulder, an act I would have much preferred being done by Nica. I wondered if she thought spoken language was the way to get through to my family or if I was being paranoid. She went back to writing.

This is not a fun time for anyone, especially those closest. We have support groups that you could join, either now or at any point in the future.

I raised an eyebrow and said nothing. Support groups. For a Deaf guy. Would they provide interpreters? Or would they write everything down for me? Or, better yet, speak and hope I picked up the so-called support through osmosis?

The last time I checked, my ears picked up nothing through osmosis, except an occasional ear infection.

I nodded and thanked Sally for her help, not willing to dive into anything else. My world continued to unravel strand by strand.

I pushed on through the warm tones of the hall towards my grandmother. Grant picked up his pace, matching my stride. *"What the hell was that? Support group? Who needs that?"*

I didn't stop walking. *"Normal people."*

"Normal hearing people."

I tapped my nose. When we arrived at Grandma's room I found her sitting up in bed, all her energy focused on her knitting. Slow-moving hands struggled to get the stitches right. Light filtered in from the hall, illuminating the subdued colors of the soft, floral bedspread, the blue walls, and the overstuffed chair for visitors. It also cast a shadow over her face. A gray tone sunk deep into her cheeks.

"When did she get so frail?" Grant asked.

Yesterday. Last month. Last year. All were part of the answer. *"That's what happens when you only show up for parties."*

"No one parties like Cassie. Get her attention—we'll have an impromptu one here."

I flipped the lights and her blue eyes registered on me, and a smile worked its way over her wrinkled face. She darted her gaze back to her knitting.

After completing the stitch, she set down the light blue yarn. *"My sweet boy,"* she signed. *"Why don't you let some other family members come and harass me?"*

I balled one hand into a tight fist and signed with the other. *"Sorry, I only called them yesterday; someone should be by soon to visit."* I hoped; if not I was going to have to force them, Deaf baby of the family or not.

"*Don't worry about me, I'm fine. Worry about your lonely self.*" She went to pick up her yarn, but checked behind me and a spark flittered across her face. "*My not so sweet boy, you visited.*"

Grant, smile on his face like we were out for a nature walk, stepped closer and gave Grandma a hug. "*Of course I visited. Any excuse to see this dazzling beauty.*"

Grandma brushed him off. "*You keeping this one in trouble?*"

I crossed my arms and leaned against the wall.

"*He found some trouble himself the other night; you'd be proud.*"

I stomped, contemplated making noise, but Grant didn't even flinch. Grandma, however, turned those knowledge-filled eyes on me. Her eyebrows raised high. She did always see straight through me.

"*I'm meeting someone for dinner,*" I admitted.

She collected her yarn again. "*A girl?*"

"*Yes.*"

"*Finally!*" she signed, raising her face to the ceiling. "*Hurry up and make up your mind about her. If she's a keeper I want to meet her.*"

"*You know her.*"

Grandma lowered her head and scrunched up her face. She scrutinized me long and hard. When her hands moved again they were in short, sprinted motions. "*Explain.*"

I inhaled a deep breath. What I said next would go straight to inflate her ego, but one glance at where she lay made it worth it. "*I met Veronica the other night.*"

Grandma laughed, her shoulders rising and falling from the motion. "*Perfect. So you knew each other before meeting here?*"

"*We didn't realize who each other was until here.*"

She laughed again. "*So you had a little fun before?*" My grandmother always knew how to make me blush. "*Smart boy.*"

Grant settled into the chair. "*Told you.*"

I shook my head. Accepting a match, especially this particular match, was not in my best interest, or Nica's. "*It's complicated.*"

"*I'm dying. It's an old woman's last wish. Give me paper, I'll write a note*" excusing *Veronica's behavior, she always said it was a conflict with her job to listen to my advice, but life is too short for conflicts.*" Grandma held out her hand, shaking as she tried to keep it steady.

"*She agreed to have dinner with me. You can hold off on the note for now.*" I wasn't sure what our dinner was. Somewhere between work and a date, or maybe work and friends. The label didn't matter, as long as I saw her. Wasn't that a conundrum in itself? I wanted to see her. Again. Both the sweet social worker Veronica who had helped me out for years, and the sexy Nica. But that didn't change certain facts. "*You know I'm not looking for anything serious.*"

Grant shook his head and signed behind my grandmother's back. "*You're in trouble now.*"

Her eyes narrowed. "*Maybe not with any woman, but with this woman? Yes.*"

I tried to find a gentle way to get out of this conversation, when Grandma waved for my attention.

"*Don't be stubborn. You think it's best to stay detached so you don't turn into your father. Not true. He chose your mother. You can choose someone who will support you, not suffocate you. Someone like Veronica.*"

I studied her. She seemed so full of life, full of energy. Up until six months prior she was always involved in a conversation while knitting. There was a familiar dance to the yarn being picked up and put down as she signed. Except for being in a bed she was the same grandmother I had always known.

"*Why Veronica?*" I asked.

"*She's a very hard worker. Same as you. Determined to get things right. Oh, she tries to keep her personal life private, but that girl wears her heart on her sleeve.*" She paused and gave me a good hard glower. "*Veronica deserves to be loved. She will give her all but needs the same in response.*" She narrowed her eyes. "*Don't hurt her.*"

"*Easier to do if you don't set us up.*"

Grandma picked up her knitting but couldn't get her hands around the next stitch. "*You know who the first couple I set up was?*"

Yeah, I knew. I'd been told this story so many times I could repeat it with my brain half off. But her fumbling with the needles reminded me where we were. *"Grant doesn't know."*

He gave me a smile that said to watch my back—he'd also heard this too often.

Grandma tossed the yarn to the side. *"Liar."* She grinned. *"I saw his grandfather on the first day of high school. He was a junior, so cute in his crisp white shirt. One look, and I knew. I walked over to him and told him I had the perfect girl he should go out with. He thought I was a fourteen-year-old brat. He challenged me and asked who. I lost my nerve, for a minute, and told him it would be a blind date. He agreed."* A faraway gaze melted into her eyes, softening at the memory. *"He wasn't surprised it was me."*

Her spark returned, the same I had grown up with, and I forgot about her struggle with her knitting.

"I'm right about you and Veronica," she signed.

"Give it time."

"Time." She shook her head and reached for her knitting. Before her hands could grasp the blue strands she turned back to me. *"Time will steal everything from you if you give it a chance. Time stole your father from me, and nothing I could ever do would get that back."*

I swallowed the lump in my throat. The closest thing to a relationship I had with my father was the memories my grandparents held on to. The man hardly ever interacted with me unless my mother told him to be the disciplinarian. I leaned forward and placed one hand on hers. *"That's why I don't want a relationship."*

Grandma shook her head, her brow creased in determination. *"It's not the relationship, it's the who. That's why I want to set you up, to find a match to be good to you. And you won't find a better one than Veronica."* Grandma turned to Grant. *"You help him out, this Veronica is good for him. He'll need her."* She faced me. *"Make sure she visits me before I go."*

I had a sneaking suspicion her will to fight just grew stronger.

Chapter 5

Cam

"*Don't you have a gym to get back to?*" I asked Grant as we stood outside the restaurant, waiting for Nica. Every shifting object had me glancing down the street, checking for the blond beauty I had to stop thinking about. So far only the green, yellow, and red leaves blowing around the sidewalk had been the culprit.

"*I have staff. And Cassie's instructions were clear. I need to help you out.*"

"*By crashing my meeting?*"

"*By making sure it's a date.*"

Movement had me looking over Grant's shoulder, this time not due to leaves. A woman headed our way from across the street. Petite, dark hair, not Nica. But as she grew closer something appeared familiar.

Grant nudged my arm. "*That her? She's hot.*"

I shook my head as recognition hit, slithering down to my stomach like a sticky substance. Nica's friend from the bar. Nica wasn't coming. Relief should have followed—it didn't.

The woman held out her phone when she approached, a message written on the screen.

I'm Lexie, Nica's friend. She's chicken and trying to stay true to her ethics, which is a load of shit if you ask me, one life and all that. But the social worker in me gets it and also understands you need someone to help who hasn't seen you naked.

Grant laughed. I handed Lexie back her phone.

"This is Grant, ignore him. Nica's not coming?" I spoke and signed.

Lexie shook her head and typed.

No clue how you want to communicate. Nica suggested I type. And she feels bad due to the communication issue. But, like I said, ethics.

Lexie stood with adequate lighting on her face; she'd be easy enough to lip-read. It would be simpler than writing, and not a big deal if I missed something she said, unlike at Hospice. *"You can try speaking, I catch some, and so does Grant. Ethics?"*

Lexie shoved her phone into her back pocket. "... psychologist dating... patient."

"His grandmother's the patient," Grant said and signed.

Lexie scrunched up her face. I missed the first part of what she said, but figured out the gist, patient or not, this was still a problem. "... Nica should be here... ban, if...?" She gave us a crooked smile.

I shook my head, my lack of sleep affecting my lip-reading more than I'd expected. Without me saying a word Lexie collected her phone out again and began typing.

Grant nudged my side. *"I like her."*

I did, too, but not in the way Grant was thinking.

Lexie's smile shot up a notch, so Grant must have voiced. She handed over her phone.

I think Nica should be here. I have a plan, if you are up to a little deception?

"What did you have in mind?"

I tell Nica we can't communicate, and she needs to get her ass down here.

Grant started signing before I handed Lexie's phone back. *"Starting a relationship with lies..."* He shook his head. *"I'm so proud of you both."*

Lexie showed teeth when she smiled at him. My head spun, from sharp let-down to pathetic hope, to the basic fact that I needed a social worker and would have emailed Veronica if she hadn't turned out to be Nica for details that Lexie wouldn't have.

Deep down, I wanted to see her, the sexy woman who made me forget about my problems for a while. And I knew damn well the other social workers didn't know my grandmother's case the same way she did. Grandma wanted this meeting; a little deception would put a smile on her face. I'd give her as many more happy moments as I could manage.

"*One, not a relationship. Two, a white lie never hurt anyone.*" I hoped, at least. Grandma might whack the side of my head, but she'd also approve of me seeing Nica.

Lexie typed while nodding.

So what's it going to be?

A smile worked its way across my face. "*No, I don't think we can communicate.*"

*****

Nica

Guilt crawled up my spine. I let Cam down and roped Lexie into my mess of a situation. I wanted to know how things were going, to the point where I held my phone in my hand. But didn't dare. Lexie would be using her phone to talk with Cam, the last thing I needed was a pathetic message from me scrolling across her screen.

Meow. My black and white cat, Oreo, jumped up onto the couch, paw raised for attention.

"*What am I doing?*" I signed, since Oreo happened to be deaf, the main reason I adopted her from the shelter.

But, as usual, my cat had no desire to communicate. Instead, she used my moving hands to rub her face on my nails.

"Silly girl, you're no help."

She moved into my lap and curled up, small body purring against my legs. Should have helped my anxiety a lot more than it did.

My phone vibrated, and I jumped to get it. Oreo meowed in protest at the movement, and then curled up on one leg as if to say, "Stay, human."

A new text message waited for me.

Lexie: He can't understand me and I can't understand him, so you better get your ass down here.

I groaned and leaned back until my head hit the top of the couch.

Nica: You know that's not a good idea.

I tapped my thumb, waiting for a response. None came. I switched to my phone app and dialed Lexie.
Voicemail.
"Shit."
If Lexi truly struggled with communicating, she'd have answered her damn phone. Which meant she only accepted this favor to set me up.
Oreo stared at me.
"I shouldn't go, should I? It's a bad idea. Just let Lexie handle it."
Oreo hopped off my lap and headed to the kitchen. The cat was more the devil on my shoulder than angel. I tried Lexie again. Another voicemail. I switched to my text folder.

Nica: Some favor you accepted.

I pushed up, ready to grab my stuff and get this over with, when I caught a glimpse of myself in the mirror and nearly shrieked. Mascara smudged around my eyes, and not in a good smoky effect. My hair had turned from curly to frizzy. Half curly, half straight strands stuck out in multiple directions. My nerves looked like they'd given me an electric shock. With no time to lose I doused my hair with frizz spray, flipped my head upside down, and scrunched my curls back into shape. Then I wiped down and reapplied my makeup. I rested against the sink, staring at myself, wondering why I went through this much trouble. This wasn't a date, not even close.
Ten minutes later I walked up to Salem Beer Works, the cool night unusual for early September. Being the witch capital of the world meant the area already had witches, black cats, and other spooky artifacts on display as the tourist season approached. Tonight

was another quiet weeknight for the locals. A few cars drove past. A hint of the nearby salty sea mixed in with the overflowing cooking smells from the restaurant.

I turned to the restaurant doors and plum forgot how to breathe when I spotted Cam. His neatly combed hair called out to my fingers to revert him back to that messy state of two nights ago. His jeans lovingly cupped his thighs, making it damn hard to keep my gaze off his crotch. When I succeeded the green polo did little to help, stretched tight across broad shoulders. I shuddered and it had nothing to do with the breeze floating past. I was still attracted to him. The complications hadn't dampened any of my desire. *Damn.*

I struggled to keep my breathing under control as I came closer. Our eyes locked. A slow smile formed on his face. I broke myself from the trance and realized he was alone. Where the hell was Lexie?

He must have read the confusion on my face. "*She's inside at a table, with my friend who had joined to visit Grandma.*"

Something smelled fishy, and it had nothing to do with the nearby sea. "*And they can communicate?*"

A light pink tone warmed his cheeks. "*My friend's hard of hearing.*"

I crossed my arms. And waited.

"*It was her idea.*"

I nodded, willing my anger to boil up and take over. Instead, I laughed. "*Sure it was. But this still isn't appropriate.*"

He stepped closer, and I had to fight not to take a step back. Not because I wanted to get away, but because I wanted him nearer. I knew how he felt, and it tempted more than chocolate. "*Explain.*"

I glanced up at the sky, the glare of the streetlights blocking out the stars. "*This is a conflict of interest. The minute we discovered who we were, my relationship with your grandmother, my ability to give her unbiased service, changed. This blurs the boundary between us and with your grandmother. I should lose my job.*"

I sucked in a breath, praying he understood.

He ran a hand through his hair, that one motion bringing a flash of the other night to mind, with him over me, those strands out of place, as our bodies moved together. I tried to banish the thoughts from my mind as he scanned left, right, then finally settled on my face. *"I hate myself for this thought, but you do realize she's been given two weeks to live."* His eyes grew glossy. *"And for the rest, I don't give a shit. I'm the only one caring for her. My friend is the only other person to visit her. So, yes, I want to talk with you about what is going on. I need it."*

Here I'd been lost in the other night, and he thought of his grandmother. *Dammit, Lexie.* This was why I needed to stay away. Because standing here in front of him my resolve faded to ash. The urge to help him overpowering all rhyme or reason. *"OK."*

His shoulders relaxed. *"You've saved me, the social worker at Hospice wants to set me up with a support group."*

"Support group? With what communication access?" The last I checked, there wasn't any in the area, and I'd been checking ever since Cassie started Hospice services.

His smile turned into a grin. *"I didn't ask. I see now why Grandma likes you."*

And what about you? I wanted to ask. Yet the answer was as obvious as us having this conversation. *"Well, don't count your chickens before they've hatched, I might have to agree with the social worker."*

We shared a small laugh, and the air between us changed, ignited as though our connection had turned flammable. He opened the door for me, and I moved past him into the restaurant, catching the subtle whiff of his cologne. He smelled like a tropical island, like a vacation from reality.

A man a few tables in with tousled light brown hair waved, and I noticed Lexie sat with him. I narrowed my eyes as my friend gave me an innocent expression. Lexie was many things, innocent not on the list. "You're dead meat," I voiced only once we were close enough.

Cam's friend laughed. "This is going to be fun," he said in both languages.

Lexie held up a finger. "One, I don't know the case. Two, I don't know the caregiver. Three, there are four of us here, pull up your big girl panties and chill."

I groaned but settled into my seat, not missing how close Cam felt next to me and how much I liked it. And it occurred to me my resistance to this meeting had more to do with my personal self-preservation than anything else.

It also occurred to me that Cam's friend, who seemed to be able to understand Lexie, hadn't interpreted our exchange. And Cam didn't appear to be lost or confused. I placed an elbow on the table, studying him. "*You understood her?*"

I got half my answer with Cam's friend speaking. "Uh oh, Nica's onto your ploy."

Cam didn't flinch. "*Yes. Her idea, but communicating with you is easier than playing guessing games with mouth patterns.*"

Introductions were made, and I learned Grant was Cam's friend and had been since they were in college together. The way Grant joked and teased, he appeared to be very much like Lexie, and it came as little surprise the easy comradery passing between them. Which made this feel more like a double date than an innocent business meeting.

I buried my face in my menu, reading each word twice and still not comprehending. I needed to get a grip on myself, and fast. Cam put his menu down and leaned closer. "*You OK?*" His warm eyes offered comfort like the hazelnuts they resembled, all dangerously sweet and irresistible.

I forced a smile. "*I'm fine.*"

He settled his elbows on the table, leaving very little space between us. "*Liar.*"

"*One night and you think you know me?*"

He shrugged. "*I don't know why, or how, but, yes, I know something is bothering you.*" He leaned back. "*Then again, it could be your concerns over being here.*"

The cliff between professional dinner and date threatened to throw me over the edge. Never had anyone understood me that quickly, mostly because I didn't want anyone to. "*I thought you needed help?*" I signed quickly.

"*I do. I was enjoying the distraction.*"

I didn't dare make eye contact with Lexie as the waitress approached our table with her head in her notepad and began rattling off specials. I was prepared to interpret, but I didn't have to. Cam either followed the waitress or didn't care. When she finally turned to him he spoke his order. His deep, gravelly voice was surprisingly clear for his hearing loss. The waitress paused, not writing anything down. As clear as Cam's voice was, it was still obvious he was deaf. Cam lowered his eyebrows and opened his mouth to speak again, but the waitress snapped out of her haze and wrote on her notepad, collected the rest of our orders, and left.

"*Friendly,*" Grant signed, his face full of sarcasm.

I laughed.

"Is that normal?" Lexie asked.

Grant rocked a hand back and forth. "Depends on the day, the mood, and whether we speak. Once I speak, forget it, they assume I'm hearing."

They continued chatting, but Cam turned to me. "*Where did you learn ASL?*"

I wanted to ask a similar question about his speech. It wasn't normal, especially for a man with Deaf grandparents. "*My childhood neighbor was Deaf. I picked up signs interacting with her and then took formal classes while in college, minoring in Deaf Studies. Does the rest of your family sign?*" I unfolded my napkin and placed it on my lap.

Cam hesitated and rested his elbows on the table. "*Depends. My aunts remember enough. Their husbands and kids learned some. My brothers are skilled but Grandma raised me. I was the youngest and my mom went back to work. So Grandma watched me and gave me my language.*"

I read between the lines, and the crease between Cam's eyebrows. And I hated it. More so because the confirmation would invest me more fully into him, and I was already in danger of straddling the line from the wrong side.

"*What about your parents?*"

"*Dad never really learned ASL; he was the youngest and his sisters handled the communication. My mother,*" he said, rubbing out a kink in his neck, "*never approved of ASL. She feels oral is best, and Dad didn't do anything to stop her.*"

Hard to stay detached now.

"*That's awful*," I signed before I could stop myself. Poor Cam couldn't communicate with his parents unless he spoke their language. I imagined his childhood wasn't an easy one. "*Thank God you had your grandmother.*"

The stress vacated his shoulders, landing somewhere far away in the dim restaurant. He held my eyes captive with his own, electricity pulsing between us. I had the sudden urge to curl up inside those hazel depths, and the scarier thought he'd let me. *Crap, definitely moving into date territory.* I tried to remember we weren't alone, but Lexie and Grant were lost in their own conversation.

Cam resumed signing. "*Grandma wants to see you again. But a warning, she's in matchmaker mode.*"

My cheeks flushed. "*She always tried. I distracted her with work.*"

"*I didn't have any work to distract her with. Instead I had to listen to her pleas. I'm the youngest of the grandkids, and the only one single. She's been on my case for years.*"

"Same as your mother." Grant leaned forward, still using both languages. I had all but tuned out the other voices at our table and nearly startled. "She thinks he needs to settle down."

Cam shoved Grant's shoulder. "She thinks I need to be taken care of. Grandma wants me to be happy." Cam copied Grant's communication style, using both languages.

"True. But if you start dating someone, maybe your mother will back off."

"That didn't work for my brothers. And I stopped living my life according to my mother when I was still a kid."

"Parents are overrated anyways," Lexie said, the only one of us speaking-only. "Sounds like your mother is a bit of an asshole, no offense."

"Grade A asshole," Grant confirmed, and the two went back to their own conversation.

A light flashed on our table, vibrating across the wood grains. Cam read the message lit up on his screen.

"*Oh good*," he said, putting it away. His shoulders relaxed and he faced me. "*Sorry, text message. My parents live in Florida. They were downplaying this whole situation. I threatened to buy their plane tickets for them. Somehow common sense prevailed, and they booked a flight up. I think they would have preferred Grandma to give them her date of death in advance so they could prepare."* Cam rolled his eyes, and I knew he was the one handling everything. It weighed on his shoulders, in the depths of his eyes. It blurred the lines further, breaking my resolve, human need eclipsing every rational thought in my head. His hand rested on the table, and I reached over and grabbed it. The fuse from the first night sparked to life at the simple touch, seeping into my veins.

"Sorry you're dealing with this alone," I signed one-handed.

He shrugged, his eyes drifting to our intertwined hands. *"Your family messed up?"*

His thumb had started stroking mine, slow and smooth, reminding me of that night, the bar, and everything that came next. Reminding me I played with fire. I snatched my hand back. *"My parents divorced when I was five."*

Cam furrowed his thick eyebrows.

"Don't worry, they had the perfect divorce. I grew up with two parents that loved me and were friends with each other."

"No stepparents?"

"Nope, neither remarried." I didn't view divorce as a bad thing. It wasn't. My parents taught me marriage didn't always last. And that was okay. I did my best to end my relationships like they did, parting as friends. It didn't always work, life and human emotions not always going according to plan, but thus far I'd avoided any big dramatic ending.

Cam fiddled with the metallic saltshaker. *"What do I expect from here?"*

I studied his face, wondering how much he could handle, but I didn't know him well enough to make an appropriate assessment. Through e-mail I didn't have to gauge a reaction. I opted to go with the simple, gentle, truth. *"She'll get weaker, more medicated. They'll take good care of her."*

He raked his fingers through his hair. *"She still seems so alive."*

"She's a fighter, she's going to go down kicking and thrashing." We both let

out a small chuckle.

Cam caught my eyes, his own deep and solemn. "*I can't do this alone.*"

Moisture built in my eyes, and I had to blink in quick succession to keep it from leaking over. My heart ached enough over the thought of losing Cassie, but seeing Cam's pain did me in. It shattered through me. I held his gaze and signed, "*You don't have to.*"

*****

Cam

At the end of the meal we stood outside in the crisp night air. Grant and Lexie clearly playing wingpeople as they were still inside, checking out the beer menu, even though I knew damn well Grant wasn't drinking another. The yellow streetlights picked up the lighter tones of Nica's hair. I wasn't ready for the night to be over. Regardless of my desire to stay unattached, I enjoyed Nica's company. With all the stress and shit in my life, I'd take whatever enjoyment I could get.

"*Thank you for meeting with me.*" I stood close, the narrow sidewalk allowing me to intrude on her personal space. Her full lips called to me. One touch and all my troubles would be forgotten. Not going there. "*I needed this and it was nice seeing you again—*" I smirked "*—sober and without any burst pipes.*"

"*You had two beers, I wouldn't be so sure about the sober part. Walk in a straight line and touch your nose before I let you get into your car.*"

I laughed but demonstrated. I backed up then walked directly towards Nica, her cheeks high and round as she continued laughing, until our noses almost touched. I stopped, retaining the closeness, wondering why all this damn chemistry lingered. She bit her lip and shifted away. The much-needed cool air filtered between us, but her eyes remained on my lips. *Right there with you.* We both knew this was wrong, and yet here we stood, our gazes all but making out.

Nica stepped back. "*I'll find some time to check on your grandmother. But beyond that, this really needs to be it."*

Funny how even though I agreed, her words contracted a vibe I felt deep down in my gut. *Get a hold of yourself, Thompson.* This connection screamed giving up control. One thing my mother taught me by being her bitchtastic self: never give up control. So even though everything in me demanded to do something different, I stood there, like an idiot, as she backed up. She waved somewhere over my shoulder, then turned and walked away.

A hand landed on my shoulder. Grant. *"You let her go?"*

"I had to."

We both turned to Lexie. She waited until Nica rounded the corner. The shadows blocked her face, but Grant understood and translated. *"She's right in what she's doing for her job. Just maybe not for the chemistry you two have."*

"That's comforting."

Grant yanked out his phone from his back pocket. *"Then maybe we take Nica out of the equation. What do you say we force these two—"* he signed in my direction and the empty space where Nica would have been *"—into close quarters?"*

I tried to interject, but Lexie's wide grin matched Grant's, and it occurred to me that perhaps Nica and I weren't the only two with some chemistry. Since they didn't have the obstacles we did, it was best I stood back as they exchanged numbers and let things fall as they would.

But that didn't feel right. Not at all. Running down the street and tugging Nica back into my arms felt right. Never had anyone made me feel this way. From the stories my aunts told me, Dad acted like this when he met Mom, back when he didn't shun his Deaf parents. Back when he had an opinion. Which meant I had to listen to Nica.

We had to stay apart.

Chapter 6

Nica

On my lunch break I headed over to Hospice House. I removed my ID and signed into the Hospice book as Nica instead of Veronica. After everything with Cam, I had to treat Cassie as a personal appointment, not work related.

Since Cassie didn't have a light doorbell here, I opened her door and flicked the light switch. Cassie lay in bed, watching television, looking as though a slight wind could break this usually strong woman. Her knitting lay lifeless on her stomach. Needles crossed at an awkward angle while a dwindling roll of yarn snuggled against her hip. Until the past few months Cassie was always up and moving around her apartment when I visited. Now her short hair stuck out in multiple directions, the curls she always had done unraveling. She wore a housecoat, blankets bunched up around her. The wrinkles on her face appeared more prominent in the dim lighting.

Cassie's blue eyes found me, and the dullness morphed into a shine. She smiled, the sides of her mouth crinkling, and waved me in.

"*How are you feeling?*" I asked, sitting down.

"*Tired.*" She eyed me, her wise eyes taking in the situation in its entirety. "*C.T. told you to visit?*" C.T. Cam's sign name, those two letters tapping the chin. His grandparents would have given him this name. Mine had come from my Deaf elders when I started working with them. If we had used our sign names when we first met things would be very different.

I nodded as I checked out the room, namely the pictures brought from Cassie's apartment. I found one of Cam; he wore a graduation cap and a huge grin. I wasn't sure if it was high school or college, but it was certainly several years ago. I recognized him but would never have put two and two together, even sober. I always thought he was a nice-looking grandson. Except now I knew his face well, and that huge grin made my stomach flip. My attempt to stay away, to stay detached, wasn't going well.

I turned back to Cassie, the matchmaker—even though she had nothing to do with our initial meeting.

"I'm here on my lunch break," I signed.

"You didn't have to do that."

"Not appropriate for work."

Cassie brushed me off. *"Nonsense. I told C.T. I would write a letter, excusing you of any problems with your work. Give me paper."*

I laughed and held onto Cassie's shaking but determined hand. The hand was cold, the skin paper-thin. I signed one-handed. *"It's OK. Though when you get better, I can't be your case manager."* Maybe if I never did any further official work on her case I could somehow handle this mess of a situation.

Cassie jerked her hand away. *"I'm not getting any better."* The feisty woman had lost her spunk just like that. *"C.T. will need you."*

I fought against the tears threatening to blur my vision. *"I can't be the one to help him."*

Cassie smiled, the fight burning in her eyes. I knew it wasn't the fight to live. *"I know you two. You will be my granddaughter-in-law."* As the last sign finished, Cassie's hand moved to her chest and a deep cough ravaged her. I helped her lean forward and rubbed her back. The congested, fluid-filled cough vibrated through the frail body.

I continued to rub after Cassie calmed down.

"Want to know why you two are perfect for each other?"

I said nothing. Cassie wasn't going to stop until she was ready.

"You are both determined individuals. You work hard. Solve problems when they come up. You each need someone else like that. Someone willing to jump in and help bounce around ideas."

"And no one else in the world is like that?" I teased.

"Don't be smart. You two are like my husband and me. We complemented each other in drive, in ambition. Oh, they say you need only one person in the driver's seat. That's for wimps. You need both people in the driver's seat, both people steering the relationship in the right direction. Otherwise you have one person dragging the other. I've never met anyone else who shares the type of drive C.T. has. He's not someone who wants a follower. He wants a partner. And from everything I've seen, you're the same way."

I wanted to comment on drive not being enough for a relationship. I didn't. Cassie's breathing was increasing in frequency. She needed her rest.

"Happy I'm finally listening?"

Cassie smiled. *"Are you?"*

"Yes." The honest answer surprised even me. This was no longer my client I was chatting with. I was no longer the social worker. This felt like family. Cassie was much more dangerous than I gave her credit for.

"My hearing loss is genetic. So far only C.T. inherited the gene. If any of my family can handle a deaf child it's you two."

I laughed and rubbed Cassie's hand. I was used to my client's heavy-handed and blunt conversation style. Part of it was cultural, the rest a feisty personality. All of it a wonderful woman I was sure to miss.

"Time to get some rest," I said as I stood.

With a heavy heart I made my way out of the building, giving Cassie a chance to nap. The crisp air caressed my cheeks, allowing me to fill the fall air deep into my lungs. The trees swayed and I lost myself in the dance of rustling leaves until my cell rang. I crossed the last few feet to my car and answered as I climbed inside.

"We have plans tonight," Lexie said.

I mentally ran through my calendar, but knew it to be empty. "Oh really."

"Yes, really. After seeing you fail to resist Cam you need a night out."

I studied a mark on my windshield. Bird poop. My car needed a bath. "I resisted him. You saw me go home alone."

"I saw you two practically eye fuck followed by you running."

I resisted the urge to rub the mark from the inside, since bird poop or not, it wasn't inside my car. "You were supposed to be helping."

"I am helping. Hence the plans."

I groaned and tried to figure out the location of the nearest carwash. "I should go home, and stay home this time."

"Right, because that will get him off your mind. I've never seen you like this before. Maybe you should give it a chance."

I gripped my keys so hard they dug into my palm. "Are you out of your mind? You know how bad this is."

"Yeah, I do. And I also know the biggest problem for you has nothing to do with him being a caregiver."

"Lexie," I moaned.

"You don't believe in the fairytale."

"Neither do you." Lexie never dated the same guy more than two weeks.

"True. I don't. But I'm not falling for my client's grandson."

I clamped my teeth together so fast my back molars ached. "I'm not falling."

"Hook, line, and sinker. The fairytale exists. See if your prince has a glass slipper."

"You're almost as bad as my client, it's not happening." I forced my fingers to uncurl and jammed my key into the ignition.

"Ha!" Lexie exclaimed. "Do me a favor, don't run before you get a chance to see where this might go."

I glanced upwards at my roof, wondering if there was more poop waiting for me there. "Is there a point to this call?"

"There is. Wear sneakers. I'll pick you up at six."

I hung up the phone and tossed it on the passenger seat. I should never have roped Lexie into this mess, and then she wouldn't be attempting to make things worse. I shifted the car into reverse and pulled out of the parking lot. A quick glance back tugged at my heart. Cassie's death was going to hurt, like all the good clients did. I didn't want to think about how much more it would hurt if I continued to blur the lines of professional and personal with Cam.

*****

Cam

The curved green handhold above my head lay just out of reach, but it wasn't getting the best of me, not today. I pushed onto my toes and wrapped my fingers around the holding, drawing myself up. I realigned my body with the wall and reached for another. My muscles ached with satisfaction. It felt damn good to do something normal, even if the timing was nine hours later than usual, thanks to visiting my grandmother that morning.

The rope around my waist tugged and I looked down.

"Feeling better?" Grant was on the ground, at the other end of the rope, belaying the climb. We were far enough apart that I doubted a hearing person could hear, and noted Grant's mouth was uncommonly still.

I angled myself securely against the wall and released one hand. *"Yes."*

Grant shook his head but moved both hands onto the rope. I turned back to the wall and completed my climb.

The second my feet hit the ground, Grant waved for attention. *"So,"* he signed, prolonging the *O* until his arm was outstretched. *"I saw that climb, you're becoming slow. Old man."*

I unhooked my equipment and dropped it to the ground with a satisfying vibration at my feet. *"You want to start with the 'old'? Last I checked your birthday came first."*

Grant grinned. *"True. But I'm not falling over some girl's feet."*

I had no plans to fall, especially in some pathetic display. I arched an eyebrow. *"Funny, I thought you exchanged numbers with someone last night."*

Grant's grin grew and I smelled trouble. He glanced over his shoulder. *"I did, but not for me. Not yet, at least."*

I shifted my focus to the entrance, where Lexie dragged Nica by the hand into the climbing area. Both their mouths moved—Lexie's tilted upwards, Nica's down—the facial expressions made it clear whose idea this meet-up belonged to.

Nica wrenched her hand free and held both of them up, palms out. Exasperation covered her face and all I wanted to do was rub out the crease between her eyebrows. The attraction between us begged me to cross the room. I had no idea how I was supposed to resist her. No clue if I could.

One question remained: Could she?

Arms still raised, she turned away from Lexie. I knew the moment she saw me, our eyes meeting like a live wire. Her hands slowly slid down, and it occurred to me she could have been fighting against Lexie because of the rock climbing, not necessarily because of me. I all but held my breath, waiting to see what happened next. Torn on which results I wanted more.

Grant crossed the room, arms moving as he approached. I couldn't catch his signs, but then again they were in my peripheral. I continued to hold Nica's stare, as she did for me. This had gone past surprise, past polite gaze. We had something here, something stronger than the ethics of her job.

She broke the stare, turning to Grant, and I glanced down at my shoes. I couldn't mess with her job, not when I worked so hard for my own. Still did. My job was a part of me. Who was I to mess things up for someone else?

Grant waved. *"Get over here."*

Each step had cosmic implications. My feet felt heavy, each stride held an importance or signification, or some shit. I couldn't explain or describe it. I just knew Nica was special and moments like this were not to be wasted.

She had her bottom lip between her teeth, cheeks rosy, and the image went straight to my dick. I needed to stop this train of thought now before my track pants gave me away.

"They've never been rock climbing before," Grant signed, mouth moving.

"Oh really," I asked in both languages, hoping for any excuse to get

up close and personal with Nica.

"… never… the chance, right, Nica?" Lexie said.

Nica shook her head, hand pressing on her forehead. "*No, you never mentioned. This is a set up. A trap. And I…*" Her hands lowered. Her eyes, warm pools of brown, locked on my own. Two quick breaths that did nothing for my building libido, and she turned sharply and headed for the hall.

I jogged after her, catching up on the other side of the double doors. She had stopped, leaning against the wall, those frequent breaths making it damn hard to keep my gaze on her face. But her eyes were closed, and somehow I all but felt the whirlwind of emotions floating around inside her. I barely knew her, yet this was no stranger. Not to me.

Everything in me screamed to get out now, this was how Mom trapped Dad. But leaving wasn't an option. I settled against the wall and placed a hand on her shoulder.

Without opening her eyes she signed, "*I should go.*"

I waited and when she opened her eyes I had to fight against hauling her in for a kiss. "*Probably. But I'm not looking for anything other than a good time. Stay. Have fun. Or do you not have fun?*"

One side of her mouth quirked, then fell. "*I work with frail elders, often times unable to meet all their needs.*"

"*So you need a stress release.*" I inched closer, unable to resist, wanting a much different stress release than climbing. "*Consider this a coincidence, like meeting with the elders. We climb, we laugh, we go our separate ways. Or I can leave and you and Lexie can climb. No harm done. No foul play. Just two adults meeting in odd places. Is that really against your ethics?*"

Her smile was closer to a grimace. "*Little bit. I shouldn't be here with you.*" She shook her head. "*And I sound like a broken record. I'm sorry, I really am. You visiting your grandmother tomorrow?*"

"*Not tomorrow. I'll visit again over the weekend.*" She had been full of life, sparks of her usual vibrant self that morning, no doubt due to this thing with Nica. I'd breathed a little easier all day since. A group of teenagers raced past us, creating a wind tunnel. Nica didn't move, didn't sign. She stood there, staring at me. "*What's wrong?*"

She placed a hand on my shoulder and I didn't miss this was Veronica the social worker who'd come out to play. "*I saw her at lunch. She's sliding.*"

"*No, she was showing more of a reason to fight, she was going to hold on.*" All my emotions, everything shifted enough that I could have stood on quicksand. One moment my world faced upright, the woman I wanted in front of me. The next, none of it mattered.

"*I'm sorry.*"

My mind spun in a million directions. The momentary hope vanished, replaced with the bitter dread. Reality was going to bite me on the ass. I fell back to the wall, my head against the hard surface. Here I'd been climbing and interacting with Nica, while my grandmother lay in a small bed, dying. I studied the exposed beams of the ceiling, trying to hold myself together.

Two hands settled on my shoulders, and then a soft body pressed against mine. Nica placed her head against my chest, wrapped those arms tight around me. I crushed her against me, not able to hold back anymore. Not when my world fell apart, and she was the stability I craved.

I placed two fingers under her chin, bringing those fathomless eyes up to mind. We were so close, inches apart. One shift from either of us and our lips would meet, and I knew too well how good she'd taste. The blacks in her eyes deepened, but neither of us moved, remaining in this eye lock. And even though no one moved I all but felt her hands over me, her body under me, her lips on me. With her frequent breaths, she had to feel it, too. Best damn chemistry I'd ever had, and it was with the one person who needed to stay away.

She felt good in my arms, right even. And that scared the crap out of me. For the first time in my life I understood why my father did whatever my mother said. But I would never understand the extent he rolled over, belly up, even while hurting me.

I let go of Nica. "*Thank you. Now, let me show you how Grant's gym works, it's the least I can do.*"

*****

Nica

I tugged at the rope around my waist, then on the end connected to the wall in front of me, following the different colored hand holdings until my neck hurt. I wasn't afraid of heights, but I'd also never thought I'd do something like this.

Lexie stood beside me. To anyone else she'd appear calm and cool, but I saw the slight shift in her shoulders and fingers. I pointed to the top of the wall. "You sure about this?"

She forced a smile that leaked false bravado. "Of course."

"Why don't you just admit we aren't here to climb?"

She fisted her hands on her hips. "You could be off climbing all over Cam right now, but, no, ethics, so instead we climb." She swallowed, eyes on the wall, and I knew right then and there I'd be climbing alone.

Cam and Grant came over, and Lexie pointed to the wall. "That's tall."

Grant grinned. "A small wall wasn't going to bring in the crowds."

Lexie sucked in a breath, and I turned to Cam, far too aware of his presence. His eyes raked over my body, making me tingle and want his touch in ways I had no right to do, reminding me of our night together and how good it felt. I tried to convince myself it was the alcohol that made it so good, but when standing in front of him doing nothing turned me on, I knew it wasn't the intoxication. Then he pointed and I realized he checked out my harness, and even though it made no sense, I deflated. "*That comfortable?*"

I raised a shoulder. Were harnesses supposed to be comfortable? Certainly no different than the throbbing I felt that wouldn't get any release. Not at least until I made it home.

He stepped into me, reaching to my waist to tug on the ropes, and I had to hold my breath. All the nerve endings within a foot radius of him sparked to life, practically getting off through proximity alone. I had to lock my knees before I embarrassed myself. I really should have taken him up on his offer to leave, rudeness aside; this vibe between us grew too strong. I wanted to reach out and touch him, but he stepped back, giving me much needed space and air. *"Looks good, you ready to try this?"*

No, but if I climb I can get away from you. I managed to smile and since Lexie and Grant chatted, Cam went over some rules and techniques. He held onto the ropes as I tried to figure out which holdings to grab. Somehow my attempts to stay away from this man had turned into him being the one in control of whether I fell to the ground and broke my arm or not.

Wall, focus on the wall. I grabbed a blue holding and hauled my body up, stepping on a yellow one. Then reached for the next one I could grab, this one green, before leaving the comfort of the floor. Lexie stood at the wall next to me, and I grew hopeful she'd give this a try. After all, she was the thrill seeker of the two of us.

I made it a few feet before stopping and looking down. Cam stood with legs spread, steady and sure, holding onto the rope. From my height his hair flopped over his forehead, calling for my touch.

"You okay?" he asked, removing one hand from the ropes and causing me to grip the wall tighter.

I managed to let go of a yellow holding. *"Fine."*

"You don't look fine."

"Oh, and you did so well the first time you climbed?"

"Grant's been into this since college, I still thought I was Superman back then."

I drew myself up another level and then turned back to him. *"So Superman but not Batman or Wolverine?"*

"Careful, you're mixing up Marvel and D.C."

"Is that a problem?"

He smiled and even from my position I caught the glint in his eyes. *"Depends on your nerd level. Comics aren't really my thing."*

"Same. But climbing is?"

He tugged on the rope, not enough to throw me off, but enough I felt them, and considering they went around my waist and between my legs, it had an erotic feel that I would not have anticipated. So much for cooling off.

"*Yes, climbing is. Get to the top, then you'll get it.*"

I nodded and returned to the wall, eager to place more distance between us, though I feared I could move across the ocean and still feel his magnetism.

Lexie still had a foot on the ground, and Grant was hands on showing her how to move. Another time, a different life, and that could have been Cam and me. No, scratch that; we'd be off in an office somewhere tearing at each other's clothes.

My breath hitched and I wiped my mind, focusing on the wall. Tonight the only thrill I'd feel was reaching the top, then going home alone.

Chapter 7

Cam

We climbed until the gym closed. Or rather, Nica climbed as Lexie barely made it off the ground. The momentary panic from Nica's concerns over Grandma had left, only to return like a sledgehammer when I arrived home. So I worked until the moon angled down into my view, then a little longer. It was after one by the time I fell asleep—but at least I slept for a few hours. In the morning even thoughts of work couldn't keep my grandmother out of my head. It spun until logic leaked from my ears. I struggled with putting coherent thoughts together, with making sense out of any damn thing. I skipped the gym, grabbed a large coffee, and settled into work early. Nica's warning flashed through my head.

Grandma couldn't be ready.

I wasn't ready.

The day crashed around me. Each step of my job, a job I knew so well, became a struggle. After my fourth fuck-up I had to get out of there. If I stayed I'd only produce more work I couldn't handle. I had to see my grandmother. The work would wait. It didn't have a prognosis of a week or two. She did.

That thought alone squeezed my heart tight. How was I expected to be on my usual A-game at a time like this? I wasn't and I was willing to admit that, at least to Matt.

The traffic was thankfully light and with my windows rolled down, I let the fresh air recharge my senses. I focused on the facts: my parents were flying in that day; my brothers, cousins, aunts and uncles had heeded my words and were visiting. One small victory for the baby of the family. Grandma was going to have a busy weekend. She deserved it.

Dread hit my stomach when I reached Hospice House. A sickening sensation that could make a starved man feel full. I signed in and tried not to notice the pitying gaze from the receptionist. I ignored her and entered my grandmother's room.

I almost didn't recognize her.

She sat up in her bed, leaning against pillows. Heavy eyes watched the television. Her hair was half flat from napping. One button popped open on her housecoat, a slight frown on her face. What hurt the most was the dullness in her eyes.

I sucked in some air and counted to ten to center myself before I stepped in front of the television and waved. A smile worked its way over her face, and some light shined back into her eyes. *Not enough, dammit. Nica's right.*

"*Visiting an old lady before seeing a young one?*" Grandma smirked.

I did my best to smile and sat down on the bed, resting one hand on her foot, needing that extra connection. "*You look tired.*"

"*I look awful. I've decided I want to be twenty-one when I die. That was a good age. Before children damaged my body.*"

"*I'm not ready for you to die.*" I couldn't help blurting it out.

"*It's not your decision. It's not my decision either, and I've had a good life.*"

"*Who will whack me on my head and set me straight?*" Grandma was always the voice of reason, my very own Jiminy Cricket.

"*Veronica.*"

I shook my head and started to sign, but Grandma cut me off.

"*You two are meant to be.*" At my stern expression Grandma narrowed her eyes. "*I may be old, I may be deaf, but I am not blind. Don't mess this up. She's perfect for you and you are perfect for her.*"

I glanced to the ceiling, wondering how Grandma remained so positive about love and relationships. Sure, she had the real thing with Grandpa, but when Mom stole Dad away from the family, wasn't that enough to change her mind?

A frail hand landed on my own. "*I know your childhood was difficult. I know your father should have known better, and your mother should have cared more. But they are just two individuals. Don't close yourself off when the right woman is right in front of you. She won't change you, she'll make you better.*"

"*It's not that simple.*"

"*Maybe not now. But when you truly know a person, then you'll know what you stand to lose, or gain, by being with them.*" She touched my cheek. "*I want you to be happy.*"

"*I am happy.*"

Grandma's smile was rueful. "*Somewhat. But you let those scars remain deep inside. The right love will heal you.*"

Her face filled with such determination I didn't bother arguing. I knew some scars remained, and sure as hell mine were deep enough.

*****

My phone vibrated as I made my way to my car. A text. From my mother. I unlocked my doors with more force than necessary. My mother never texted; she much preferred to speak.

Rhonda: Sarah says you never called her back.

I settled in behind the wheel. Was that the strange voice number that called? I never paid them any attention, because anyone that wanted to reach me knew a voice call didn't work.

Cam: I never got her call.
Rhonda: Then I'm going to have to give you her number again. Really, Cameron, it's like you're not even trying.

I contemplated heading back into the building and showing this to Grandma. Surely she'd see why I didn't need a relationship. I still had this parasite trying to set me up. Two women in my life, both with matchmaking ambitions when I wanted neither. Although I had to admit, Grandma's contender tempted me more than I'd have liked.

And that gave me an idea. A little last hurrah win for Grandma.

Cam: That wouldn't be fair to the date Grandma set me up with.
Rhonda: Really, Cameron, someone your grandmother chose? We all know her track record is not worth even considering.

So is yours. I nearly sent the sentiment but she texted again first.

Rhonda: And how is that fair to Sarah?

Oh, two can play this game.

Cam: And how is it fair to my date to cancel?

I tapped my steering wheel. Now I needed to follow through, otherwise Mom would find some way to get back at me, I knew it.
I switched to Nica's thread.

Cam: I need a favor. It'll make a dying woman very happy and piss my mother off. A win-win.
Nica: I'm not sure I like the sound of this.
Cam: Good thing I'm deaf. I need a date for tomorrow to throw off my mother's matchmaking attempts. *Casablanca* is playing at Coolidge Corner.
Nica: It's captioned?

I couldn't stop the stupid grin on my face. I'd kick my own ass later.

Cam: I'll buy ear plugs, you'll watch it like I did with my grandparents when I was a kid. Their plot, much more interesting.

I started my car as I waited for her response, ignoring how much I wanted her to say yes.

Nica: Okay, I'll do it. But only because I'm curious.

I high-fived my wheel then turned onto the road. Getting even with my mother had never been more rewarding.

Chapter 8

Nica

The earplugs didn't diminish all the sound, but it did make it quieter. Not that I paid much attention to the screen anyways. I spent the movie watching Cam, his lively expressions lit up by the projector light and his own enjoyment. If I thought he was handsome before I was greatly mistaken, because here, in the dark theater, he was devastatingly beautiful. He used the images on the screen to create his own story. Up until now I hadn't realized how many interpretations one scene could have.

I wanted to watch more with him, see the classics through his eyes. And then turn on the captioning and decide which we liked better. Which jerked me back from the brink. Those thoughts were of the relationship sort. This was a favor to a friend. That's it.

"You watch a lot of older movies?" I asked once the credits rolled and the lights came on.

"My grandparents watched with me, gave me their love for the classics. I have many of their movies at home." When I moved my hands he cut me off. *"And yes, with captioning."* He shrugged. *"I like some of my other versions better."*

I feared I did, too.

"Want to grab a coffee or some dessert? There's this place I frequent that has the best selection," he said as we made our way out of the theater.

"You had me at dessert," I said too late to remind myself I needed to head home and not find an excuse to spend more time with him.

Cam's smile turned knowing and he began walking. *"Chocolate is the way to your heart I take it?"*

My cheeks heated. *"I'm a non-discriminatory dessert addict. As long as it has sugar, and sometimes when it doesn't, I'm a fan."*

"Oh, I understand. No flowers, only dessert."

I laughed. *"I think you're the first person to get that without me telling them. At work we'll get flowers, or a fruit arrangement from time to time. Mostly loved ones or vendors, sometimes a family cares enough to appreciate us. What I want is a large chocolate chip cookie. Put the message on the front with frosting. Flowers only last a short time, at least food I can eat."*

"Then trust me, you've got to see this place."

Curiosity had the best of me, so I followed. We rode the train further into the city, exiting into the sunny day. We chatted about everything and nothing—the weather, the Red Sox, more old movies, until we turned down a street and Cam halted, jaw suddenly clenched tight, eyes trained across the street at what appeared to be an apartment building. Or perhaps he eyed the tall, leggy brunette who strolled up the street from the opposite direction.

Cam turned to me. *"Sorry,"* he signed before crossing the street. I checked for cars and followed.

He intercepted the woman at the building doors. "Sarah, what are you doing here?"

I stayed a few feet back, feet glued to the cement. The woman, Sarah, sized me up, eyes appearing to take in every flaw I owned, from the frizz in my hair to the way my toes tended to point inwards. Not a pleasant experience. I straightened my spine.

"Am I late? Your mother said to meet you here." She thumbed to the building, and I had a funny feeling this was where Cam lived.

Cam rubbed a temple, a slight shake to his head, and I wondered how much he could understand. Sarah's ruby painted lips didn't move a whole lot when she spoke. Heck, if this was a scene from the movie he'd probably have someone off screen talking. I received my answer when he yanked his phone from his pocket and handed it to her. She sighed, resting a hip against the exterior brick, pecking at the screen with nails that matched her lips and required several inches of space between skin and object.

She handed the phone back, and Cam's shoulders inched closer to his ears as he read. "My mother mentioned nothing to me. I'm sorry to have wasted your time."

"It doesn't have to be a waste, I'm here now." She flipped her hair back. I had no clue why she remained; Lexie communicated better with Cam than she could.

Cam's face scrunched up, clearly still not understanding her. She deemed his pause as encouragement and stepped closer. I wasn't one to be jealous, certainly not with someone I was definitely not seeing, but a twinge travelled up my spine, and if she moved one more step I'd break her overgrown nails off.

I moved in beside Cam, placing a hand around his waist as though he belonged to me. "I'm sorry you're here now, but so am I, so you'll have to find some other way to occupy your time." I signed as I spoke, hoping to catch Cam up on what he missed.

Sarah's eyes narrowed. "His mother won't be happy."

I gave her a smile, fake as hell. "I don't care what his mother thinks."

Cam's arm wrapped around my waist, holding me closer to him, and I tried not revel in the feel of him so near. Or how shockingly right he felt. "Fine." She held up a hand in a phone gesture and winked at Cam. "Call me." Then she hobbled away, hips swaying so much I worried she'd hurt her spine.

Cam's forehead met mine after she rounded the corner. My heart swelled, and I wanted to run my hands up his back, over those muscles, and bury my fingers in his hair. The intensity shocked me, and I remained still, barely breathing. His chest rose and fell, and I placed my hand over his heart, strong pectoral muscles and fast heartbeat messing with my senses. How easy it would be to forget everything, even the fact we stood outside, and give in to the magnetic attraction between us. The more time that passed the harder it was to remind myself why we couldn't do this.

Then I remembered. My job. My clients, and as much as it pained me I couldn't give in. I stepped back, bringing some much needed air between us, and didn't miss how this felt more wrong than bringing my lips to his.

He ran a hand through his hair, a slight laugh breaking the tension, but not the desire. *"Sorry about that. That's why I needed your help today, my mother's idea of a good match for me."*

"And Sarah thinks dating you is a good idea? You can't communicate."

He shrugged. *"Mom doesn't understand and would feed her lies. Now I believed I promised you dessert?"* He pointed across the street, and I noticed the pink canopy that housed the bakery. We crossed and one step inside was all it took for the sweet aroma of chocolate and sugar to attack my nose in the best way possible.

Almost as good as sharing breathing space with Cam.

"This smells delicious," I signed, taking in the multiple display cases.

Cam waved to the man standing by the register. *"Best place around. Pick your preference."*

"You have time? Because this will take a while."

I caught his smile from my peripheral as I continued to scan over cookies and cupcakes and pastries. *"Plenty of time. You helped me with Sarah, it's the least I can do."*

I nodded and then kept my eyes away from him, the desserts fading from view. For a moment, I wished we were real, a couple out buying dessert and bringing it home for a quiet afternoon in. I pushed that aside and focused on the sweets—safer territory.

"What do you like?" Cam asked, sliding up next to me.

My gaze roamed the dessert display. *"Oh, a little of everything."*

He didn't respond and I turned to him and the smile on his face I didn't quite trust. *"We can do that."*

I scrunched my face. *"Do what?"*

"Taste test. A little of everything."

I laughed, but he didn't. *"You're serious?"*

He nodded. *"There are chairs over there, and they have some great coffee."* He nudged my shoulder. *"What do you say; let's find out what you really like?"*

74

A part of me wondered if this was him trying to crack my code, but I knew my love of a wide variety of sweets would keep him guessing. *"You're on."*

Chapter 9

Cam

I left work early to visit Grandma, for no other reason than a gut-deep intuition. Many different worst-case scenarios ran through my head during the long drive. Worst-case scenarios all too close to becoming reality.

When I arrived at the front desk the receptionist held up a finger, urging me to wait. She picked up the phone and made a quick call. I kept my hands in my pockets, wearing the seams to the point where I wouldn't be surprised if the loose change fell to my socks. I prayed it wasn't too late. I hadn't seen Grandma since Saturday, giving the rest of the family time to visit. No one had warned me that anything was amiss, yet something was obviously wrong. They never made me wait before. A few tormenting minutes later, one of my grandmother's nurses approached, scribbling on a pad of paper.

She handed it to me and rested a hand on my shoulder.

Her pain has been increasing, and we've had to up her medications. She's not herself anymore and is dozing on and off. I wanted to warn you, to prepare you.

My hands shook but I managed to thank her for the warning. I wanted to ask if this meant the end was near, but she was here so the end was always near. Each step felt like a hundred, my feet dragging along the carpeted floors. When I reached the room I froze. Tempted to run, I dug in my heels and wished Nica was there to support me.

I found Grandma lying in bed, watching television. Her face

appeared thin and frail in the dim lighting. Her skin grayish, her eyes dull. She looked up at me and smiled weakly, signing "*I-love-you*" with a barely raised hand.

I fought against the burning in my eyes and talked, her listening with the same compassion she always had. I talked about how work was going, how even with all this time off projects were still running on schedule. I had a wonderful team that made me proud. I talked about Nica. How special she was. Mostly I told Grandma how much I was going to miss her.

"*I will always be with you, inside,*" she told me.

I hugged her and kissed her cheek. Then I stayed by her side, holding her hand, as her heavy eyelids closed and her breathing slowed. Through her open shades the sky shifted into shades of red and purple, day slowly turning into night. The changing colors of the leaves swayed in the breeze, the world somehow at peace and built on this damned cycle of life and death.

I don't know how long I sat there, but at some point the hand in mine slacked, growing cold. When I focused on Grandma again her chest no longer rose and fell. The same peace that existed outside spanned her face. She was gone.

*****

Nica

My lobby buzzer pulled me from reading a book. I blinked the room into focus, trying to figure out who could be visiting. Coming up blank, I pushed the button and called down, greeted by nothing but silence. An inkling gripped me, and I fumbled with my cell and noticed a missed text from Cam. I quickly buzzed him in as I loaded the message.

Cam: I need to see you.

I went cold at his words. He was always playful with his texts before. My heart pounded. Cassie couldn't be gone already, could she? I paced the apartment, waiting for Cam to make it to my floor. What felt like an eternity later, he knocked and I opened the door.

His eyes were bloodshot, not even the hint of a smile on his face. "*Oh no*," I signed. I drew him into my apartment and flung my arms around him. Once inside my embrace he broke down. With my own tears streaming I held his head close with one hand, the other rubbed his back.

I stood there for a long time, letting him fall apart in my arms. My heart clenched at the loss, at his naked emotion, and I struggled to keep myself in check, to be his support. He tested my resolve. I held onto my social worker hat with a fierceness, keeping his needs the central focus. Once he moved his head off my shoulder I grasped his hands and tugged him over to the couch. He followed without protest, his legs crumbling like jelly when I pushed him to sit.

"*Are there any calls you need to make?*"

He shook his head. "*I did that before I got here. My parents and aunts and uncles are working on the arrangements.*"

"*What can I do?*"

His glossy eyes and enlarged pupils, full of sorrow, soaked me up like a sponge. "*I don't know.*" He seemed so lost and broken. I wanted to kiss him, anything to soothe him, even for a short while. But that wouldn't be what he needed, and I had to keep the distance. Instead I found an old movie to keep his mind occupied and did my best to come up with a storyline more intriguing than the captions.

*****

Cam

The following morning I woke up to a cat perched on my chest, whiskers brushing my face. Her yellow eyes sported black circles; her paw rose for attention. I scratched her head as the ache in my chest settled back in.

My grandmother was gone.

The tears started again, and I let them slide down my face. Light bled through the shades into Nica's living room. I had no idea the time. Didn't care. The discomfort of the couch nothing compared to my insides.

The bedroom door opened and Nica appeared, hair almost a light brown with dampness. A weak smile formed over her face, coupled with a haunting sadness that matched the hole in my heart. She sat on the edge of the couch and deposited her cat, Oreo, on the floor. She brushed away my tears, her own eyes full and heavy.

"*You want some breakfast?*" She rubbed her other hand over my stubble-riddled jaw.

I shook my head. Was I hungry? Probably. Did I care? Couldn't.

"*You OK?*" she signed so small I almost missed it.

Her image blurred before me, and I forced my eyes shut to keep the moisture inside. "*I'm fine,*" I managed to sign. She touched my shoulder, and I opened my eyes.

"*You're not; don't force yourself to be otherwise.*" She rubbed her hands together. "*I need to get to work. There's a spare set of keys in the kitchen. Text me if you need anything, OK?*"

I nodded as she stood and returned to her room. My mind was numb, not thinking, not registering. I ached deep inside, feeling hollow, empty. Pointless. I wasn't going to work, couldn't put two and two together, and Matt had insisted on bereavement leave. I would meet up with my parents later on to go over funeral arrangements. Then we were to clean out Grandma's room at Hospice. All I wanted was to stay in Nica's apartment, even if Nica wasn't there.

*****

By mid-morning I needed a wall to punch. I'd been excluded from the funeral arrangements. Six adults crowded around a table, all but ignoring me. I couldn't lip-read and follow them all. When I left I thought the argument involved which caterer to use. At not even ten in the morning, with their mother dead, they argued over food. I hadn't even eaten breakfast, and I couldn't care less about my next meal.

I had been the one chosen to handle the burden of caring for my grandmother, but not to help with the arrangements. Or perhaps it boiled down to the big family joke to keep the Deaf members secluded together. Didn't they think that maybe, just maybe, I knew her wishes? No, of course not. All they cared about was what the fucking deli platter looked like.

I brought my bad attitude to Hospice House to collect Grandma's belongings. The emptiness of her room hit me square between the eyes. The small, cozy place seemed large and cold. The wide open shades let harsh sunlight into the room. The bed had been changed and made up. All that remained were a few belongings and the meteor-sized hole in my heart. Empty box in hand, I picked up the picture frames sunbathing on the mantel and placed them inside. When I made it to my own photo, my college graduation picture, a folded piece of paper slid to the floor.

I placed the picture in the box and bent for the letter. In Grandma's shaky writing I read "Veronica" written on the top of the paper. I opened it, desperate to have some contact with my grandmother again, even if not directed to me.

Veronica, I am sorry if you and Cameron cause any problem for your work. I never want you to have problems. I saw something special in both of you that work well together. I hope you have seen it. Thank you for giving an old woman some hope.

Cameron, make sure she gets this.

I had my first laugh since her hand went cold in mine. I didn't know where things would go from here with Nica, all I knew was that when I needed someone I turned to her without even thinking. Which meant perhaps I needed to see if my grandmother's death changed things.

Chapter 10

Cam

I sat in the large holding room at the funeral home. The furniture, walls, and floor came in different neutral tones, comforting yet somber. Couches and chairs lined the walls, able to accommodate a large or small family. In addition to my black suit and tie, I wore a black yarmulke on my head. Mouths moved all around me. Hands remained stationary, clutched items, or moved in non-language motions. My parents chatted with one of my aunts. My two brothers chatted with their wives, their children running around the small space; my four cousins and their spouses were in small groups talking, along with their children. I was the only one sitting, the only one mourning.

The crowd was a revolving door as other family and friends stopped by to pay their respects. I received a sad smile, nothing else. The two interpreters I'd arranged for the funeral stood in a corner, all but not needed as my family continued to ignore me. In the past I had my grandmother at family events, before that both my grandparents. Now I was the only Deaf member.

I had a sudden stab of guilt for all the family events I missed due to work. Events I knew someone had arranged to pick up Grandma. I'd left her alone in this mess. Now I'd be alone for the rest. At least the punishment fit the crime. To think I'd been absent due to my career, due to trying my damnedest to make something out of myself. To prove to some of the people in this room that I could. I hadn't meant to hurt anyone, at least not Grandma. I scrubbed a hand down my face. It had been worth it, hadn't it? Or did life intend on throwing more bricks on the house I so carefully built?

Black peep-toe shoes entered my line of vision, forcing me to scan up a long pair of legs to a short black dress, and up to Sarah's face. If this had been Nica, the view would be cock hardening. But on Sarah it left me cold.

Her ruby painted lips quirked, but she may as well have been a ventriloquist act. In fact, I'd often wondered why she hadn't pursued that as a career. I shook my head and turned to my interpreters, finding Maria already joining us. Once we made eye contact she signed Sarah's words. *"Where's your girlfriend?"*

Crap. Not the place I wanted to be discussing my personal life. Or whatever fabrication of it I needed to get Sarah off my back. "She's at work, she'll join later." Maria knew my communication style and didn't flinch at my verbal response.

Sarah eyed Maria with a heavy dose of distain, and I resisted the urge to glance up towards the heavens. The funeral of a Deaf person should not be a place to question appropriate communication access. But I blamed my mother on that one. Sarah's lips twitched, eyes still on Maria. I caught Maria explaining for her to face me. *"Then it's not that serious."*

Tiredness seeped into my bones—and the day had barely begun. I gave Maria a nod and raised my hands, time for a little show and tell. *"It's serious enough. And I prefer to date people who know ASL."*

Again, she watched Maria, as though she had her own hearing loss. She flipped her hair over her shoulder and walked away. Maria signed her parting shot. *"Discriminate much?"*

I rubbed my temple. *"She has no idea what discrimination really means."*

Maria smiled, keeping herself professional and neutral. I thanked her and she returned to her corner. Not two minutes later the couch shifted and Dan, my oldest brother, sat next to me. *"Rumor has it you're dating someone."* Dan had the same brown hair as me, though graying around the temples. With twelve years between us, he was more of a parent figure than brother.

I took in the tease in my brother's eyes. *"What did Grandma tell you?"*

"So it's true? You and the social worker?"

Only my grandmother could cause problems at her own funeral. Doubly so, because I didn't know exactly what to call Nica and my relationship. *"Sorta."*

Dan slapped me on the back. *"Finally getting some romance in now that you're thirty. Maybe by forty you'll settle down."*

I had no intention of giving someone that much control over me, but now wasn't the place. Though I had to admit, Nica made the prospect worth exploring.

Dan shot his eyebrows up twice and moved away, his motion for *"I'm getting your ass in trouble."* I nearly groaned.

Dan closed in on our mother and faced me as he spoke. "Hey Ma, Cam's finally dating someone."

I wasn't up for this. Lip-reading about my personal life was never a fun activity. My second interpreter moved, ready to assist in the communication, but I caught her eye and shook my head. In the interest of family harmony for the next few days I had to handle this alone.

My mother stood in front of me. She brushed back my hair as though I was an incompetent child. "Cameron, why... said anything?" After a lifetime of communicating with her it was still a guessing game. I focused on her lips and did my best to put the pieces of the puzzle together.

Because you never listen, and the woman that raised me was dying. "I told you about her last week." I fisted my hands by my side to keep them from signing.

Mom slapped Dan's arm, mouth flapping while she faced her hearing son.

Dan stepped behind her when she turned her head and interpreted. *"A week: that means nothing in guy language."* Then he stepped forward. "It does in Cam language." Unlike our mother, Dan knew how to speak to me and be understood. The subtle ASL shifts to his hands helped.

83

"… calling… brother a girl?"

I dropped my head into my hands and welcomed the momentary silence. I *really* wasn't up for this today.

Dan kicked my foot and forced me to raise my head. "Look at him, Ma, he looks like Ben when he brought Zoey home."

"Ben always looks… it doesn't mean…"

Regardless of anything, Nica had carved out a spot for herself in my life. I didn't know what that meant, beyond "It means something."

"… brush… Sarah."

"I never asked for or agreed to that date." What I said next would make things worse all around, but I needed to say it. "I can find my own dates." *I can take care of myself.*

Our eyes locked. She broke contact first. She always did. "… she coming… support you…?"

I nodded, even though I knew it wasn't just about me, it was also about Grandma.

They left me alone after that, back to staring at the black screen on my phone, until the couch shifted again. I glanced up at Grant in his one and only suit, a gray one. Matt and Ashley stood nearby dressed in black.

Grant crossed his arms and checked out the surroundings. He turned back to me. "*You OK?*"

I shook my head.

Ashley sat down on my other side and wrapped an arm around me. "*I'm sorry.*"

Grant thumbed towards my mother. "*She behaving?*"

I found Mom laughing in a carefree manner with a family friend. "*So far.*"

One of the interpreters waved for my attention. She stood next to the Rabbi and interpreted. The Rabbi asked for friends and extended family to leave. Grant patted my knee as he stood up, Ashley squeezed my shoulder, and Matt remained silent as the three of them left.

Once they were gone the Rabbi addressed the group. My father and two aunts, Grandma's children, were given black ribbons, placed on their clothing near their heart. They were the only immediate family of Grandma's still alive; she had outlived everyone else. The Rabbi recited a prayer as he tore the ribbons up the center, a symbolic act of tradition, indicating the torn heart from losing a loved one. My own heart ached at the process. Grandchildren didn't receive ribbons, even though this woman raised me. My father remained emotionless. My two aunts fought back tears, only one succeeding. The rest of the family was finally somber. One cousin crouched down low, talking to one of the younger great-grandchildren.

I hoped I would find some peace in the process, rather than the dread. The final pages in my grandmother's life were being written and sealed. Only the family left behind. I glanced around the room, wondering if we would all be together again. Perhaps just for big events. Though with me being the only single member, there was little in the way of weddings until the next generation became older, only a few Bar and Bat Mitzvahs for the younger children. I scanned the aging generation. *And funerals.*

*****

Nica

I had five folders on my desk and had written up two visits in the early quiet of the office. My dark suit had me overdressed for the casual office environment, and I shifted uncomfortably in the confining material. I ignored all sounds around me, concentrating on getting as much done as possible. A hand over mine stopped me.

"Relax, Nica, what's gotten into you?"

I glanced up to see Rebecca leaning over my desk. She studied me, and a frown formed on her face. She dragged a chair over.

"You've been acting off all week, what gives?"

Heat settled in my cheeks and my pulse flicked at my veins until they resembled a guitar in use. "Remember that guy?"

"You saw him again?" she whispered.

I closed my eyes against the view of my client listing. "Yes."

Rebecca clutched my chin and made me face her. "Why are you acting like a kid who got their hand stuck in a cookie jar?"

My heart had to be beating loud enough for her to hear. I glanced around, but our pod was empty. Still, I kept my voice low. "I bumped into him at Hospice." While Rebecca's eyes went wide I quickly updated her on the whole mess. When I finished she remained quiet, not even moving. "Say something," I whimpered.

"How's your client?"

I smoothed down my skirt. "Cassie passed away."

Rebecca checked me out from head to toe. "You're going to the funeral."

I didn't nod, it wasn't needed.

Rebecca leaned back and sighed. "Of course you are. The real question is who are you going for?"

I focused on the folder open on my desk, and the one under it. Yes. I wanted to pay my respects to Cassie, as I'd often done for clients near and dear to me. But even Rebecca knew Cassie wasn't the main reason. I rubbed my temples. "I know, it's bad."

"That's putting it mildly."

"But what would you do?"

Rebecca raised her eyebrows. Of course, not see Cam again. A fact getting harder and harder to follow. She straightened up, but her eyes were on me, reminding me this was my friend beyond coworker. "You really do care for him, don't you?"

More than I had any right to. "If I didn't, I wouldn't be in this mess."

"Then go, but perhaps go as Cassie's case manager, not, whatever you are with Cam."

"Friends. Only friends. And thanks."

Rebecca moved back to her desk, but I didn't miss her slight head shake that doubted my proclamation. I knew Cassie would hurt more than Vinny, but I didn't expect it to hurt this much. It was like losing my own grandmother, which was exactly what Cassie wanted. The old woman should have had a career in matchmaking.

I continued plowing through my work. I was down to my last file when a phone call about a missing homemaker delayed me. Once the worker was located I raced out and made it over to the funeral home. By the time I arrived everyone was already inside. I snuck in the back, half listening to the Rabbi speaking. I quickly found Cam sitting up front, eyes trained on the interpreter, shoulders slouched forward. My heart ached. I wanted to go to him but knew that wasn't a good idea. Instead I went to take a seat in the back. A waving hand caught my attention.

June sat with a group of Deaf elders, also watching the interpreter. I slid in next to her.

"*So sad, poor Cassie,*" June signed.

I wrapped my arm around her. "*Nice that you are all here,*" I said.

"*Same.*"

I turned and found Cam again. He glanced my way and caught my eyes. A half smile formed for a second before fading. He sat separated from everyone else. All others were at least a couple, with several kids babbling around parents desperate to keep them quiet. The group was almost lively. Cam wasn't. My heart constricted further.

June poked me. "*C.T. is cute.*"

I held in a laugh, too emotionally distraught to think about what I should, or shouldn't, be signing. "*Are you taking over Cassie's matchmaking?*"

June smiled. "*I saw that look.*"

"*What look?*"

June ignored me and turned back to the interpreter, and I wondered how much Cassie had to do with that exchange.

*****

Cam

The September breeze swept a lone leaf across the cemetery,

providing a break from the sun that was a tad too hot for suits. My grandmother's casket lay low in the deep ground in front of me. I held the thin, folded paper in my hands. Flipped to the back, the Mourner's Kaddish was face up. The words meant to offer comfort to the suffering. Half Hebrew, half English filled the page. I knew how to vocalize the words, and would be expected to do so. I didn't want to. The words were meant to be spoken softly in unison, a skill I didn't have much control over. What I wanted was to sign the words, in my language, in my grandmother's language. Or not have them spoken or signed at all. I dreaded having to make this any more real than my grandmother already lying in the dirt.

A hand rested on my shoulder. I wished it was Nica but accepted the comfort from Dan as the Kaddish began. I stood still, watching the interpreter but said nothing. Signed nothing. Instead I found some peace in watching the signs, in the ASL interpretation of Hebrew words no one there could understand.

My father was the first to shovel dirt onto the casket. I turned away, unable to watch his emotionless face. My aunts followed, the dirt and some stones sliding off the shovel and disappearing down the large hole. Family continued the tradition, making a dent in the large dirt pile. My vision blurred as I took my turn, hating the sense of finality the act brought.

People returned to their cars and prepared to head to my aunt's house as the last few people moved the dirt. Soft fingers enfolded my bicep. From touch alone I knew it was Nica. She squeezed before taking her turn with the shovel. When finished, Nica wrapped her arms around me. I settled into her embrace, fighting a losing battle with my tears, as her soft hair blanketed my face.

When I shifted back, she brushed my cheeks dry. *"I didn't think you were Jewish?"* I asked at her unusual level of knowledge of a Jewish funeral.

"I'm not, my father is. Mom raised me. I have to return to work."

I squeezed her hand, not giving a damn what anyone else thought, not when the only comfort I had truly felt had been this moment right here. *"Can you join me later?"*

Nica hesitated, but when she looked at me, really looked at me, all hesitation faded. "*Sure.*"

I nodded and released her hand, making my way back to my family. Nica paused by some of my grandmother's friends, giving them all hugs as they chatted lively with her. I caught June eyeing me and then Nica carefully. I hoped the next generation of matchmaking would at least be kind.

*****

Nica

It was after six in the evening by the time I made it to Cam's aunt's house for Shiva. I liked the ritual—after the funeral, family and friends stop by the house of one of the mourning to pay their respects and support the living. Tradition had Shiva lasting a week, but many people sat for shorter amounts of time. Cam hadn't mentioned how long the family would be sitting here to honor Cassie's life.

When my grandmother died, there had been more laughter than tears, due to all the antics she'd gotten into. And food, so much food. Tradition was for visitors to bring food with them, so the mourning family didn't have to cook for themselves. In that regard I held a package of chocolate chip cookies and hoped Cam would eat as he'd barely touched anything when he'd been at my apartment.

At the front door a pitcher of water and paper towels sat on the step, for those who entered to wash their hands, but I never learned why. My father hadn't done so at any of the funerals I went to with him. The front door stood open, and I stepped inside without ringing the bell as my father had done.

The loud noise of chatter and dishware hit me. People milled about in the open dining room and living room. I checked for Cam but couldn't find him. Instead I was met by a woman in her sixties, with short brown hair.

"Hello? Did you know Cassie?" the woman asked.

I nodded. "I was her case manager at elder services." I held out my hand. "Veronica Anders." I paused and then added, "Nica."

The woman shook my hand. "Nice to meet you, Veronica." *So much for nicknames.* "I'm Rhonda, Cassie's daughter-in-law."

I studied the woman. I had no clue if this was Cam's mother or aunt. Cassie spent most of her time chatting about Cam, not her children. Somewhere in the recesses of my mind I knew the answer, but my mind wasn't working. My stomach lurched. Ethical landmine going off in three, two, one…

"The rest of the family's in the living room." Rhonda gestured behind her. "You can drop off the sweets on the way."

I thanked her and made my way into the house. I'd never made a business-related Shiva call before. Not that my being here was exactly business as usual. I could fool myself about attending the funeral for Cassie. But now? Now was for Cam, consequences be damned.

The dessert table overflowed with goodies. I rearranged a few in order to add my cookies to the mix. I wished I had time to bake something more personal. At least the cookies were from a bakery and not the food store. In the living room almost everyone had plates in their hands. They were talking, laughing, back and forth. Children ran around. Cam sat with his phone in his hands, no food.

I sat down next to him and smoothed down my skirt. "*You need to eat,*" I signed when he faced me.

He put away his phone, a small ghost of a smile crossing his lips. "*I will.*"

"*I don't like that statement.*"

"*Are you going to tell my mother I need to eat?*"

"*Right after you point out who she is.*"

He leaned back and put an arm around the back of the couch; his unbuttoned suit jacket slid to his hips. "*So now you want to meet my family?*" He grinned, his first real one in over forty-eight hours.

"*Might be nice. Your grandmother did tell me a lot of stories.*"

The grin turned cocky. Then he stiffened. Rhonda and another woman with gray hair, who appeared a little older and a lot like Cassie, approached us. The torn black ribbon on the older woman's shirt confirmed she was an immediate family member of Cassie's, must be her daughter. "This is Mom's case manager, Veronica," Rhonda said.

I glanced at Cam for any reaction to the lack of signing from a family member and found none. I had a feeling I was about to understand Cassie's complaints about the family more than I wanted to.

I stood, an uneasy twinge settling low on my spine. The Cassie look-alike turned to me. "I wanted to thank you for everything you did with Mom. She always spoke very highly of you. I know you made things easier. Cameron has always said how easy things were with elder services involved." The Cassie look-alike signed as she spoke, a smile on her face as she glanced back and forth between Cam and me.

I glanced over at Cam, who'd also stood, a bit of color to his cheeks. "Come on, Aunt Kat, stop beating around the bush," Cam voiced, no signs, placing one hand on my back, out of view from the others. He moved his fist in a slow circle and I pegged the sign: *sorry*. "You know what Grandma was always saying, and I know she was talking while at Hospice."

Queasiness bloomed in my gut.

Kat laughed. "Oh yes, Matchmaker Cassandra," she addressed me. "You'll have to excuse my mother, that's just the way she was. From the time I was sixteen she pointed out prospects for me." Kat laughed. "Each one worse than the rest. I joke I married just to force her to stop."

"She really was awful at setting up matches," Rhonda began, her lack of signing grating on me like nails on a chalk board. "I'm much better."

"Don't you start." Kat turned to Cam. "How did you deal with this from both your mother and grandmother?"

So Rhonda was mom. I had a bad feeling about this.

Cam moved his hand off me. "I tuned them both out and found my own dates."

"And yet you followed your grandmother's deathbed advice." Kat smirked.

A lump formed in my throat. I hadn't had a chance to mention to Cam what my role here should be, not that Cassie gave me much of a chance. I needed to find a way to diffuse this problem, but all my thoughts ran blank.

Rhonda shifted to her son. "So that new relationship your brother was picking on you about?"

Cam nodded, the hand signing *sorry* once again on my back. I bit my lip, a wide-eyed doe taking in everything and doing nothing in self-perseverance.

Kat smiled at me. "You made a dying woman very happy."

The conversation soon swayed in other directions, but I caught Rhonda scrutinizing me, and not with a friendly expression. *Landmine partial explosion: check.*

*****

I tugged Cam down a hallway and stopped once we were far enough out of view that any signers wouldn't understand us. *"What the hell was that?"* I asked, all my nerves coming out more as anger than fear.

Cam rubbed my arms, as though he understood. Scarily, I suspected he did. *"I'm sorry. Sarah asked where you were before the funeral, and I had to keep her at bay. I tried to describe the truth to my brother but there wasn't time."*

I placed my head against the wall. *"Of course."*

Cam eyed me, those dark eyes always full of knowledge. *"I can set things straight, but it will ruin your attempt at helping me with Sarah. And turn my mother into a matchmaker again."* He stuck out his bottom lip an inch. Instead of appearing sweet and innocent I wanted to bite it. Hard. Then soothe the sting with my tongue. *"Help keep them out of my love life, at least for a short while?"*

One of these days I'd be able to resist this man. Maybe. I studied the way the hall light created a shadow on the side of his nose. Probably not. *"Fine, but—"*

My hands ended up squashed between us when he kissed me, and my knees weakened to putty. I gripped the lapel of his suit coat, kissing him back with everything I'd been trying so hard to bottle up.

He stepped back, allowing much needed cool air between us.

I struggled to catch my breath. "*Why did you do that?*"

A small smile quirked his lips. "*Just keeping up appearances.*"

Dammit. He had a point. And I'd do it again if it made him smile.

Chapter 11

Cam

Nica had handed me a plate filled with food before leaving for the bathroom. The food had the appearance of sawdust, and I was grateful she wasn't here while I picked at it. The kids ran around the room, but mostly up and down the stairs to the basement, where the XBOX 360 was set up. The adults stood in small groups talking, a sea of black with little to differentiate between individuals. Hands held plates, or cups, or hung limp. Mouths moved. No one signed. I was tired and my head hurt from the constant lip-reading. Each mouth I focused on was the equivalent of trying to lip-read a puppet.

I sat alone, realizing what had always gone on around me and my grandparents. Inaccessible communication. There was no one left in my world.

Made the hole that much bigger, that degree stronger.

I managed to eat a third of the plate by the time Nica returned, a splash of blond hair against all the dark tones. A welcome contrast to all the people ignoring me. Or was that people I was ignoring? Hard to tell. She made her way over, joining me on the couch. A slight dip in the cushion and my mood shifted to a happier state. She held my hand, a thumb rubbing over my knuckles. People continued to chat around us. Nica studied the crowd and then turned to me.

"Tell me your favorite story about your grandma."

I caught her eyes, surprised that she understood what I wanted: to remember the deceased.

"I was eight when Ben went off to college. Dan had already been gone for two years, and now it was just me and my parents at home. I was lonely and isolated and stuck without communication. I complained to my grandmother, and she picked me up one Saturday, brought me to a Deaf event. I can't even remember what the event was for. I remember feeling at home. My grandmother made sure to ask each person we met what their childhood was like. I heard so many stories of not communicating with parents, or forbidden signs, stories from adults comfortable in who they were. On the way home my grandmother told me her own stories. Up until then she had only shared with me the good, now she shared the bad, an almost mirror image to my home life. And I knew I could survive."

Nica brushed away a tear.

"Your turn," I said.

Nica leaned back, one finger tapping her lip. A smile soon worked its way over her face. She glanced around then leaned in.

"About four years ago I had been dating this guy for a while. My nosey Deaf clients knew because they pried the information out of me."

A strong jealous twitch threatened to crawl up my spine. Not a sensation I was used to.

"When we broke up I saw Cassie first. Before I could even open up my papers she forced the story out of me. She then took my paperwork from me and told me all about meeting your grandfather, how sometimes the right person comes along and you need to fight for it." Nica's brown eyes burned into mine. Her cheeks reddened. She angled herself so only I could see her hands. *"Then she pulled out your picture."*

She leaned back, searching my eyes. Cheeks still red. *"I, of course, grabbed my paperwork and got us back on track. For the next ten minutes she answered every question with facts about you."* Nica shook her head.

The smile stretched across my face. *"I think she's very happy right now."*

"No, she's pissed we didn't listen." Nica pointed at my plate, still two-thirds full. *"Eat. You've barely touched any of the food."*

I stared at the plate with disinterest. *"I had some food before you showed up."* I contemplated it, at least. The day was such a blur I had no idea if I'd managed to eat or not.

Nica narrowed her eyes. *"And I've been here for a while. Eat."*

I dug my fork into a piece of pasta. "Yes ma'am," I vocalized, before taking the bite.

Nica laughed. "*Oh please, I work with M-A'A-M's, I'm still a baby at thirty-one.*"

One side of my mouth curved upwards. "*I'm thirty and my mother did teach me to respect my elders.*"

Nica stole a carrot from my plate. "*A year doesn't make me an elder. Don't fight elder age games with an elder service case manager, you will lose every time.*"

I kept my head down. "Yes ma'am," I muttered. Or I thought I muttered. I dared a peek through my eyelashes and saw a slight smile on her face. Muttering accomplished.

"*You don't get along well with your family.*"

I shrugged. "*I'm different, Deafness not included. I'm ten years younger than my middle brother, and he's younger than our cousins. Mom went back to work when Ben started school. I was a surprise and she was enjoying her career. So Grandma agreed to watch me. For the life of me I can't figure out how they came to that arrangement. It certainly worked for the better when my hearing loss was discovered.*"

"*Your parents really don't sign,*" Nica said to herself more than me.

"*Not one word.*" I'd been told Dad knew some signs once upon a time, if not able to express himself he at least understood his parents. Meanwhile I couldn't even use the alphabet with him.

"*Why don't you sign to your mother?*"

"*To prevent WWIII.*" I laughed but Nica didn't smile. "*She feels ASL is a crutch and forced me to speak.*" I contemplated telling her of my hands being taped behind my back but thought better of it.

"*Your brothers?*"

I glanced around but they had to be in a different room. "*They sign. They already knew some ASL from my grandparents, then both kept at it when I was born. My grandparents told them how important ASL was for me. They used to hide with me in our rooms, signing with me, teaching me.*" I still remembered those days. The afternoon light shining into the room as my brothers taught me everything from the alphabet to division to Shakespeare. I learned how to read from their textbooks and homework. "*I missed them when they went to college.*"

"*I'm sure you did.*" Her eyes traveled to the table. "*You finally ate.*"

I followed her gaze to my empty plate. "*I guess I was hungry.*"

"*Told you.*"

She collected my plate and moved it towards the large trash setup near the kitchen. Her curly hair brushed against her shoulders, contrasting against the dark jacket. Her black skirt molded to her curves, curves I knew by touch and taste—gazing at her stirred more enjoyable emotions than I had all day. I had the sudden desire to get the pity out of her eyes. I hadn't been searching for this, never wanted to risk losing myself in a relationship. But I couldn't deny Nica didn't feel like she would manipulate and control like my mother. Nica felt like, well, what my grandmother claimed. A dying woman's last wish. I owed it to her to at least consider it. It wouldn't go anywhere, not yet, but she was fun to tease, fun to be around, especially after the day I had. When she returned, I spoke. "Yes ma'am."

Nica's eyes widened. "*What did you*—" She paused when she saw me, eyes traveling to my lips. I'd convince myself it was the smile, but she lingered, heat shining in those dark eyes of hers. Fate had an interesting way of handling things. Took my grandmother. Gave me Nica.

"*You tease,*" she finally finished.

"*Guilty.*" I lowered my hands, resisting the urge to reach for her. To kiss her. Wrong place, wrong time.

"*I should have known. Your grandmother was a big teaser; of course her grandson would be the same.*" Nica joined me on the couch again.

"*Grandma's favorite trick, or perhaps it was mine, was hiding my hearing aids when I was a kid. They did almost nothing to help me, so we made it a game.*" I laughed at the memory. "*We played hide and seek with them, but we often left the batteries in. Made it really easy for my brothers to win when they played, due to the sounds they made.*"

"*I guess I don't need to tell you the time she somehow managed to get one of your pictures into my paperwork. She didn't even look perturbed when I brought it back.*"

I laughed again, even if a bit shocked at the extent my grandmother went to try to get us together. Not that I really had any reason to be surprised. Nica understood. She understood me and my grandmother, and even if just for the night, I was glad she came.

*****

Nica

I stayed with Cam until his two nephews ran over, yelling, "Uncle Cam, Uncle Cam," their suitcoats flapping behind them. I cringed, expecting them to continue speaking once they arrived. They didn't. They signed, begging Cam to help them with the XBOX. Cam hesitated but I sent him off, the boys jumping up and down and each tugging on a hand as they left.

The room grew airy and cold. I tried not to feel awkward. I was the only person who wasn't family. Like Cam, I was all but ignored and I couldn't blame them. I was surrounded by people I knew only from the bits and pieces of stories from Cassie. Not all of them pleasant. I did my best not to focus on the unpleasant tales and found myself smiling when happy shouts of "Cam's here" echoed from downstairs.

I struggled to keep my smile when Rhonda walked over. The tight-lipped grimace on her face telegraphed bitch. She wore pressed black pants, a white shirt, and a black jacket. She settled in next to me, her movements indicating a desire not to create a single wrinkle. "You're dating Cam."

I didn't know what to do with that sentence. It wasn't a question. It wasn't friendly either. And thanks to the Sarah situation I couldn't correct her. Not that I wanted to with her attitude, much.

"Yes."

"Isn't that a conflict of interest?"

More than a conflict. I had to find some way to diffuse the situation without causing issues for Cam. *Time to deal with the shrapnel from landmine number one. Remember, honesty is the best policy.* "Yes. I was embarrassed when I realized who Cam was. The bottom line is that neither Cam nor I realized who each other was before meeting at Cassie's door."

"I see," Rhonda muttered, her tight-lipped glare increasing.

I mustered up the rest of my strength. "I'm sorry if this is unsettling for you. I've wrestled with the complications. There's something very special about Cam. Your mother-in-law was very excited about us." *And you should know your own son is special.*

I caught her eye. The blues remained crystal cold and threatened to shoot frozen daggers. "I'm only going to say this once so listen well. I don't let just anyone date one of my sons, especially disabled ones. There is a standard to be met, and I expect it to be met. A social worker is not that standard."

I blinked. Of all the possible responses I wasn't expecting that. I clenched my hand into a tight fist. "I believe it's up to Cam who he dates, not you." What I wanted to say was not appropriate for a Shiva house. Heck, it wasn't appropriate anywhere. Did Rhonda really see her Deaf son as disabled? "The person you chose can't even communicate with him. What type of relationship is that?"

"I see then." She stood up, again cautious not to disturb a single fiber on her suit, and walked away.

I placed my head in my hands and focused on my breathing. In and out. In and out. Calm the racing pulse. Was this woman for real?

A few minutes later a hand touched my back. I jumped at the contact before the warmth penetrated, letting me know it was Cam and not Rhonda. I raised my head.

"*You OK?*" he asked.

I knew a white lie was appropriate here, but I also knew nothing I said would surprise him. "*Your mother really doesn't approve.*" Still, I couldn't, *wouldn't* share the rest of what was said.

He rubbed my back. "*That's Mom. You could be everything she would handpick for me, and she still would find a fault. Don't take it to heart.*"

Well, at least we both agreed I wasn't going to be handpicked. But it made me wonder what fault she would find in Sarah, or if that was the proverbial unicorn exception.

"*She did handpick someone.*"

Cam glanced around before leaning into me. "*Someone I'm not interested in. Never have been with any of her non-signing dates. Same with my brothers. We've never humored her enough to see her turn on her own picks. The only person I'm interested in right now is you.*"

My pulse pressed hard against my neck, all but pushing my hair aside. I didn't know what to say. Staying away from this man demanded all my strength. And I was tired. I wanted to curl up with him and let my guard down.

Not yet. Not while surrounded by my former client's family. But the crack in my willpower had solidified. Cam shifted, his island scent luring me to him. I could claim we were just friends as much as I wanted to, but it wouldn't last.

My morals were screwed.

*****

Cam

Due to the late night, and another day left of sitting Shiva, Nica allowed me to spend the night. I did my best to stay out of her hair, my head bent over my phone, handling a few work emails. More than likely confusing people thanks to the pesky "out of office" message Matt had set up. Work didn't wait, not even for bereavement.

Nica moved about in the kitchen in curve-hugging yoga pants and a matching tank top that had my blood pumping. I tugged at my collar, grateful to be out of my tie and down a few more buttons than decent, and kept my eyes on my phone. Work. It had always been my escape, now it would keep me from what I couldn't have.

I sent another email when my phone was ripped out of my hand. Nica dropped it on the other end of the couch as she set down an apple pie in front of me.

"*I wasn't finished with that,*" I signed.

"*You are now.*" She dug a fork into the pie. "*It's store bought, not my favorite but it'll do.*"

I accepted the bite, the sweetness and Nica's interaction making it damn hard to care about my work interruption. *"You saw me eat today."*

Nica dug the fork back into the pie. *"This isn't about food, this is about you taking a much needed break. And about me dealing with your mother."* She took a bite of the pie, determination on her brow.

"I'm sorry about her."

She waved her fork in the air and then dropped it into the pie pan. *"Don't be. I'm glad she wasn't the one taking care of your grandma."* Nica shuddered. *"She would have been the caregiver from hell."*

I couldn't argue with that. *"And what was I?"*

Nica paused while picking up the fork before digging it into our dessert. She fed me a bite. *"You were one of the better caregivers. Concerned and involved, which was strange since you were never around during the day."*

"You don't have to be around to be involved."

"True, but I never knew quite how much you were."

Her eyes held mine, and I struggled to swallow my food, barely tasting it with her right there, looking at me like I was important.

Nica set the pie on the coffee table and shifted closer. She placed a hand on my cheek, eyes large and welcoming. A few more inches and our lips would touch. I wanted to close that gap but kept my spine straight, waiting on her. Her thumb stroked my skin but she didn't retreat. Eyes flickered between mine, as though she had a lengthy conversation in her head. Her lips moved. "I can't fight… anymore." Before I could figure out if she meant for me to understand her or not, she leaned in and brushed her lips against mine. Mixed in with the apple pie, Nica's sweetness created an intense sugar high. I wrapped my arms around her, grateful she initiated and didn't leave me hanging in lust by myself. She melted into me, her curves against my muscles, as though we were two puzzle pieces fusing together. No doubt about it, this woman felt right in my arms.

I ran my hands up her sides, angling my head, licking at her lips, wanting more of her taste and texture. She opened for me, ratcheting up the heat, until I didn't care about anything but her in my arms. How we managed to resist this, to refuse us, I'd never understand.

But none of that mattered, not when she straddled me, taking the kiss deeper, eradicating any thought that didn't involve her. I clutched her hips, the curves that were heaven to me. Familiar, too, like coming home from a long time away—that's how she felt.

Nica drew back, staring down at me, her curls framing her face.

I released her hips so I could sign. *"I don't want to fight this, either."*

"I shouldn't be here. You shouldn't be here. But—" she licked her lips "—*I can't deny I want you."*

I yanked her to me, kissing her with everything I had. She settled against me, body to body, squirming against my overeager erection. My broken heart fused back together at the sight of her so enraptured, so taken with me, when we'd just started.

She shifted up, slow moving fingers working at unbuttoning my shirt, determined to drive my patience. She leaned forward, kissing and licking as my skin was exposed, igniting that raging inferno our chemistry wouldn't let die out. Even with all the space circumstances kept placing between us.

I caught her wandering hands and sat up. I didn't want this to be a stolen moment. I wanted an honest chance with her. *"What are we doing here?"*

She glanced at the outline of my dick with a coy smile.

I tipped her chin up to mine. *"We are more than sex."*

She settled beside me. *"Yes. We are."*

"Date me." My heart pounded in my chest, the intensity of my need for her foreign and unfamiliar and wonderful and scary.

A world of matching emotions swam in her eyes, the now familiar internal struggle I brought out in her. I waited her out. *"All my ethics somehow go out the window whenever you are around."* She brushed her fingers over my cheek, tangling them in the ends of my hair. *"I can't stay away from you. Yes."*

I claimed her mouth again and nothing else mattered. Not my grandmother, not my parents or the funeral or even my job. Just this wonderful woman in my arms. She clutched me to her, hands moving with desperation over my shoulders and under my shirt. I scooped her up and headed to her bedroom.

Once there I deposited her on her bed. I stole a moment, soaking in the site of her. Those blond curls framing her face, the curve of her hip, the way her shirt separated from her pants, exposing a strip of delectable skin. I started there, kissing her stomach, raising her shirt as I moved higher, before taking a cotton-covered nipple into my mouth. Need pulsed deep in my veins, a near tribal beat to claim. But she wasn't a conquest. She was light and joy and pleasure. And life. She arched into me, hair tumbling behind her, so damn beautiful. It wasn't enough. Needing her, all of her, now, I stripped Nica out of her clothes before shedding my own to the floor.

"*Impatient much?*" She signed, propped up on her elbows, naked body enticing every last ounce of my control. Her gaze slid down my body, stopping where I pointed and throbbed in her direction. "*I guess so.*"

She shifted on her knees, kneeling in front of me, before taking me deep into her mouth. I shifted my feet, needing some grounding, before I fell over at the pure pleasure of her lips on my dick. She sucked and licked, as though I were one of her desserts. My balls pulled up tight, every nerve ending I owned trained on what her talented mouth did to me.

But I wasn't coming in her mouth; I had plans for tonight. Big plans. I tapped her head and she let me go, a shit-eating grin on her lips. I claimed her mouth with my own, angling her back against the bed. Then I kissed a path down her body, returning the favor. Her taste the best damn thing I'd eaten in days, and the way her body squirmed under me my own proverbial frosting.

She writhed, her hands fisted in the blankets, head back against the pillows. A damn angel with the powers to stop my heart. I could look at her, only her, forever.

I paused long enough, soaking in the sight of her, that she grabbed hold of my shoulders. "*Now.*" She hauled me to her, kissing me so deep I felt it straight down to my toes.

When I broke free of her clutch—that one was sure to leave scratch marks on my back, *lucky me*—she reached for her nightstand and collected the box of condoms. I rolled one on. She had her bottom lip in her mouth, denting the plush curve. My job. I leaned over her, taking the lip in mine instead. Her body rose up to mine, part invitation and part seductress.

She was flush, her body almost trembling with need. *Mine.* I had no right to think such thoughts. No right to assume, not with my own issues. Yet I wanted to. I moved over her, sliding inside, closing my eyes at how right she felt. Her legs wrapped around me. I stayed there, fully in her warmth.

I lowered my head and ran circles with my tongue around her nipples. Her nails dug into my back, again, as her body shook around me. I knew I was lost in her. All the stress and sorrow of the day, of the week, vanished. There was only me, only her, only this erotic moment.

I moved within her, her face flush, a slight smile on her lips. The age old dance different with her beneath me. Our bodies moved as one, each writhe of hers pushing me harder and faster. I needed this more than I needed anything else, needed this moment with her. Pleasure mixed with comfort, in that strange something we created together. I tried to slow down, make the moment last. Her hips urged me on, coaxing me to give her what we both needed. And I did until the pressure building inside was too much to resist. I burst and fell down into her arms, resting my head in the crook of her neck.

She held me, running her fingers through my hair. I shifted up and pressed my forehead to hers. *"Better,"* she signed.

Yes, this was better. I rolled to my back and held her close.

Chapter 12

Nica

The following morning I awoke on my stomach with an arm around my middle and my feet against a sturdy, hairy leg. Cam. I lifted my head and found him fast asleep beside me. Mouth half open, dark eyelashes brushing his cheeks, a sense of peace on his face. I waited for the guilt to creep in, for this feeling of rightness to evaporate. It didn't. Of course, I still knew it was wrong to tangle with Cam, but with Cassie gone and our attraction only growing stronger, I had to give us a try. In Cassie's honor.

I could all but see her grinning down at us. Which was really creepy so I shook that thought aside. I needed to move and get ready for work, but being so close to Cam had all my good parts nearly purring. On the thought of purring I sat up, finding Oreo curled up between Cam's legs.

At least she approved.

I placed a hand on Cam's shoulder, trying not to get lost in the texture of his skin and all the many reasons I could be late for work, and gave a little shake. His eyelids flickered and the grin he gave me would have melted my panties if I wore any.

"I need to get ready for work, you going to be OK?"

He blinked, and I saw the moment reality hit him, that there were two reasons he was still in my apartment. He rubbed his face. *"I'm fine, you get to work."*

I nodded but didn't move, not wanting to leave him. One side of

105

his mouth quirked, and I knew he got it, he got me. I leaned forward, giving him a quick kiss, before sliding out of bed and heading to the bathroom. I all but felt his laser gaze track my every move and did my best not to sway my hips, too much.

My happy mood faded the minute I arrived at my desk and saw the afghan covering the back of my chair. Cassie had given it to me. I hadn't accepted it, not at first. Took until a third visit which had the afghan being passed back and forth like a hot potato. I wasn't supposed to accept any gifts due to my job. But every once in a while I had to weigh the impact the gift giving would have on my client. In Cassie's case she loved to knit and reported that each family member had too many of her afghans to accept any more. For Cassie, it was important to give something back. Her persistence had the afghan laying on my chair, and her grandson in my apartment.

This whole situation was going to bite me on the ass.

Rebecca dropped her bag on the floor the minute she saw me. "How did yesterday go?"

A shuddery breath worked through as I paused with my fingers on my keyboard. "His family thinks we're dating thanks to a matchmaking attempt. His mother isn't amused." Well, we were dating, now, but I couldn't summon the strength to admit that, not yet.

"Yikes." Rebecca scrunched up her face.

I swiveled my chair and faced my friend. "Cam claims his mother hates all dates he or his brothers bring home, but this is worse." It didn't help the feeling was mutual.

Rebecca sipped from her travel mug. "You don't have to tell me. Question is, does she know how problematic this is for you?"

I sucked in a breath. "Let's hope not."

As I continued working I caught Cassie's name in my system. I let out a long sigh. The case was still active. I forgot to close it down.

Dammit. I clicked open the file and went into the notes. I titled it: *Case Closing.* In the body I typed a simple message: *case closing effective for date of death.* I called Cassie's homemaker vendor to update her. I cancelled all future services and went through the tedious twelve-step process of deactivating Cassie in the system.

In my drawer, I found her file in the section roped off for suspended cases. My thumb brushed over the name on the tab: *Cassandra "Cassie" Thompson*. Absently I opened and flipped through the pages. Services from the last six years were chronicled here, Cassie's shaky signature at the bottom of several forms. Cam's information listed several times, both as emergency contact and caregiver. I closed the folder and rummaged around my desk until I found Cassie's obituary. A picture from several years ago, of a younger and vibrant Cassie, graced the newspaper clipping. I attached the obituary to the front with a paper clip. The folder weighed heavy against my heart as I placed it on my supervisor's desk.

One hand lingered as I parted with the folder, parted with my professional connection.

Back at my desk I stared at my screen for a while, unsure what I was feeling. Numb was the closest I could come up with. Cassie's name was now italicized. When I hit refresh the name would disappear. Cassie was really gone. She was no longer a client of elder services. Did that make things any less complicated between Cam and me? I wasn't so sure.

Desperate for comfort, for a confidante, I grabbed my cell phone.

"Hello?" came a groggy voice.

I cringed. "Sorry, Mom, did I wake you?"

"No, you didn't sweetie, making my coffee now." An elongated yawn came over the line that had me following. "What's wrong?"

"You'll still love me even if I play with ethical landmines, right?"

"What?" She laughed.

I verified my pod was empty. "Your daughter, your flesh and blood, your only child…has found herself in an unethical situation."

"Veronica, you're scaring me, what happened? Are you having problems at work?"

I should be. "Not quite."

"Veronica," the stern voice prodded.

I lowered my voice. "I accidentally…dated one of my client's grandsons." It wasn't a date, per se, but I wasn't about to tell my mother this fact.

"So you went out on a date with a guy and then learned he was related to a client?"

"Yup."

"I'm waiting for the problem."

"His grandmother passed away."

"I'm sorry, sweetie."

"His mother doesn't like me."

"She's grieving, don't read too much into it."

I shook my head, a pointless thing to do during a phone call but one I did anyways. From everything I knew about Rhonda, grieving didn't appear to be her thing. "Cassie was her mother-in-law, I don't think she's grieving too much. And with her stance against ASL I doubt the two ever got along."

"What do you want me to say, Nica?"

I leaned back and sighed, the italicized blue lines from Cassie's deactivated case taunting me. "I sat Shiva last night with a man I've known a week and a family that knows how complicated we are."

I wasn't expecting Mom to laugh. "A week? You really are smitten."

It was pointless to deny the inevitable. "Yes."

"In times of sorrow, in times that are difficult, a person's true colors are shown. You're showing yours. If his mother doesn't like you, then at least you know now and don't have to play footsies with niceties."

Anyone who played footsies with Rhonda probably ended up stabbed. "It's worse than that. Cam communicates in ASL, but his mother forces him to speak to her. Who does that? Would you do that?"

"Sweetie, you've told me stories like this from your studies, from your Deaf friends. Why is this any different with Cam?"

I opened my mouth but no words escaped. I did know many people who grew up like Cam. Those stories didn't infuriate me like this one did. "Because he had Deaf grandparents. His father knew better, his mother should have known better."

"Do you have any idea how invested you sound?"

I paused and thought over my words. How did I end up so invested in Cam? I'd been holding back, knowing I shouldn't have tangled with him at all. Somehow he snuck in, between any protective barriers I placed. And I gripped on tighter than I ever had before. No longer safe territory, not even close. I lay my head on my desk. "I'm in over my head, aren't I?"

"Yup. I'll be waiting on my invitation to meet this man. I think I remember a few of those signs you taught me, so you better not complain. Besides being a grandson of your client, tell me about this guy."

I leaned back. What did I know about Cam? Turned out I knew a lot. I told my mother about his job, and those long work hours that kept us from meeting. About Cassie raising him and him caring for her in return. About his two brothers who were a decade older and either picked on him or got him into trouble.

But my mother wanted to know other details. "Good looking?"

I squeezed my eyes shut and saw Cam's smiling face. "Tall, brown hair the shade of a rich caramel, deep hazel eyes…"

Lips more bitable than brownies. My breath kicked into choppy beats. I forced my eyes open and away from lust-filled daydreams.

"You only use food references when you really like someone. And you seem to know an awful lot about him in such a short time."

Yeah, yeah I did.

*****

Cam

I wandered around my aunt's house, investigating all the pastries on the table. Scones and muffins in multiple flavors had the intrigue of sawdust. Shiva was supposed to be a time to heal. All I wanted to do was get this over with. Maybe if anyone else appeared truly affected by Grandma's death, then I would feel some sense of belonging. Instead I felt more like an outsider than ever before.

My father, with his bifocal glasses and his suit that tugged on his expanding waistline, walked over with a lazy gait Grandma claimed we both had. "*Same legs, same walk*," she used to sign.

It was the biggest connection we had.

Dad placed a hand on my back. "Where's that…?"

I blinked, trying to put the words together, enough to guess, and failed. "Where's what?"

"… that girl…"

Nica? "She's at work."

"Nice that she…" Dad always mumbled the end of his sentences, drove Grandma up a wall. Me too, if I was honest. I wanted to use my hands. The man understood ASL at one point, why did I have to play the speaking guessing game?

I wasn't quite sure what he said and didn't care. "She's grieving, too." I focused on the torn black ribbon Dad wore. It was *my* heart that was torn. I should have a ribbon. Instead Dad would probably stop wearing it once Shiva was over, rather than the month custom dictated. As it was we were only sitting for two days, ending before Friday as required and not resuming for the rest of the week, although I welcomed the quick end to get away from my family.

"Your mom… interesting… dating Grandma's…"

I squared my shoulders and looked Dad in the eye, an easy enough task as we were almost the same height. The fact that he brought this up meant Mom had gone on a rampage. I went on the defense. "As I've said before, I met Nica at a bar, we didn't know who each other was."

"But… didn't stop…"

No, no it didn't. "That's my fault. My own parents delayed flying up. No one was visiting Grandma. Nica understood what I was going through. I convinced her to go out to dinner with me." *With a little help from Lexie.*

"And…?" Dad raised his eyebrows.

"There's something there between us. Grandma knew what she was talking about in regards to Nica and me."

Dad's eyes shone with the start of a fire, a fire ignited by Mom. I wondered what he would think, on his own, but had given up hoping for a miracle. "… professional that worked for Grandma.… conflict between the two of you…? Be careful not to fall…" He shook his head and walked away. As unusual as this situation was, this was the standard response I received from him. I would introduce a girlfriend to my parents, my mother would find a flaw, and my father would try to talk me out of it. And the family wondered why I was still single? Not only did they steer me away from whoever I held an interest in, but they were proof that the wrong match destroyed a person.

For the first time I wondered about the right match. What my grandparents had. What Dan and Ben had.

The pit of my stomach burned with a rage ready to rumble. Complications and all, I knew I cared deeply for Nica. My family would have to deal.

Chapter 13

Nica

"You finally stopped resisting Cam. Good. Except I owe Grant ten bucks. I thought for sure you'd hold out for another week," Lexie said on Saturday as we sat at a local coffee shop. The interior was nothing special: off-white walls, off-white floors, wooden tables. But the coffee could not be beat. We each had pumpkin spice lattes and commandeered a table by the window.

I resisted the urge to throw my head on the table, especially with the few lingering crumbs. "You bet on my sex life?"

"Of course we did. When it's obvious to anyone who sees you that you two are meant to be. Just pissed I lost to him." A sly grin swept over Lexie's face.

"Wait, what was that?" I asked, pointing at my friend. "I know that smile."

Lexie sipped her latte. "I don't know whatever you mean."

I narrowed my eyes. "Are you and Grant hooking up?"

"Not yet. We're toying with the idea. Waiting to see what happens between you two. We're not commitment people. So if you two are good, we'll need to be cordial. But if you two crash and burn, then hey, why not."

I shook my head. "Don't let my sex life mess with yours."

She waved me off. "I'm good. The question is, are you?"

Thoughts of waking up to Cam in my bed that morning swept

over me, along with the way he took me in the glow of the morning light. "I'm powerless to resist him."

"You needed some action, why did you fall in love?"

I stared at my cup, but only saw Cam's face and his infectious grin. "I didn't mean to." The full meaning of my words hit me, and I nearly spilled my drink. "Did I really say that?"

Lexie sipped her coffee, tipping it back further this time. "Yup."

My heart hammered out a frantic SOS code. "I didn't mean that."

"Well, which one didn't you mean?"

I studied the clock behind Lexie, trying to find the truth. After such a short amount of time I truly cared for Cam. And I had no clue what that all meant.

Lexie snorted before I summoned anything resembling words. "You've got it bad."

I had the urge to pace. Damn Cassie for being right.

"So," Lexie said, mischief in her voice, "I think pulling a Nica and messing up this relationship is out of the equation."

"This situation is messed up enough on its own."

"Exactly. Normally Nica would be running by now, not falling. Which has to be scaring the crap out of you."

My head finally met the table, crumbly particles scratching at my cheek, but I didn't care, not anymore.

"Head on table, yup, you're scared. So that leaves 'The Veronica.' I think Cam's got a few more weeks before you pull that, on account of the dead grandmother and all."

I lifted my head and brushed the crumbs away. "Are you putting a time limit on my relationship?"

Lexie leaned back and flipped her hair off her shoulders. "Do you want a time limit?"

No, I didn't want a time limit. I clutched my foam coffee cup until the sides dented. Talk about deep and scary thoughts for a Saturday. I didn't want to stop seeing Cam, that much I knew. But could I open up my heart and allow him to demolish me when, years from now, we stopped working? That day would come, sooner or later. At least with sooner I could dust myself off with ease.

"Okay, deer in headlights look. I've officially freaked out Nica."

I snapped back to attention. I focused on my surroundings again, the aroma of coffee, and Lexie's concerned face.

Lexie leaned forward. "Stop overthinking it. Just enjoy. You obviously are dealing with the big stuff as far as emotions go."

And wasn't that the problem. I was dealing with emotions I'd never expected to experience.

A twinkle of amusement appeared on Lexie's face. "So, I'm thinking of getting a tattoo."

I let my tight shoulders sag in relief. "Thank you for shifting the conversation." I recognized a life preserver had been tossed.

Lexie shrugged. "You needed it."

"A tattoo? You hate needles."

Lexie rolled up her sleeve and admired her arm. "I think I'd look good with a little ink on my skin."

"You. Hate. Needles." I poked Lexie's arm with a pink fingernail.

Lexie jerked back and rubbed her arm at the minor poking. "It would be worth it."

"You'll get a tattoo when I willingly admit my feelings."

"No fair, that's when hell freezes over."

"Exactly."

Lexie's grin turned mischievous. "Except you just admitted there was something to admit."

Not willing to divulge anything, I pointed a finger at Lexie. "If I sterilize a needle will you let me near you?"

"No."

"Then no tat."

*****

Cam

My grandmother's apartment used to feel cozy. Today it was downright suffocating. The small space held my parents, my aunts and uncles, and two of my cousins. There was no place to sit, no place to stand, and no place to escape. Mouths flapped in a place where ASL was the norm. No one here had been able to lend a hand in caring for Grandma, not even when Hospice first became involved. Now their hands were silently outstretched as they picked through her items as if it were a cheap yard sale. I was ready to punch someone.

I moved into my grandmother's bedroom and rolled my tight shoulders in the open space. After a moment of solitude I found the little wooden box by her bed. The box was decorated by a child's hand in markers and stickers. My hand. As an adult I begged her to retire the box, something I spent a few minutes scribbling on decades ago. She refused, telling me she remembered my face filled with pure joy upon giving it to her. I pushed aside the memories clenching my heart like a vise. Inside the box I seized the piece of paper we'd written up together years prior. She didn't believe in a will, much to my chagrin, but she did have certain wishes on how her property was disbursed.

Back in the living room I banged the wall for attention. "Grandma had some wishes on how she wanted her belongings taken care of," I voiced, my throat dry and stiff.

"She didn't... will, Cameron." My mother rolled her eyes.

I needed a moment to process her lip movements and decode her words. Between my eyebrows throbbed, a sure sign of a headache brewing. "But she did have wishes. We wrote this two years ago, when her health took that first big decline."

"Let me..." My father held out his hand. Sucking in some air, I handed the paper over. Hands clasped behind my neck, I walked into the bedroom to get a little breathing space.

I studied the pictures on the wall, ranging from black and white to faded color to vibrant color. Black and white pictures of my grandmother's family back when she was a little girl. They showed a different, simpler time. A black and white wedding picture of my grandparents hung in the center. They appeared young and scared in their formal clothing. Pictures of my father and aunts growing up, color slowly appearing in the photographs, then their weddings, the grandchildren, depicting the vibrant color of modern times. These were the pictures that represented a lifetime, her lifetime, a lifetime now gone.

The lights flickered on and off. I turned to see my cousin, Grace, standing in the doorway. She pointed to the living room. *"Fighting."*

Vultures. *"What's new?"* I said in both languages.

"Your mom's upset over a *name* on the *list,* they *need you,"* she said, her lips moving and using what signs she could.

I glanced to the window. The frame had a tendency to stick. But we were on the first floor. If I could pry it open I could—

Grace shuddered and closed her eyes. *"Your mom screamed your name. Sorry."*

I made my way back into the living room, Grace close on my heels, using me as a shield no doubt. I caught Mom's beady eyes moments before my aunt caught mine.

"Calm down, Rhonda, let the boy explain," Aunt Kat signed and spoke, one of the few willing to go head to head with Mom when necessary. Also one of the few willing to sign and speak in front of her.

Mom said something before she turned and faced me, clutching the paper in her fisted hand. "... write this?"

I sighed. "Yes."

"And Veronica... here?"

I blinked. Did I read that correctly? I stared at her red lips, running the movements over again. "What?" I grabbed the paper and smoothed it back out, scanning the list until I found Nica's name. Sure enough, Grandma wanted to leave her favorite brooch to her. I laughed. "I forgot about that."

When I glanced up Mom still fumed. "Relax, Mom. This was written two years ago."

"She's trying to..."

I rubbed my eyes. I needed some pain meds and an interpreter. Or my own damn mother to sign. "What?"

She gave me a condescending glare. She hated any time I needed something repeated. I sent the glare back.

Mom pointed to the paper. "She's. Trying. To. Get. Items. From.

Frail. Elders." Over enunciating. No one would ever know she had a Deaf son. Well, at least she gave me time to figure out what the fuck she said.

I fisted my hands. "I highly doubt that. Grandma did this because she wanted to." I scanned the list. "She also has a few items for the woman that cleaned her house and the one that helped with the shower." I scratched my head and wondered how I was going to get in touch with them. I hadn't contemplated any of this when we wrote up the list, but that was years ago. I didn't even know if the same women were still involved. I'd have to ask Nica.

The floor vibrated, and I caught Aunt Kat tapping her foot with a great deal of force and nodding towards my mother.

"… isn't appropriate, Cam," Mom seethed. I checked my family and no one made eye contact. A few of my relatives found their shoes particularly interesting. I guessed they were debating how quick of an exit they could make when Mom went into full blowout mode.

"It was Grandma's wishes. That's all." I faced the rest of the room. "If anyone wants it grab it, I know Nica wouldn't feel comfortable taking anything anyways."

"Oh really… two weeks you know…?"

I stomped to my mother until I towered over her. "Yes." By my sides I fingerspelled the word, out of her view. I knew Nica had a good soul, felt it in the depth of my being. Heck, I'd have known her stance on the brooch even before we met in person.

The fire in my mother's eyes didn't diminish. *This is ridiculous. This is how we celebrate a life, by fighting over Grandma's wishes?*

I checked my own rage and reached into my pocket for my keys. I learned a long time ago that I shared Mom's temper, and if we ever went head to head, an explosion of cosmic proportions would ensue. "I'm leaving. Anything on that list for me, put aside. I'll be back next week to finish cleaning up. The leftover furniture can be donated to the building if no one wants them."

With that I pushed past my family, slammed the door, and headed to my car.

*****

Nica

Lexie continued staring at her bare arm. "Perhaps you're right. I don't know what kind of tattoo I would get anyways."

I tapped the side of my coffee cup. "Your dad has tattoos, ask him if you can handle the pain."

Lexie tugged her sleeve down. "Larry wouldn't know."

My phone buzzed, vibrating along the table. I saw Cam's name and snatched it up.

Cam: I left the vultures to their own devices.

My gut clenched.

Nica: Want some coffee?

He texted his order and I had it waiting for him, ignoring Lexie and her "good little housewife" teasing.

Ten minutes later a prickle of awareness hit the hairs on my neck, and I turned to Cam making his way over. The long, easy strides were in contrast to the stiffness in his shoulders. Those bitable lips were squashed into a thin, grim line. His hair more messed up than the first time we met. I knew the instant he found me as his shoulders relaxed and his lips quirked upwards. My heart skipped a beat. To have that effect on him turned my insides into a gooey marshmallow.

"Hi Lexie," Cam signed as he spoke, his voice scratchier than usual as he came close before all but falling into the chair next to me, head in his hands. I rubbed up and down his back, hoping to smooth out the tension.

Lexie grabbed a napkin, dug a pen out of her bag, and scribbled a note. She slid it across the table, in-between Cam's elbows. Through his bent arms I read: *Sorry about your grandma.*

He raised his head and leaned back. "Thanks. And thanks for writing. My brain's a bit fried on lip-reading from my family."

Lexie sipped her coffee. "Nica can interpret then."

I moved my hand to Cam's shoulder and signed with the other. "I'm guessing it was pretty bad?"

Cam nodded. "Turns out Grandma wanted to give you something. Mom's pissed."

"So I don't take it, what's the big deal?"

He let out a laugh and kissed my cheek. "That's what I said. Mom still wasn't happy."

"What was it?" Lexie asked.

I glared even as I made sure Cam understood Lexie. "That's hardly the point here, is it?"

Cam sipped his coffee. He started signing then stopped and waited until he could speak and sign. "It was a brooch she always wore."

The color drained from my face. I turned to Cam, the room tilting off its axis. "What?"

Lexie leaned forward. "He said—"

"I heard him. She wanted me to have that?" I clutched a hand to my chest and willed my eyes not to tear up.

"What's so important about this brooch?" Lexie asked.

I caught a half smile on Cam's face as he awaited my explanation.

I sipped my coffee before answering, letting the memory wash over me. "Cassie always wore her brooch. It was something that was a part of her, like the shape of her nose. One day I was visiting her, years ago. She was having a tough time. Her health was declining, she was feeling old and defeated. So I asked her about the brooch. My own grandmother always wore one and it reminded me of her." I shrugged. "But when my grandmother died my cousin swooped in and grabbed the brooch. I suspect she thought the diamonds were real and wanted to sell it. Whereas I wanted it for sentimental reasons."

I turned and faced Cam. "I never expected her to leave it to me. You have a large family, it should go to someone else."

"But she wanted you for family," Lexie said.

"Shut up, Lexie." I never left Cam's eyes and didn't bother interpreting.

"I suspect you'll appreciate it more than anyone else. I'm sure that's why Grandma wanted it this way."

I broke eye contact. "Well, I will always treasure the thought. The rest isn't worth causing problems."

"*We'll see.*" Cam groaned and grabbed his phone out of his pocket.

I glanced at the display, an incoming text from "Dad." I nudged his arm. "*Answer it.*"

Cam scraped his chair back and headed outside as he tapped his phone. Lexie leaned forward.

"You two are cute together. I haven't seen you this enraptured with a guy since senior year."

"Shut up." I peered through the window and watched Cam pacing outside. The breeze ruffled his short hair. His jaw set stiff. I knew his hand would be clenching. He turned, and I received confirmation as the white knuckles relaxed, only to scrunch up again. Less than forty-eight hours after giving this thing a try and I was in too deep.

*****

Cam

Cars passed by on the busy street, bumper-to-bumper as they inched along. The minute my phone vibrated I knew it would be my father and knew it would be about the battle I'd walked out on. It never mattered the size of the battle; Dad always took Mom's side. I'd spent too much of my childhood praying he'd stick up for me, gave up years ago. Only my brothers would stand up for me, or act as buffers. In this case we were arguing over a brooch that my factory-working grandfather had given to my grandmother upwards of fifty years ago. I doubted the brooch cost more than twenty-five dollars. Hardly worth this fight.

Dad: You know it's not appropriate.
Cam: It was written before Nica and I started dating.

If my parents didn't fly back to Florida in the morning I was going to pretend a restraining order had been issued.

Dad: That doesn't change the inappropriate nature of the request.
Cam: Is it inappropriate because we're dating, or because of her job?

I stopped in front of the large window of the coffee shop and squinted through the metal blinds, where Nica and Lexie laughed. I wanted to be laughing with them rather than having this ridiculous conversation.

Dad: Cameron.
Cam: Look, it doesn't matter. If someone else wants it it's theirs. Nica wouldn't dream of accepting something from her clients, not like this. So continue picking through a dead woman's belongings like it's a grand old flea market and leave me out of it.
Dad: Cameron!

The downside to text messaging, my parents now had a way to effectively yell at me. Messages filled with capital letters would be coming next. I didn't expect any reaction beyond yelling; Dad always played Mom's games. It was one thing to turn his back on his parents, but Mom had him so controlled he never even bothered getting to know me.

Cam: What?

No one had acknowledged this was a life they were arguing over. A life now gone, with only a few belongings, a few memories, and a few ungrateful family members left behind.

Dad: I'm sorry Grandma's gone.

The first ounce of sympathy the man had shown in years. A rare glimpse at the man inside and not the puppet.

Cam: She was your mother.
Dad: Life's convoluted, son.

Like having a Deaf son. I was really tempted to type my thoughts. What would Dad say to that?

Cam: After arguing with me over my complicated relationship with Nica, you come out with that line?
Dad: We've all gotten off on the wrong foot. Why don't the four of us get dinner before Mom and I fly back home?

I peered through the window again at Nica. Her eyes caught mine, and she gave me an encouraging smile.

Cam: Only if you promise Mom will behave.

Chapter 14

Nica

I shuffled through the hangers in my closet for the tenth time. Maybe if my hands stopped shaking I could concentrate on finding an appropriate outfit. One that said, "Please don't hate me for being Cassie's case manager and sleeping with your son." *No, don't go there. Pick a damn top.*

I grabbed one and turned around to face Cam. *"What do you think?"*

"It's fine, they're all fine."

I shook my head. *"No, it's not. Your mother already hates me. I need to be on my best behavior."*

He tugged me close, my shirt squashing between us. *"Just be yourself."*

I sighed and yanked the shirt free. It was a long-sleeve blue top in a silky material. *"This one isn't right,"* I said before making my way back into my closet. I grabbed a long-sleeve black top, with lace trim and a tie at the waist. Black wasn't my first choice after a funeral, but it looked good and sent off a professional yet casual vibe.

Finally dressed I stepped out of the closet and faced Cam with my hands held out.

"Beautiful, now come here." He collected me in his arms, melting me with a devastatingly sweet kiss, like always. Only now I realized how dangerous he was, how dangerous *we* were.

I shifted back. *"I've never been so nervous about being judged before.*

123

Normally when I meet someone's parents it's amusing to see how they react to my job."

"Why?"

"Either they think it's wonderful, they think it's going to be too stressful, or they are convinced I do charity work." I thought for a moment. *"They might be right about the last one."*

"You help people."

"By working for pennies. What language do I use with your parents?"

"What do you mean?"

"You only speak with them, no sign, your brothers sign with you but not when your parents are involved in the conversation. I refuse to make communication difficult for you, but I don't want to cause any problems."

He smiled. *"You answered your own question. Sign and speak. They'll have to deal."*

"But why don't your brothers sign and speak at the same time?"

Cam's smile faded. *"ASL was banned. Mom didn't want me using it as a crutch. They know Dan and Ben sign now, but it's habit to put the hands away at the dinner table."*

The temperature of my boiling blood rose higher with each of Cam's signs. *"That's horrible. Absolutely horrible."* I paced in a circle, trying to calm my trembling hands. *"I'm really sorry I didn't commiserate with your grandmother more."*

"It's normal. Sad but true. I had my grandparents. I had my brothers. I had it better than most."

"I don't care. They should have known better. They should have—"

He stopped me with his lips, a hand pressed into the small of my back, soothing the raging fire inside me. *"Let it go or you'll never get through dinner. Remember they go back to Florida in the morning."*

I sucked in some air and nodded. Was it too early for a drink?

*****

Cam

I had to admit, dinner started off better than expected. Even Nica relaxed as the conversation stayed determinedly on current events, and my parents didn't flinch at her signing. Mom kept conversation light, smiling at appropriate intervals, even allowing her face to crease at one point. I couldn't remember a time when she'd been this nice to any of my dates. The sudden change of heart worried me.

Empty dishes were waiting to be cleared when, without warning, the conversation shifted. "Do you have… clients, Nica?" My mother's face was cool and calm. It wasn't a good sign.

Nica's cheeks turned pink. But she held herself confidently. "*I have almost a hundred clients.*" Whether my parents realized it or not, Nica did her best to find some way to work the question into her answer, no doubt to make sure I hadn't missed anything.

Dad's mouth movements were gibberish, but his face telegraphed bafflement.

Nica relaxed a bit. "*I do what I can to manage them all. It's not easy. The caseloads have been getting larger and larger in the past few years. The clients are also getting frailer. It's a juggling game. I only see my clients once or twice a year. At any given time I have quite a few who are quiet, giving me time to devote to the rest.*"

"You help them…?"

I understood the sentence to be a question, based on years of studying Mom's face. Pain radiated from the back of my eye sockets as I tried to piece together the rest of her words. I hadn't recovered from the past few days. How had I ever survived the constant lip-reading of my childhood?

I rubbed my temples, grateful Nica insisted on signing as she spoke. "*Not quite. All my clients are receiving services in their homes. These services range from cleaning, to shopping, to personal care, and beyond. The goal is to take an elder that would otherwise be at risk for nursing-home placement, or struggling to meet their daily needs, and keep them safe at home.*"

She turned to Dad. "*Your mother started off having trouble with cleaning, her body unable to perform the tasks. She never had an issue with food shopping, thanks to Cam. Closer to the end she no longer could bathe herself, and we started with a personal care worker. At that point I shared the case with a nurse, who wrote the care plan to make sure Cassie would be safe in the shower. Then we stepped back once Hospice started."*

My parents stared at me. Dad's eyes bulged while Mom scowled, both perplexed by what had gone on. I held up my hands. "Don't look at me. I was there for the whole thing."

"It was Cam who noticed showering was becoming an issue. He e-mailed me and I was able to step in. Then we both had to talk Cassie into accepting it."

I remembered Grandma's dramatic plea to die *"smelling like a cheap whore."* "She was stubborn. Nica worked hard to get a worker Grandma would like."

Nica nodded. *"Yes. I knew I had one chance. I called my favorite vendor and made a very specific request. It worked."*

I glanced across the table and found my parents dumbfounded. Well, they were out of the loop by choice. I tried talking to them about all of this; they told me to deal with it, part of the lifelong insistence of lumping the Deaf family members together. This lumping had worked for me and my grandparents until now.

"You two... a lot of communication..." Mom said as she eyed us both. I held in the urge to roll my eyes. *Here we go again.*

"Yes, we did have a lot of communication over the years, he was very involved," Nica said, her spine stiffening.

"..." Dad gestured between us. "Is new?"

This time I did roll my eyes. I let a grumble escape before catching myself. "Yes. We emailed maybe a few times a year. We never met or used our nicknames. It was business only."

Nica placed her napkin on the table. *"Excuse me."* She left for the bathroom, and I wondered how she knew I needed a moment to smack my parents.

Once she was no longer visible I spoke. "I thought you were giving her a chance?"

"We are... If... handle the complications..." Mom's perfectly manicured eyebrows rose.

The throbbing increased. "Then stop interrogating us, especially Nica." They could chastise me all they wanted, as long as they left Nica alone.

"It's interesting... how much you knew... over the years."

I held in a groan. "Professionally. She helped me out when no one else was there. I couldn't turn to any of Grandma's children for support. The rest of the grandchildren were busy with their own families. It was just me. Nica was the only person I could contact and get help from. Even now." I was two steps away from up and leaving.

"It... too perfect," Mom said with all the cultured air she could muster in the tilt of her chin.

"Perfect? As in Nica doing her job when the rest of you forced me to handle Grandma on my own?"

Mom bared her teeth. "... impossible for you two to know each other... stemming back... years... worked with Grandma."

"You have no idea what you're talking about." I clenched one hand under the table.

"... don't... Nica until... Sarah."

I rubbed one temple. "Not this again."

"Yes... Sarah... better match. None... social worker crap. She'd... need... look normal."

I blinked but I knew deep down I saw that right. "You mean not Deaf?" I purposely moved my hands with my voice, tempted to not speak at all, give them a taste of their own ineffective medicine.

Mom picked at something invisible on her sleeve. Dad refused to make eye contact. I yanked out my wallet, threw some money on the table, and stood.

I grabbed Nica's belongings. "Have a safe flight back to Florida." It was better than telling them to have a nice life. But I meant those sentiments with every fiber of my being. I had no parents. The two slack-mouthed humans sitting at the table were not my family. My family was dead.

I pressed my free hand to the ache in my chest. In a family filled with aunts, uncles, and cousins, I was alone. I never truly realized it until this moment. I used to think I was special to be like my grandparents, to be the only other one like the matriarch and patriarch of the family. Now I knew better. Special wasn't the label, freak was. Disabled. Less than. For thirty years my parents had looked down on me. No more. If Dan and Ben wanted to stay in touch, so be it. But not the baby of the family. Not the unwanted third son.

Family. What I wouldn't give for a family of my own. Where I wasn't an outsider, regardless of the hearing status of the other members. I needed a place to belong almost as much as I needed my next breath.

In the narrow hallway that housed the bathrooms I leaned back against one wall, knee bent, eyes trained on the stick figure with a skirt on one door. Family. The woman behind that door was mine.

*****

Nica

I splashed cold water on my cheeks in the ladies room, trying to tone down the pink coloring and burning sensation. I stared at my face and attempted to soothe my racing pulse. My stomach clenched and tumbled. The face stared back at me, offering no words of comfort or support.

I'd known it wouldn't be easy interacting with his parents; I didn't expect to be put under the spotlight. I certainly didn't expect for them to focus on the reason I held back for so long: the ethics of my job. It connected with my own internal struggles. I had to either let Cam go for good or accept that I couldn't walk away from him, regardless of the complications.

My reflection stared back at me, knowing one option to be cowardice and the other to be true. My stomach clenched tighter. Leaving wasn't an option.

I couldn't hide in the bathroom forever. I filled my lungs, gathering air up from my toes. The image in the mirror straightened and appeared confident. One more deep breath and I grasped the cool iron handle and stepped into the hall.

The door hit my back when I found Cam waiting for me.

"What happened?" I asked as I collected my purse and coat draped

over his arm.

He raked his fingers through his hair, tugging on the ends. Steam practically puffed out at each breath, even though he did his best to hold it in. *"They wouldn't let it go, so I told them to have a safe flight."*

A piece of my heart tore for him. *"I don't want to come between you and your parents."*

His expression softened but his body remained stiff. *"You didn't. We've been strained since birth. This is the perfect ending to that text I received seven years ago: Grandma isn't doing well, go check on her. And that was the last time they or anyone else were involved. They don't get to be surprised by a situation they know nothing about."*

"I'm sorry." I gathered him into a hug. The stress had his body fused straight.

"Let's go."

I followed him to his car and slid in. We drove in silence for a while, me trying to find the right thing to say. When in doubt, ask.

I pressed the button for the interior light of the car and waited for Cam to glance at me. *"What can I do to make you feel better?"*

A slow smile formed over his face, and his shoulders loosened. Fluid movement returned to his body. *"Being with you makes it better."*

I melted, my earlier decision reinforced. *"Would dessert help?"*

His deep voice laughed, filling the car. *"Always with the dessert."*

"I suspect there would be fewer problems if other people would follow suit." I smiled.

"Right now I want a punching bag."

"We could punch some dough? No, that won't work. Dessert and an old movie?"

A slow smile formed over his lips. *"That sounds like an excellent plan."*

Chapter 15

Cam

Monday morning I fought against the emptiness swelling inside my chest. Grief wrapped its prickly fingers around my throat. I focused on the tiny bumps on the ceiling, barely visible in the dim light struggling to infiltrate the room. Every fiber in my being wanted to collapse, wanted to stay right here in bed. Fuck the world. The emptiness spread, threatening to envelop me in a deep black hole.

I rolled to my feet and gripped the edge of my bed. I needed to get back into work. My bereavement leave had ended. I was expected. As co-director I needed to not play any stupid games. With strength I didn't know I had, I ripped those prickly fingers aside and forced myself up.

It didn't occur to me I hadn't even waited for my alarm clock to go off; not until I stood outside Grant's gym and the locked doors. Lights were on inside. Grant's Jeep was parked in the lot. Only a little lock stood between me and what I needed.

Cam: Let me in, I want to use your weight room.
Grant: Why aren't you lifting yourself off of a sexy blonde?

My friend watched me through the closed glass doors.

"Funny," I signed. The doors remained closed, posing no barrier to a visual language, only a barrier to me and a punching bag.

130

Grant didn't move but his face held none of the teasing his text message had. *"You OK?"*

I held out my hands. *"I'm here, right?"*

"Not an answer."

I was so far from okay I didn't have a word in either language. *"I need to punch something. Either it's a punching bag or your window. You choose."*

Grant shook his head but opened the door and let me do my thing. He didn't follow, sensing the serious *"back off"* vibe rolling off me in waves. In the small room I didn't even flip on the lights. I let the morning sun cast a yellow glow over the equipment and walked over to the punching bag. It hung motionless in the dim light, dead weight hanging from the ceiling like a useless lump.

I ran a hand down the smooth material, transferring the black hole in my chest to the black bag. Then I clenched one fist, sending the lifeless bag jerking on the chain in an attempt to get away. That one motion soothed and calmed and spurred me on to attack the bag again, and again. And again. The brutality of the action was in stark contrast to the sense of peace I found in beating the hell out of the thing. It became my parents, my pain, and my loss. When my arms ached and I could barely catch a breath I collapsed to the floor. Try as I did, not one of the punches eased the ache the way I needed. The hole remained.

The floor vibrated, and I glanced over at Grant by the door. *"The answer is time. In the interim it sucks balls."*

I let my mouth turn upwards before pushing to my feet. Brutal exercise didn't help. But going back to work might. It was still early, so I went back home, showered and changed, before walking into 409 Marketing. I was still the first one there.

I booted up my computer and started on my work. My e-mail inbox was near exploding, even with all the work I'd snuck in, and I relished the big to-do list. There were no phone messages to attend to, as Matt handled any voice calls. My inbox was down to fifteen when a hand on my shoulder forced me to stop hunching.

Ashley squeezed before releasing, a slight frown on her face. Matt was already leaning against his desk, taking me in with a similar expression.

"If either one of you ask if I'm OK I will throttle you," I signed.

Ashley squared her shoulders, ready to go to battle, but turned to Matt. I didn't see any lip movements but would have bet my salary I missed something verbal. Ashley nodded to Matt and left for her own desk.

Matt raised a finger in the air. *"Don't kill yourself."* He turned and grabbed a stack of papers off his desk. *"Get started on this."*

I gave a salute that might as well have been a one-finger gesture not found in ASL and returned to work.

I vaguely remembered lunch being delivered and eating it while continuing my mad game of catch up. By the time I found the bottom of the pile the outside world was dark and the office empty. I leaned back, rubbing my eyes. Never before had I managed a work trance that long. The emptiness of the office seeped in; I needed to stop the spread. I picked up my cell, only to have a different type of internal ache.

Nica: I guess that date isn't happening tonight.

Shit. I scrolled back over the ten messages I'd missed from her and felt like a royal ass.

Cam: Sorry, a lot of work to catch up on.
Nica: So you are alive, good to know.
Cam: Tomorrow?
Nica: You OK?

No, I wasn't. It was after 7pm and I'd been working for almost twelve hours. Worse, I'd been more than happy to continue until the following day. Usually that thought meshed with my drive and ambition. Today it left me cold. I stared at my keypad, thumbs poised to respond, clueless on what to type.

Nica: Do you need me to come over?

Cam: No. I'm going to finish up here, then get some rest. Tomorrow?

Nica: Tomorrow.

There was plenty left for me to do, but I shut down my computer. *Time to go home, Thompson.* A good night's sleep and I'd be back to normal.

*****

Nica

"So, I guess you have plenty of time to finish that drink," Lexie said once I put down my phone.

"Guess so." I picked up my drink and gulped. It was a Lexie special, with some name that sounded like a bondage act. A harmless-looking fruity drink filled with potent alcohol. I set my glass down and pushed it into the center of the table, the scraping noise drowned out by the chatter and music.

"What's the matter?"

"The last time you presented me with a drink like this I took home my client's grandson."

Lexie laughed. "I'd ask if you were afraid you'd find another one, but the truth of the matter is you are spoken for. You're not even looking at the potential."

"I've been stood up, have some compassion."

Lexie cocked her head, dark hair cascading over one shoulder. "Yeah, you've been stood up. But you don't care. Why is that?"

"Because I already know he's a workaholic."

"Well, there's that, but you'll just end up yelling at him for that one. It's because you're in love with him."

I paused while reaching for my drink, a shiver freezing my limbs. "I'm not in love with him. I know about his hours. If they become a problem we'll part amicably."

Lexie threw her head back and laughed, clutching onto her side. "Oh no, you two will not part amicably, not at all. You can't pull 'The Nica' when you're already head over heels."

I took another gulp and what do you know, the bottom of the glass was now visible. "We'll part one day, that's how all relationships end. But I refuse to lose him as a friend." He was too special to me, too important.

"Nope, you're not getting out of this one; you're going to have to fight to keep him, not let him go." The bar lighting created a halo that was 100% not true to Lexie's personality.

This conversation was too much for my alcohol level. I needed to redirect this and fast. "Sorry I'm putting a damper on your sex life."

Lexie leaned forward, elbows on the sticky tabletop, eyeing me in ways that I had to resist a squirm. "There's still the chance one or both of you will fuck up royally. My money's on both."

I copied her stance. "Is there a second bet going on?"

Lexie settled back in her chair. "Perhaps."

I pointed an unsteady finger at her. "Stop betting on my sex life."

"But it's so fun."

I groaned and searched for a waiter. This conversation required another drink.

*****

I was still buzzed when I made it home. I scratched Oreo, who stood by her food bowl, meowing expectantly.

"Oh, all right, I'll feed you." I reached for the can of wet food and popped the lid. "You know, you're loud for a deaf cat." I spooned out the food into the bowl, and Oreo dug right in.

I sat back on my heels, watching her eat. "Why is it all the deaf individuals in my life are vocal?" I shook my head and tossed the can in the sink before leaning on the porcelain, lost on what to do next. Sleep wasn't an option, not when my skin felt tight and itchy, and my mind raced with all the changes in my life. I gathered a brownie batter mix, oil, eggs, and a package of Oreo cookies. I removed one cookie, smirked at Oreo the cat licking her lips from her dinner, popped the entire cookie in my mouth, and went about pouring the oil. I closed my eyes to savor the much-needed chocolaty goodness. The past two weeks had felt so long it could have been a mini-series. Episode one: meeting Cam (big ratings on that one). Episode two: Cassie moved to Hospice House. Episode three: Ethical landmine. Episode Four: Cassie's death.

I dumped the batter mix into the bowl and assessed the mess on my counter, the now empty carton of eggs, and the open package of cookies. Episode five: gorging on junk food.

I ate another Oreo—and dropped a piece into the bowl. *Shoot.* I dug my clean hand into the batter and picked up the broken piece of cookie. "Gotcha. Now what am I going to do with you?" My cell phone chirped and a text flashed across the screen: Cam.

Shit. Even with my finger in my mouth, and my taste buds in chocolate heaven, I was in no condition to check the message. I licked two fingers clean and woke up my phone.

Cam: I'm here. Can I come up?

My heart skipped a beat. What was he doing here? I glanced at my sweat pants and oversized T-shirt. What the hell, he'd seen me naked. He'd have to deal with the crappy clothes.

Nica: Sure. I'll buzz you in.

A clean finger and auto correct saved me from sending a garbled message. The same finger pressed the door buzzer. I held it down for a minute, hoping he felt the vibrations. Then I cracked the door open and resumed grabbing the ingredients for the batter.

A few minutes later Cam knocked, and I turned, mixing the wet and dry together as he entered.

He was still dressed for work, in clothes that appeared tailor made for his fit body. Once I peeled my eyes off the maroon shirt stretched across his firm chest my lust nosedived. His hair appeared as though he had run his hands through it several times, his face somber, eyes heavy, mouth downturned. I cursed myself for not washing my hands so I could hug him.

"*Rough day?*" I asked one-handed, holding the bowl with my other so I could face him and continue mixing.

Cam nodded and ran his fingers through his hair, increasing the out-of-place look. "*I'm so sorry about tonight. Work had piled up and I lost track of time.*"

A lump formed in my throat at his naked grieving, but I swallowed it away. He didn't need my concern. "*I understand. Make sure you take care of yourself before work.*"

Cam nodded and glanced at the bowl, but I caught the moisture in his eyes before he blinked it away. "*What are you making?*"

"*Brownie covered Oreos. The cookie, not the cat.*" I tried to avoid touching my face with the sign but bet I failed.

A half-laugh choked its way out of him. The cat slept on a chair, and he scratched her head. Oreo let out a startled yelp, stretched, saw she was being petted, and relaxed back into a curled up position.

"*The dessert sounds delicious,*" Cam signed.

I smiled as he washed his hands. He unbuttoned his cuffs and rolled them up to his elbows, revealing his strong arms. Once the muffin tins were full, Cam set them in the oven. I stood by the counter, licking one of my hands, and I caught that glint in his hazel eyes, the same glint he had before kissing me. I held out my other brownie-covered hand to him. "*Want?*"

A slow, sexy smile worked its way over his face. He stepped towards me and grasped my arm. His eyes hot on mine, he sucked my entire thumb inside his warm mouth.

My legs wobbled. I stumbled backwards, leaning against the counter. Cam followed, pressing our bodies together, all those hard muscles against my softer ones. He continued to ravage my fingers, sending carnal thoughts straight to my core. I all but forgot about my own snack on my other hand, fighting the desire to climb him like a tree. Before he could make it to my pinky, I gave up the farce and wrapped both hands around his neck and kissed him with everything

I had, reclaiming some of the batter with my tongue.

He shifted back, his chest rising and falling in quick bursts. *"Do you have more?"*

I nodded. *"There's supposed to be another batch of cookies—"*

"I'll buy more."

Cam dipped a finger into the chocolate batter and brought it to my lips. I licked the batter off his finger with my tongue, the sweet taste of brownie mixed in with the salty texture of his skin. He grumbled and yanked me against him, mouth to mouth, body against body, his hard length pressing against my belly. Between my legs throbbed with want.

I wasn't the only one. Cam removed my shirt then grabbed the bowl. The sexual haze started to crack, until he drew a brownie-covered line on my skin, and then licked it off. Then he drew another, and another, until all that mattered was his tongue and where the batter would land next.

Cam trailed batter across my stomach. The timer beeped. I tried to sit up, but he placed his lips just under my ribs. One touch of his mouth to my stomach and I couldn't remember what had startled me, could barely remember my own name. I leaned back against the cool floor as my body continued to overheat. The second beeping broke into my sensual bubble. I jerked myself up and shoved him off.

"The timer," I said as I found my oven mitt and removed the brownies from the oven. The nearly empty batter bowl sat on my kitchen floor next to Cam. Shirt half unbuttoned he had brownie fragments streaked from his collar to his sleeves, spiked in his hair, smeared around his mouth, and trailed down his bare chest.

I collapsed on the floor, laughing. *"You're a mess."* Hair clung to my face, and when I went to brush it aside, I found dried brownie chunks. *"I'm a mess, too."*

He breathed heavy, smiling wide at me.

I stood again and turned off the oven. *"Well, there isn't enough for another batch. Shall we finish this off and shower?"*

Our clothes fell to the floor as we stumbled into the bathroom. Once there I reached for the water to turn it on, hard to do with Cam still attached to my lips. I twisted the knob, the sounds of running water filling the room, guessing at the right spot. When Cam finally broke free to collect a condom, I managed to turn the temperature down from scalding to comfortable. I was bent over, checking the water temperature when he wrapped around me, trailing hot kisses down my spine. Before I could straighten up, one hand slid around to my front, not stopping until he rolled a pebbled nipple between his fingers. I let out a moan and gripped the edge of the tub for support. Steam filled the bathroom. I had to remind myself it was from the hot water and not us.

"If you don't stop we're never making it into the shower," I said, breaking free to step back into the tub.

Cam followed, our bodies sliding together under the falling water like a lock and key. I needed this man, now. I wrapped my arms and legs around him, licking water droplets off his muscular shoulders as he nibbled on my neck, hitting damn near every nerve ending I owned. I worked my way back up, gazing into his fathomless eyes. A small voice inside said this would be the last man I would have sex with.

The intensity of the moment hit me. All the questions of what was really happening between us surfaced. In the heat and steam of the shower, with Cam's lips on my neck, a long buried yearning stirred. The shackles cracked and for the first time in my life I contemplated the fairytale.

I closed my eyes and pushed the feelings aside. Too many emotions flitted through me: from fear to joy to ecstasy. I reminded myself this was way too fast. I'd known this man, in the flesh (and what glorious flesh he had) for two weeks. Cam nibbled my collarbone and brought me out of my torment, back to the present. I threw myself into the action, into him, shutting off my brain, letting my body handle the rest.

Cam pinned me against the cool shower wall. I wasn't cold, not with the warm water, the even warmer body against mine and between my legs. Heat consumed me so fully that I couldn't register anything except for what I felt and what he made me feel. I almost missed him reaching out of the shower for the condom. Then he slipped inside me and any chance of my brain turning back on vanished. Only the sound of water, and flesh against flesh, filled my ears, my inner voice lost in pleasure. Each thrust, each kiss pushed me higher and higher, until my head thunked against the shower wall and I came hard around him, shuddering as the water continued to hit my skin. After his own release I opened my eyes. He pressed his head against mine, breathing heavy, smiling.

I struggled to gain footing on the slippery ground, but Cam held me close. I couldn't figure out if he was trying to steady me or if he wasn't ready to let go. Instead of grabbing the soap, I pushed my lips to his, not ready to leave the moment.

Chapter 16

Cam

I sat on the end of Nica's bed, blinking her bedroom into focus. Beside me she slept, stomach down, curls covering her face and pillow. A bright band of light skimmed across her, peeking in from the side of the shade. I had hoped her presence would make a difference, but the morning brought with it all the heavy weight on my chest. Too much flittered through my mind. Thoughts of my grandmother tried to break through, but I kept focused on work and everything I still needed to catch up on there.

Best plan was to arrive at work early again, leave on time and live up to my promise of baked goods. So why wasn't I moving?

I shook my head and found the will to push myself up and moving. After collecting my clothes and freshening up, I found Nica sitting in bed, covers clutched over her chest, watching me. *"You OK?"* she asked.

I forced a smile and crossed the room to kiss her. *"I'm fine. Going to head home and get ready for work. See you tonight?"*

She placed a hand on my cheek, and I contained all my turmoil deep inside, not wanting her to see I barely held myself together. *"You'd tell me if you needed something. Or Grant or someone, right?"*

I nodded and kissed her forehead. *"Of course."*

Once home I headed straight for the shower. The water hit my back, taking away all my stressors and troubles, soothing with its repetitive pitter patter. By the time I emerged it was too late to hit the gym. Instead I made my way into work, realizing it was much later than I thought when I found most of the staff already there.

Matt and Ashley regarded me, concern clear across their faces, but were smart enough not to ask stupid questions involving the letters *O* and *K*.

"*You got a phone call.*" Matt gestured to the written message on my desk.

I ran a hand through my hair. How late was I? Not willing to find the answer I read the note and provided Matt with the information needed to respond. Matt picked up the phone and made the return call, stopping as needed to receive clarification from me.

The brisk start urged me back into action mode and plowing through my work. I stopped when Grant sat down on my desk, trapping papers under his jean-clad ass.

"*Missed you threatening to break my door this morning.*"

I rolled my eyes, not liking Grant's serious tone.

"*You see Nica?*"

"*Yes.*"

"*Did you talk to her or just have sex?*"

I narrowed my eyes, and Grant held up his hands in a peace offering. He glanced beside him to where Matt and Ashley stood wearing twin expressions of worry. "*OK, you've got two options: one, we get your ass drunk; two, you talk to the social worker. Pick one.*"

"*Work, I need to work.*"

I turned to my computer, only to have Grant bang on the desk. "*You always work. It's the answer to everything. Which means it's not going to be enough. Not this time. And your grandmother would kick your ass if you bury yourself in work and not real life.*"

The ache in my chest tightened at the mention of Grandma.

"*Work is real life.*" I was leveled with a stern glare from all three friends.

Ashley shook her head. "*No. You've always buried yourself, trying to prove your worth. Look around…*" She gestured to the room where others were hard at work. "*You've proved it. Now focus on the rest of your life. What do you want besides work?*"

I studied the space. When we first started it was an empty room with a few desks and a conference table. We'd grown, we'd thrived, and Ashley was right. I wasn't carrying the weight on Matt and my shoulders anymore.

What else did I want? The same thing Grandma wanted for me: a pretty social worker with a heart of gold and a hot body.

*****

Nica

I had a difficult case I needed to review with Tess, but my supervisor's door had been closed for almost a half hour. After the first ten minutes an uneasy feeling bloomed in my stomach that had nothing to do with my case. Tess was meeting with the other supervisor and the home care director, Sharon. Not a normal situation.

Rebecca scooted the center chair over to my desk, also watching the closed-door meeting in process. "Something's going down."

There had been an odd vibe in the office from the senior staff for a full day now. "Something" was an understatement. "Do you think it's more budget cuts?"

Rebecca rolled her head back, hitting it on the small ledge of the window. "Ugh, we can't handle more of those. I'm lucky I only have ninety clients. How sad is that? My caseload was seventy-five when I started. And even that was brutal."

"We can't afford to cut services back any further." I tried to catch an expression from one of the women in the meeting through the narrow side window but couldn't. "Whatever it is, it can't be good. The length of time alone they've been in there spells one of those impossible situations."

Rebecca stood. "I don't know what it is, but something bad is brewing. I can feel it." She moved back to her desk. I tried to resume working but kept being drawn to the meeting.

"I hope it's not a staffing issue," Rebecca said softly, also not returning to work. "I always wonder what would happen to Finn and me if my job was eliminated."

I eyed my friend, her brow creased in worry. I had similar fears myself, but I wasn't a single mother. "I'm sure your former in-laws would help."

Rebecca smiled a sad smile. "They did back when I first started this single parent life. They already do so much for us, I don't want to abuse their generosity."

I gazed at the framed picture on Rebecca's small ledge—Finn's pre-school picture and his adorable little smile. There wasn't always much to smile about, especially with closed-door mystery meetings.

My phone vibrated from within my pocket.

Cam: Why don't you come here tonight? I'll cook.

I glanced at the meeting in process, unable to shake the bad omen. I could definitely use a break from all this, and I hadn't been to his place yet, just the bakery across the street.

Nica: OK.

Rebecca nudged my shoulder. "He cooks, too? Hold onto that one."

My cheeks flushed. "What happened to the warnings?"

"Meetings like that? A reminder we get one life and sometimes right and wrong are not always clear cut. He makes you happy? Keep him."

I returned to my desk as Tess's door opened. Those inside did indeed appear somber. Sharon paused, caught my eye, and with a slight shake of her head resumed walking. A sense of foreboding washed over me. I had a feeling whatever was wrong had my own neck on the block.

*****

Cam

I had my sleeves rolled up to my elbows, and three of my four stove burners working. One had the sauce reduced to a simmer, another boiled pasta, and a third browned chicken. My mother, for all her faults, made it her mission that her three sons knew our way around a kitchen.

No, no thoughts of my mother. This was me moving forward, creating my own family where I wasn't the black sheep. A family Grandma would be proud of. I pushed through the pain that thought caused, grateful for the multiple burners keeping my mind occupied. Forward, the only direction to go.

I was draining the pasta, thoughts flickering back to Grandma complaining about how the pasta needed to be rinsed, not drained, when Nica arrived. About damn time, my brain was about to drag me under. Still holding the pot I let her into the condo, taking in her light-hearted smile as though the sun itself broke through the dark clouds. She set her bag down as she examined my apartment. I tracked her gaze over the exposed ceiling vents and beams, the open kitchen and living room, and the collection of old movies by the television. I replaced the pot on the burner as she joined me in the kitchen, nose pointing upwards.

"What are you cooking?"

"Chicken Alfredo."

She rested her chin on my shoulder, her luscious curves pressed against my back. She reached a hand around to sign in front of me, using my head as her base rather than her own. *"Smells delicious."* An intimate motion that felt completely natural.

I turned around and kissed her. *"Thank you."*

Her dark eyes roamed over me. *"You seem OK, better than this morning."*

I nodded as I poured the sauce over the pasta, breaking eye contact. The ache stirred inside and I quenched it. Not going there, not now.

A hand on my bicep forced me to gaze in her eyes. No longer was this Nica. Now she was Veronica, in full-on social-worker mode, able to see through me faster than any of my friends. Or maybe her ability to see through me was due to what simmered between us.

"*You're not OK.*"

I shrugged and returned to the food. "*It takes time.*" She didn't need to know I was stealing Grant's words.

When I stopped to check on her again she was hands on hips. "*Don't lie. Tell me how you really feel.*"

The empty void inside filled with her vanilla scent, chipping at the walls I struggled to keep upright. A reminder that I was going through the motions by pure stubborn will alone. "*I feel like nothing's normal.*"

Her furrowed eyebrows and glossy eyes radiated with concern. "*There is no normal. Not after a loss. Especially not after having your whole world turned upside down for almost two weeks.*"

Too tired to protest, I dropped my forehead to hers before shifting back enough to sign. "*I always thought my family would be more affected. Would finally see what they had missed out on.*"

Nica rubbed my arm, the motion more soothing than I expected. "*Grandma had you, she loved that. Sure, she had issues with the rest of the family, but she also had good stories as well. She knew her great grandchildren— that speaks volumes.*"

I fought the knot in my chest, the knot threatening to send up waterworks.

"*Is there anything you need?*"

My heart skipped and jumped, pointing like a damn pointer dog. "*You.*"

"*I'm here, but that's only a temporary fix.*"

I shook my head, the impressions she left on me were far from temporary, but she held up her hand.

"*Don't fight with me on this. How much training have you had on grief and loss?*"

I kept my hands still.

"*That's right. You need to deal with what's on the inside.*" She tapped a finger to my heart. "*Otherwise I'm a mask and the problems remain.*"

The struggle welled up inside, and I knew I couldn't dig deeper, not yet. And I didn't want to. I wanted the momentary bliss her presence brought.

She flattened a palm against my heart. *"As I said, I'm here now. But you've got to give yourself time to work through this. Understand?"*

I nodded and wrapped a hand over hers, holding her close to my chest. The hole in my heart healed, and I knew it was the mask, but at that moment, I didn't care. I gave her hand a squeeze. *"Let's eat."*

During dinner I noticed a slight frown to her face. Had that been there when she arrived? She avoided eye contact and picked at her food as we talked. After the dishes were cleaned up I collected her into my arms and she rested her head against my chest. With her in my arms my heart felt normal. She belonged there, a part of me. Only her back remained stiff, and she didn't melt into me. I released her.

"Something is obviously bothering you, what's wrong?"

"Nothing." She sighed. *"Everything and nothing rolled into one. Why can't you be a typical guy and let me have secrets?"*

I lowered my head, as close to her as I could get and still sign. *"Because you have seen me in my darkest moments. I can't be a typical guy when you've seen me cry more times than I would like to admit."*

A small smile graced her lips. *"Nothing wrong with a little emotion."*

"Nothing wrong with being worried about the woman I'm dating."

She shifted backwards, slight but I caught it. *"Work related stuff. Something's going on and we're not sure what it is yet."*

Everything inside of me wanted to dump my own issues and work on hers. *"What is it? What can I do?"*

Her lips curved upwards. *"We don't know, just a lot of stress vibes, rumors, and meetings. Nothing you can do when I don't know what's going. Probably nothing you can do after. Government-funded jobs get hacked, a lot."*

I felt helpless standing there, unable to do a damn thing. Except for the pain in her eyes I related to. That I could fix. I kissed her, seeking, searching. Loving the way she felt against my mouth. I pushed our bodies together, loving the way that felt as well.

But like the punching bag, it wasn't enough. I wanted more of her, all of her, in a way that had little to do with sex. Even though I'd been playing with the concept of forever it still hit me hard—forever with one woman. The black hole deep inside wanted to devour her, take her in. Fill the ache. Was it my heart or my grief?

I stepped back, catching her off guard. She leaned into me, eyes closed, lips wet and swollen from my kisses. The rest of me joined the black hole—devouring her seemed like a damn good idea.

She opened her eyes. Enlarged pupils radiated intense feelings for me. Yet I knew her demon plagued her, just as the hole remained in me. I yanked her back to me, mouth to mouth, body to body. We could exorcise our demons together.

Cautious of the open windows I backed her up to the bedroom. Once inside I yanked her shirt off, needing all that creamy skin exposed to my eyes, and my eyes only.

As if she read my mind, her hands glided down to my pants and tugged off my belt. A moment later she slipped the pants down. How convenient I was commando. Served to relieve the pressure of cramped quarters. I had no trouble being naked, but she still had on far too many clothes. I wanted her, needed her, naked and burning up from my touch. I unclasped her bra and threw it aside before taking the heavy weight of her breast into my palm, teasing one pink nipple with my thumb. When she closed her eyes I replaced my hand with my mouth, sucking on her sweet skin. Blood pumped through my veins, the battle between grief and heart momentarily topped by a very hard body part with an agenda little to do with emotions. I kissed a path down her body, using my teeth to undo the button and zipper on her jeans.

Flesh against flesh, our hungry mouths searched each other. I slid my hands down her front, over her belly button, until I reached that warm and wet place ready for any part of me. She threw her head back, her cheeks flushed. She was more than grief, much more. "You're beautiful," I spoke.

A wicked grin spread over her lips as her eyes raked me up and down. She bit her lip like maybe she liked what she saw. "*I want you. Now.*" I didn't need to be told twice. I grabbed a condom and slipped it on. I angled over her and she met me halfway, raising her hips, pushing herself around me.

I sunk in deep, all her warmth surrounding me, infiltrating me, completing me. Her nails dug into my shoulders, her hips meeting each thrust. Together like this there was no grief. Only heart when she was in my arms, burning up, fueling a climax that damn near had me out of my mind.

I let my body fall on top of hers, both our breaths heavy. Nica smiled, all signs of tension gone. I wrapped my arms around her, not wanting to move and lose the connection. My heart swelled, and there was no place else I would rather be than right there, with her. Knowing without a shadow of a doubt I was in love with her and never letting go.

*****

Nica

The following morning, at an ungodly hour, a light flashing from Cam's side of the bed woke me—his alarm clock. I buried my head into the pillow. Cam flipped the switch and the light stopped ravishing the bedroom. I moved the pillow to see him smiling.

"*It's early, but you seem OK,*" I said.

"*You help.*"

I lifted up on my elbows, the cool air reminding me I was naked. "*So I'm a drug? An antidote?*"

He kissed my shoulder. "*Something like that.*"

"*I'm worried about your co-dependency issues, but I'll let that slide for another week or two.*"

He laughed and climbed out of bed. The sound made the early morning bearable. I had the best view in all the city. Cam tugged workout pants on his muscular legs, and an old T-shirt over his broad chest. I snuggled back into his bed, enjoying seeing things on his turf during the week.

After breakfast we went our separate ways. Due to the early morning start I savored the blues and oranges of the morning sky. I envisioned Cam walking to the gym in this, able to enjoy the same majestic view. The early start was more than worth it for that reason alone.

The atmosphere at work remained tense. Rumors of the closed-door meeting had spread and the theories were building. Anything from budget cuts to a letter threatening an employee. Someone should've started a pool—might as well make some money off a no-win situation.

To make matters worse, Tess was out sick. I still hadn't discussed my difficult case, and now I couldn't even attempt to get hints on whatever calamity threatened us all. Instead I continued about my day, burying myself in work as usual. On my way down to the nurses' pod to discuss a referral, my director stopped me.

"Nica, can I speak with you for a moment?"

Dread snaked through me. Sharon was using her "you'll do as I say or else" voice. I prayed whatever came next had nothing to do with the closed-door meeting. But I had a feeling my prayer was not going to be answered.

I walked into the office. A bold oak desk sat against one window, cleared of everything except for one small pile of neatly stacked papers. A small tree stood in the corner. I sat down at the round conference table, and Sharon sat across from me, with no papers in her hand.

"I want to talk with you about one of you clients. Cassandra Thompson."

Panic froze all my limbs, and I wanted to crawl under the table, or hide behind the tree. This couldn't be what I feared, could it?

"I understand that you've been—" Sharon cleared her throat "—seeing her grandson."

A string of profanities flew through my mind, none of which I could speak out loud. I tried to push those aside and remain calm, but probably appeared about as guilty as I felt. "Yes, that's correct. It was unintentional, we didn't know who each other was until a day after we met."

"And you continued the relationship?"

Shit. I couldn't come up with a way to explain that I hadn't, not at first. But nothing could erase the fact that I had spent the previous night with Cam. "Yes." I spoke in a soft voice, my heartrate pumping rapid in my veins, making it hard to hear. I wondered if there was a defibrillator in the building.

"You overstepped your bounds. You know it. I know it. Tess knows it. We should bring this to the Social Worker's Association's attention, but that would risk your license and your job. I don't approve of this situation. However, I will admit that until now you've been a stellar case manager."

Sharon paused, and I waited for the other shoe to drop. I hadn't a clue how she'd found out. Before I could theorize an answer, she resumed speaking.

"We need to minimize this issue as much as possible. Keeping you with clients that knew Cassandra is a problem. All your clients in the same building will be transferred to Rebecca."

Sharon kept talking, but I couldn't hear her over the ringing in my ears. "All those clients are Deaf and communicate in ASL," I managed to squeak out.

Sharon clasped her hands together. "I'm aware of that."

"Rebecca doesn't know ASL."

"I'm aware of that as well."

"I'm the only one who can communicate with them. You can't take them from me." I tried to remove the desperation from my voice. Maybe I would have succeeded if I hadn't stood up, scraping the chair back in the process.

"Sit, Veronica. I can do whatever I have to do to minimize the impact of your personal choices. I suggest you calm down before I remove all your clients from your care."

I sat, helped in part by the dead weight in my thighs. I attempted to swallow and nodded.

"Good. Tess had planned to talk with you and Rebecca, work out a swap so that her caseload doesn't become overburdened. In the interest of time I want you two to take care of the switch on your own. E-mail both myself and Tess once completed so we can track the transfers. And let Rebecca handle all further correspondences. Am I clear?"

Unable to speak, I nodded. My head spun. My director's cold face glared, and I willed the ground to open up and swallow me whole. Embarrassment seeped in, spreading to my cheeks.

Another ethical landmine hit, this one direct and full. I wasn't sure there was any recovery from this.

I stood up and smoothed down my pants. "Yes, you're clear." My knees shook, and I locked them into place. Now was not the time to shake, not in front of Sharon.

"One more thing. I strongly suggest you end this relationship before it causes any further damage."

Her words punched the air out of my lungs. I wanted to protest that I tried to avoid the relationship, but that would've made me appear weak and shallow. Instead I gave a curt nod and managed to get to the door without making more of a fool of myself. The nursing consult would wait for another day. I headed straight to my desk. Each step felt like a million. My mind raced in too many different directions. If anyone passed me in the hall I didn't realize it, I could barely see.

At my desk I settled into my chair. A slew of swear words traveled through my head. That meeting was confirmation I never should have seen Cam again, never supported him through Cassie's death. The walls closed in on me, ripping me off my foundation once again.

"You okay?" Rebecca stood next to my desk.

I shook my head. "I think I discovered the meaning of that meeting."

"Yeah?" Rebecca sat down.

I blinked, fighting the sudden urge to cry. "Me and my wonderful dating choices."

Rebecca gasped and reached out for my hand. "What happened?"

"Sharon cornered me." I tried to focus. "I have no idea how she even knows." Rebecca was the only one I worked with aware of the situation, and the shock on my friend's face proof enough this didn't come from her. "On the plus side: do you have seven clients you want to get rid of?"

"Why?"

"I need to give you my Deaf clients." The words physically hurt, as if they were pried from my chest.

"You lost your Deaf clients?" Rebecca whispered.

"They're Cassie's neighbors." I swiped a lone tear trailing down my cheek.

Rebecca dragged me into a side hug before we worked on swapping clients.

Chapter 17

Cam

I spent some quality time with my old friend, the black-hole punching bag. Still wasn't quite able to pulverize my demons. They remained hiding, waiting for me to crash, for me to fail.

Like my parents.

The push of spoken English was due, in part, to me not being able to accomplish anything worthwhile without it. Which was a bunch of bull. Sure, Grandpa was a factory worker. Grandpa was also raised oral, without access to appropriate language or education. I had both. The spoken English helped, but it wasn't why I succeeded. My own drive and smarts were why.

And now the black hole had little faith in me. Ready to consume me. To swallow me up and spit me out like a useless piece of shit.

I stopped punching and grabbed onto the wobbling bag. *Let it go, man.* Some holes were destined to remain.

Grant walked into the weight room. Arms crossed, he studied me. *"Well, you've had sex two nights in a row, so that's bound to help."*

I beckoned Grant forward. *"You want to fight?"* It wasn't the sex, it was Nica. Without her I'd be even more of a bear.

"You missed your chance when we were roommates, sorry, sunshine."

The ribbing was a normal I wasn't ready for. I wiped sweat off my forehead. *"I have to clean out Grandma's apartment."*

"Want a drink afterwards?"

I wanted about twelve first. *"I can wait a week, but they need to move in someone new in the beginning of the month.*" I rubbed my hand to my chest, grateful I could follow that up with de-sticking the shirt from my sweat.

"*Treat it like a band aid. Rip it off fast. Don't dwell.*"

I shook out my hands. Grant was right. It didn't make the thought any easier. "*OK. Tomorrow night you have one job, get me drunk.*"

A sinister grin crossed over Grant's face. "*What I do best.*"

*****

Nica

"Write back and forth. But use simple language. ASL has a different grammatical structure which will make it difficult for both of you." I gave Rebecca pointers in preparation for her first visit with one of my clients. Sharon had no idea the trouble posed by her sudden and drastic decree. I had a visit scheduled with one of my Deaf clients for that afternoon, a client who rarely answered her TTY—Teletype phone.

An interpreter would have been ideal, but there was no time. Without going to the building and meeting the client face to face there was no other way to communicate. An interpreter would take at least two weeks to secure.

"I'll figure it out. Is there anyone in the building that can help?"

"The office manager is hearing, but her hours are sporadic." I tapped my former client's folder. "This is ridiculous, my clients are the ones suffering."

"With any luck this will all be temporary. Once Tess comes back we can talk it over with her. Until then, wish me luck."

I watched Rebecca leave, then grabbed Cassie's afghan and made it into a pillow. What would the matchmaker say now? *Sure, I'm dating your Deaf grandson, but now I've lost all my Deaf clients.* I suspected even Cassie would see the error in this.

Here was my exit visa, via Sharon's other drastic decree. Cam wasn't completely out of the woods, but he improved each day. And

I had pushed my luck too far. Time to pull the plug, and return to my hunt for companionship.

Or adopt a few more cats, because after Cam I feared no one would satisfy me.

I dug my head into the soft fibers of the afghan. A rip started in my heart that would continue as I moved onward with this plan. I had no choice. It wasn't about my heart alone anymore. It was about my job. But why did it have to hurt so much? This wasn't what I wanted. These emotions were too deep, like trying to slash a hundred-year-old tree from its roots. If I didn't go through with this now, it would be worse later.

And there it was, the silver lining. Pain now, no pain later. I held onto that as long as I could. Turned out it was long enough to arrive home, pace my apartment waiting for Cam, and start up a batch of cookies I didn't need.

I dipped my spoon in the large metal mixing bowl and scooped out a heap of cookie dough. The sweet gooey mass filled my taste buds. The aroma of chocolate chip cookies wafted through the air. I lay claim to the other half of the dough, devouring it as if it was my life force.

Oreo was perched on the coffee table, trying to use a book edge to scratch her face. In desperate need for comfort, I scooped the cat up in my arms, petting the feline to keep her content. Her small body purred softly against me. I absorbed all I could from her, but the ache deep in my chest lingered and no amount of purring would stop the rift. I let go of her and placed my head in my hands. Oreo pawed my hair, trying to comb through the curls. I nearly cried, even my cat knew my distress level. And like her owner, provided no answers.

I didn't want to hurt Cam. Couldn't. I should have never let Lexie drag me to that dinner. Lesson learned. The one time I let my guard down, I let a lover in, complete disaster.

The timer beeped, and I brushed my cheeks dry as I headed for the oven. This would be the worst thing I ever had to do. Worse than telling my high school boyfriend his breath smelled too much to kiss him, worse than being the one to call a family member to tell them a client had been found unconscious. Worse than simply admitting I had fallen in love with a caregiver.

I pulled the cookies out of the oven. How was this conversation supposed to go? *"Sorry, I love you but I can't lose my clients over you."*

The cookie sheet banged and clattered as I tossed it on top of the stove. No, love was not on the table. I was not in love with him, and I certainly wouldn't tell him if I was.

The gooey cookies called to me. Without thinking I reached to grab one and singed my fingers. "Ouch." I stuck the throbbing fingers in my mouth.

Another tear rolled down my cheek. *"The conflict of interest is too much, I can't continue seeing you."* God, this was going to suck. But the alternative was my clients, my job. I had no choice.

My phone vibrated. I forced myself together and let Cam into the building. With my sleeves I patted my cheeks to try to appear normal. I knew the moment Cam entered that I failed.

"What's wrong?" he asked, kicking the door closed.

I shook my head and fought to keep more tears from falling. The words were there, right there, and yet refused to come. I detoured. *"Long day. You're familiar with those."*

He had the decency to cringe, considering he was an hour late. *"Still catching up from my time off."*

"I'm always playing catch up." I moved into the kitchen to grab some water. When I was hydrated I caught Cam eyeing the cookies.

"You baked?"

I raised one shoulder. *"Like I said, long day. I'm bringing these into work tomorrow."*

Cam moved to the sink and eyed my empty bowl. He raised an eyebrow. *"No batter."*

I blew out some air, moving a curl off my face. *"Co-workers need cookies, too."*

The mood shifted between us, the distance beginning, and I hated it. A small voice whispered, "Maybe the fairytale is real," before being gagged and hog-tied. Divorce was real. Fights were real.

What I was feeling was made-up notions of love and romance

pumped into humans. All in the name of procreation.

Well, one didn't need love for procreation. And against my better judgment I was not ready to let this man go, not yet. *"Sorry about the batter. How can I make it up to you?"*

Cam remained where he was, eyeing me like I was a freak. I could understand his reaction. I was at the end of my rope. He was the reason I lost my Deaf clients, the one person who had managed to claim my heart. It wasn't fair. Why did he have to be Cassie's grandson? Why couldn't we have had friendship first?

I moved towards him. *"Sorry, sorry. I'm drained. Make me feel better."*

A small smile formed on his lips. The urge to bite them hit me with such intensity I didn't wait for him to respond. I sunk my teeth down on his lower lip before kissing him with everything I had. He took over the kiss, wrapping me in his arms. It felt right to be with him, he felt right. I tried to push those silly thoughts aside, but my heart was trying to climb out of me and into him. Which proved I wasn't falling—I'd fallen. Not even my silly relationship rules could save me now.

Cam's hazel eyes searched mine as he brushed back a lock of hair. I swallowed my emotions, tried to shove them back into a box.

"I think you need a drink," Cam signed, the tease eradicated by the seriousness in his eyes.

"Always trying to get me drunk?" I needed to tease back, needed to lighten the mood before I ended things.

He smirked. *"You think better with chocolate."* He moved towards the kitchen, leaving me dumbfounded at how he knew me so well. He bent to my liquor cabinet. *"Let's see what you've got to work with."*

I almost missed the signs because I was watching the way his dress pants cupped his ass. Great, something else I wanted to bite.

He waved for my attention, one eyebrow quirked. Dammit, caught with the hand in the cookie jar. *"You have any liquid chocolate?"*

I placed my hands on my hips and tried to copy his quirked eyebrow.

He laughed. *"I guess that's a yes."* He bent again to rummage through my refrigerator, and I went back to watching his ass. Well, there was one good thing about not ending things too soon.

I gave up trying to not peek at him as he mixed the ingredients together and filled a small glass. I eyed the substance. *"Chocolate martini?"*

"Yes, a specialty of mine."

Damn, damn, damn. How was I supposed to resist a man that looked that good in dress pants and made chocolate martinis? I accepted the drink and let the chocolaty wonder soothe my throat. The sweet buzz had me closing my eyes and for a minute I felt good. Full of chocolate and alcohol, tension evaporated into thin air.

"You keep making these and I'll love you forever." The words slipped out of my mouth, and I opened my eyes as fear snaked its way through my body. No, no, I didn't say that. I couldn't have said that. Not here, not now. I darted my eyes to Cam and put down my drink. *"You didn't see that,"* I signed.

He held my gaze, eyes twinkling, as one corner of his mouth inched upwards. *Shit, he did.*

"I didn't mean that." My cheeks burned. *"Not in the romantic sense. The kind of thing you tell a bartender."*

"Of course. You were thankful for a good drink." Cam's grin turned into a teasing curve. A confident air surrounded him. I was in emotional trouble now.

Which, when it all came down to basics, wasn't fair. My job was on the line. I had known Cam all of two weeks. Love should not have been involved. Not even on the same football field. Heck, the same country. Yet it was there, hanging in the air, threatening to make a complicated mess even more complicated.

*****

Cam

I juggled my cards, trying to figure out how to follow up with her verbal declaration. I needed to let her know I was there, all in, and I needed the same from her. But the fear on her face demanded kid gloves. Her brown eyes watched me. It pulsed between us. How one little word could hold so much power baffled me. Yet I felt it. It consumed me. I wasn't one to fight emotions. At least not like Nica.

I walked over to her and ran one hand through her hair, stopping before tugging on the tangled curls. The rise and fall of her breasts increased, but her eyes remained scared. I had to ease the tension.

"*You either like my martini skills a hell of a lot, or me,*" I signed.

"*You know how I am with sweets.*" Her hands moved slow and deliberate.

"*You also speak your mind.*"

"*I can lie.*" Her sign swiped against her determined chin.

"*Prove it.*" I placed a hand just above her ass and yanked her flush. Nica glanced up at her off-white ceiling. "*The ceiling is pink.*"

"*Is that true?*"

"*And your eyes are blue.*"

"*Right.*"

"*And I can leave you anytime I want.*"

I held her gaze, searching deep inside for the answers she was desperate to avoid. Her clear eyes were wide open and full of emotion. If pushed, how would she label those emotions? Only one way to find out.

I moved my head down to her lips until I almost touched them, keeping my eyes on hers. "And you don't love me?" I spoke only, copying her slip.

The blacks of her eyes deepened and she jerked back. "*That's a trick question.*"

I pressed my lips against hers, taking, wanting. Claiming. Everything I felt for her came to the surface. I trusted she felt it too. The air crackled with our electricity, and I couldn't keep it in any longer. Her lids were half closed from the kiss, and that was the kicker to let the words flow free. "*I love you.*"

She wrenched back, out of my grasp, and paced. "*You've known me all of two weeks.*"

"*Plus a few years on e-mail consultations.*"

"*Two weeks.*"

"My grandmother needed a lot less than two weeks to pick my grandfather."

She stopped and stared at me for a full minute, her body stiff. *"You're serious."*

I had never been more serious about anything in my life. I nodded and took two steps towards her.

"This is too much."

"Isn't love too much?"

I caught her again and kissed her. She didn't fight me; she never did. She melted in my arms. Timid hands reached up for my shoulders, clutching at me as if I were her life support.

"Admit it, you love me."

"I don't."

I stepped back. My heart paused for a second, just a second, and resumed as I noticed the playful glint in her eyes.

"I told you I can lie."

I remained where I was. Confidence was a nasty beast, and she'd managed to knock mine off its ass. I knew her, felt her within the depths of my soul. Or so I thought. She'd turned my emotions into a game, and more than a flicker of doubt grew. For the moment I was floundering and unsure of myself. *"So which is true?"*

She closed her eyes and breathed deep. After letting the breath out, she faced me. *"I can't go there. Not now. Not yet. I'm sorry."* Those fathomless eyes dug at my heart, revealing the hole once again.

For the first time in my life I played my cards wrong.

Chapter 18

Cam

I parked my car in front of my grandmother's apartment building, the engine idling gently beneath me. I had the day off from work to finish cleaning up. For years I'd visited here weekly or biweekly. Now I was done, a final chapter in the memory of my grandmother.

My hands gripped the wheel, needing to prolong the inevitable, but even wishing on a falling star wouldn't bring my Grandmother back. I forced my grip to relax and marched my ass into the building. At Grandma's door I was hit with the smell of cranberries. Grandma always had a candle burning, but how was it possible the scent lingered in the air two weeks after her move? I shook off the sensation and glanced around the apartment. My family had done a good job cleaning it out. Most items were gone. Photos removed from the walls, the computer and television missing. The remaining tabletops sported only dust outlines of the items they previously held. Another final moment that hit me in the gut. Her life was over.

On the counter that divided the tiny kitchen and living room was a box with my name on it. I opened it and checked inside, noting some of the items appeared to be things my grandmother had requested for me. I left the box open and continued surveying the area.

The bedroom was empty except for the closet. Wire hangers held Grandma's clothes, untouched since I rummaged through for her stay at Hospice House. I fisted my hands in my hair, tugging at the roots. Of course my family couldn't be bothered to do any of the work. All they did was take what they wanted, letting me handle the rest. How did the youngest become the one with the most responsibility?

A red haze obscured my vision, and I counted to ten before I punched a hole in the wall. Once the haze diminished I grabbed a garbage bag and shoved her clothing inside. I continued checking drawers and countertops, throwing away anything I had no use for. In the kitchen the cabinets were still full. This time I threw away anything perishable, and piled the cans on the counter for neighbors to take. The elders here were on limited incomes, so a few extra cans of food would surely help someone.

An hour after I arrived, everything but the furniture was accounted for. Emotional exhaustion seeped into my bones and had me ready to go back to bed. Grandma would have scolded me for that thought, telling me to rest when I was dead.

The joke wasn't funny now.

I collected my box and rummaged through a little more thoroughly, taking out each item. Her knitting needles burned in my hand, never to help her with another stitch. A small framed picture made me smile. It was of Grandma and me when I was around eight years old. She was hunched over and the two of us signed "I Love You" to the cameraman, Grandpa. This was how I wanted to remember her, back in the days when she picked me up off the school bus. Back when I did my homework over fresh baked cookies. Back when she was alive and vibrant. I held the picture to my heart, grateful my family put these items aside for me, even after my dramatic exit.

The wooden box I had decorated waited for me in the corner. I figured someone would have trashed it, since the box screamed "designed by an eight-year-old." I flipped it upside down and my shaky childhood handwriting filled the bottom:

I love you, Grandma!
Love,
Cam

Not once did she mention this message when I complained about her still having the box, not once. Now it became obvious why she kept it for twenty-two years.

Under all my grandmother's belongings I found a small box with a note attached to it. My name was on the paper, in my mother's handwriting. I moved to the couch and sat down in the sagging cushion. After a deep breath I opened the letter.

Dear Cam,

Your father and I are sorry for the way things ended at dinner. Nica does seem like a nice young lady. It's hard for me to comprehend the situation.

That is no excuse. You needed us to be there at Grandma's end. It didn't affect us like it did you. I'm sorry I didn't see this until now. Grandma loved you. She would want you to be happy.

It was her wish that Nica have her brooch. It was wrong of us to get in the way of Grandma's wishes. We have left the brooch. Please tell Nica we are sorry and want her to have it.

Call us when you get this letter.
Love,
Mom and Dad

I opened the box to find Grandma's brooch inside. I threw my head back on the couch and smiled towards the heavens. No more complications.

On my way out of the building I bumped into June.

"*How are you?*" she asked, one hand on her cane for support.

I smiled. "*I'm fine. I have some of my grandmother's leftover items if anyone needs anything.*"

"*How sweet, we'll have fun shopping.*" She eyed me up and down. "*How's Veronica?*"

"*She's good.*"

"We've all been worried since we found out she lost us as clients."

My fingers went numb, the box slipped before I tightened my grip. Instead of succumbing to a shaky mess I placed it by my feet and gave myself a moment before righting myself. *"What?"*

"You don't know?"

I shook my head. What a fool, not knowing something this important about my own girlfriend.

"Isabella had a visit scheduled with Veronica. Only someone new showed up. Sweet lady, very willing to write back and forth. But not the same. After some prodding she admitted the cases were taken from Veronica." June shifted her cane beneath her elbow. *"We don't blame you too much."*

My mind spun. Why hadn't Nica told me? What else had happened? My gut bottomed out. No wonder she had fought so hard to stay away. I thought my grandmother's death would solve things. Deep down, I knew something else had to have happened, and I needed to figure out what. But I also needed Nica to confide in me, to let me help her like she did for me.

I turned to go, needing to find the bottom of this, when June stomped on the floor.

"I have something for you, but it's not ready. Make sure you come back in a few weeks."

I wasn't so sure about coming back, but I nodded and made my way out of the building. I threw the box into the trunk before sliding in behind the wheel. Complicated be damned at this point, I needed to see Nica.

*****

Nica

I pulled into my work parking lot and called myself a coward. A spineless, lust-filled coward. I didn't end the relationship and I hadn't mentioned the problems our relationship was causing at work. Not even when he took me for a second time and made me come my brains out. He was feeling better all right. Which meant I needed to end our relationship, and fast. He already said he loved me; I needed to run like hell in the opposite direction. Or give up my job. I could survive on orgasms for a few weeks at least, right?

The answer to that was a most definite "no." I scolded my libido to take a long, cold shower and headed into the building. Head down I mumbled a hello to the receptionist, hoping the cold fall air would be blamed for my rosy cheeks. I glanced at the memorial donations—*down libido, think of death*—and mumbled a hello to Rebecca, refusing to make eye contact. At my desk, I grabbed Cassie's afghan and dared my libido to think of sex while holding Cam's grandmother's knitting. The soft fibers and memories cooled my racing pulse.

Thank God—the horny bitch got the hint.

I pushed myself into work to keep my mind off my dilemmas. Distracted by my phone vibrating, I glanced at the screen and stopped short at the text from Cam.

Cam: Finished cleaning out Grandma's apartment, you free for a few minutes?

After my director's complaint I didn't feel I could allow Cam to be seen here. But I didn't have the heart to turn him away. Especially since I didn't know how affected he would be. I also couldn't leave to meet him elsewhere, so I either had to turn him away or take a risk.

Nica: Sure. Let me know when you get here, I'll meet you outside.

It was the easiest compromise I could figure out. As much as it pained me I wished I had never gone to that bar, never met Cam. Then my life would be simple. *And lonely*, I reminded myself. He was going to leave behind a meteor-sized hole.

What felt like a few minutes later he texted again, and I stood from my desk and ventured outside. The late September weather had turned chilly. I wrapped my cardigan around my body as the cool breeze nipped through me. I found him near the side of the building, leaning against his car.

"*How was the apartment?*" I remained a few steps away, out of reach. His tropical cologne crossed the distance, tickled my nose, and begged me forward. A strong reminder of why I found myself in this predicament to begin with—resisting him required more than I had to give.

"*The apartment was fine. I'm more concerned with something I heard from June.*"

My pulse ticked. "*What's wrong? Is she OK? Does she need help?*"

His eyes narrowed and a funny feeling bloomed in my gut. "*She's fine, but you wouldn't be able to help her out anyways, right?*"

Crap. I bit my lip, all the walls crashing down around me.

"*When did you lose your Deaf clients?*"

The concern on his face spurred on the growing fear we were doomed. "*Two days ago.*"

A flash of pain crossed his face. "*Why didn't you tell me?*"

Now was not the time for sabotage, but the sabotage had presented itself. At least I recognized what I was doing at face value. "*Not your problem.*"

He uncrossed his ankles. "*Not my problem? Why did you lose them then?*"

"*Because this—*" I gestured between us "*—should never have happened. It's not appropriate.*"

Cam scrubbed a hand through his hair, the strands golden in the early afternoon light. "*Then why did you agree to date me? And why couldn't you have shared this information and let me help?*"

Warning bells rang in my head. *Tuck and roll, Veronica, you can't save this.* "*It's complicated.*"

He raised his eyebrows but kept his hands on his hips.

"*I agreed because…*" My hand trailed off. *Because I love you.* But I couldn't express that sentiment, not here, not now. I feared not ever. "*Against my better judgment I can't seem to stay away.*" At least that much was true.

"*And the second part?*"

My hands shook and I did my best to keep them steady. "*It's not your problem, it's mine. Involving you will just make things worse.*"

"*So I'm part of the problem but I can't help?*"

"*The less involvement you have the better at this point. You shouldn't even be here right now.*" All I wanted to do was fling myself at him, but I had to keep going, I had to make this the last time he'd be tempted to show up at my work. "*The amount of knowledge I have about your grandmother, about the case, makes this, us, a dangerous situation. I have information that could harm your family and jeopardize the care your grandmother received.*"

He shook his head and I felt the frustration starting to simmer. "*Grandma's dead.*"

"*Some pains linger long after death.*"

"*Prove it, make me understand.*"

My heart beat wildly in my chest, pieces chipping off from every pulse. *Keep going*, my mind urged. I had the proof, the one thing Cassie never shared with Cam. I had all the power in the world. The question remained: could I use it? Or would that be worse than dating a caregiver?

Start small; embarrass him, maybe that would be enough.

"*I know you wet your bed until you were seven.*"

Cam shrugged a shoulder. "*Ask around, Grandma told most people that.*"

I rubbed my sweaty palms against each other. "*Your grandmother lost a child before your father.*"

"*She always said she had four children, not three.*" He glanced at the building, then back at me. "*You aren't giving me anything that proves why your clients would have been taken away. Or why you refuse to let me in. I thought we had something here.*"

Me too. "*You don't understand.*"

His jaw tightened. "*Is this the pity the Deaf guy?*"

I shook my head. "*What? No, of course not!*"

"*Then why won't I understand?*"

"*Because you aren't a social worker, not because of your ears.*"

"*So explain it to me.*"

I paced in a circle, the emotional turmoil inside bubbling until I felt sick. "*I have. I have tried. I stayed away, I explained. I tried to do everything right and somehow it still came back to slap me in the face.*"

"So let me fix it."

"You can't. You never could. This was all on me."

"Because my grandmother told an embarrassing story about me from twenty plus years ago?"

He held my stare, challenging me. The words bubbled up inside. Only my heart screamed not to share this, not to crumble him. I could run into his arms, apologize, work it out. And then what? Suffer pain worse than this in a few years for both of us?

No, do it now.

"Your grandmother got her cancer diagnosis two years ago."

Cam's arms fell to the side and the challenge melted away. *"She got the diagnosis six months ago."*

"She only told you because Hospice became involved."

I wished the ground would open up and swallow me whole. Then I wouldn't have to see the look of pure devastation on his face. Then I wouldn't have to remember five minutes too late that Cassie had begged me never to tell Cam. That I had promised not to share, as a social worker. Hell, I even had a fucking note in the system stating all this. But the lines between professional and personal were forever blurred.

Two years ago I had visited Cassie for a post hospital visit. Cassie had revealed she had lung cancer, stage two, and was refusing all treatment. Her husband had cancer himself and chemo had been brutal on him. Cassie didn't want the same. She was old, she had a good life, and she wanted the remainder of it to be good.

I worried Cassie didn't have all the facts. I called Cassie's doctor, discussed the diagnosis and prognosis in depth. Then I visited Cassie again, going over all I'd learned. Cassie had remained adamant, sitting across from me, pictures of her family dotting the wall behind her. *"No. I'm not getting treatment. And my family will never know. C.T. can't handle this. Losing his grandfather was hard enough on him. He needs the love of a good woman to help him through. To remind him that he's not alone. Someone like you. The two of you would be perfect together."*

Well. Her family knew now. I couldn't stop a tear from escaping. I really did mess this all up. Cam remained frozen.

"*I'm so sorry,*" I signed, another tear escaping. "*This is why we can't work. Why it's not appropriate for me to be with you. Why I lost my Deaf clients. I shouldn't have said that. Don't you see? My director told me to stop seeing you because of situations like this.*"

"*She was stage four for two years?*" Cam asked, stopping my dash into the building.

"*Don't make me answer that.*"

He stomped, the sound a loud vibration. "*Answer me. Two years ago, what stage?*"

I held up two fingers by my thigh.

He ran his hands through his hair, again, messing up those strands to bedhead level. "*My parents kept things from me as a kid. I never expected my own grandmother to do the same, for you to do the same.*"

"*I did what my job required me to do.*"

"*Always a game or a hidden agenda, isn't there?*" Then, without another word, he slammed his car door shut and drove off.

I remained glued to the spot. What had I done? Hurt Cam, that's what. Without a second thought I grabbed my phone and fired off a text to Grant.

Nica: Had a fight with Cam, said some things I shouldn't have. Things related to his grandmother that has got to hurt like hell. Please look out for him?

I clicked send and prayed he'd get the message in time. I'd needed to end the relationship, but not by hurting Cam.

Chapter 19

Cam

I stared at the beer in front of me. My head rooted to the table. The slight sway of the liquid coaxed me. *Come on, Thompson, float on the Eye-Level River.* Where life would never be half full or half empty again.

Five bottles littered the table. No, wait, six bottles. Grant set his one measly little beer down. *"I'd say drink more, but you and alcohol don't mix well,"* I signed with my head still on the table, using the sticky brown surface for my supporting hand. If anyone ever wanted to know if one could slur in ASL, all they had to do was look at me.

Grant sipped. *"Right now you and alcohol don't mix well. You're cut off. Last one."*

I shook my head, more of a dragging motion across the surface. Something stuck to my cheek. *"Hands not numb yet."*

"Tell that to your signing. You're plastered."

It wasn't enough, not yet. The shattered remnants of my heart still bled.

"Thanks to you I've won a second bet with Lexie."

I blinked, unsure of how many bets were in play here. *"Bet?"*

Grant ran a finger over the top of his beer, swaying it back and forth and making me seasick. *"We've been betting on your love life. She thought Nica would have waited another week. Ever the optimist."*

"Bet?"

"Yeah. I'm up twenty bucks. And thinking I need to bet something that

170

involves removing clothes next time. After all, if you two are on the outs Lexie and I can crash and burn all we want."

I couldn't put together what he was babbling about. "*Bef?*"

Grant collected my beer. "*OK, you're done. I've never seen you this shit-faced.*" Grant held up his hand. "*How many fingers?*"

I tried to focus on the psychedelic digits, but couldn't. "*Somewhere between two and five thousand. I understand, that counts?*"

"*Not when your grammar is worse than mine. Come on. Time to head home. You've got a roommate for the night.*"

I didn't remember anything beyond that. The next thing I knew Grant was shaking me awake, making sure I was alive before leaving for work. The emptiness returned, all-consuming this time as it swallowed my heart into the black hole. Outside was another normal day.

Inside a void raged.

Grief's prickly fingers stretched around my throat, sinking deep into my flesh. Sunlight peeked through my shades, taunting me. At least it sent shards to my skull, a nice leveling of the internal pain compass.

The time ticked by. I focused on a knot in the wood floor. The image blurred and warped into a pixilated gibberish image. I sat. My foot twitched as I tried to move, tried to get up. My heart weighed me down like lead, the image of the wood knot reappearing in my vision.

I tucked my feet back in bed and tugged the covers over my head. *It's a good thing I'm alone*, I thought, as the tears dampened my pillow.

An unknown amount of time later the light for my videophone flashed and flashed. And flashed. I ignored it and yanked the pillow over my head to welcome the darkness, but the light still managed to peek through. "*Whoever you are, go the fuck away.*" They didn't listen. Tired of the damn flashing I summoned the strength to roll over and answer the call.

Matt appeared on the screen. "*Thank God, you had us worried.*"

"*Bad day,*" was all I could muster.

Matt studied my appearance. I guessed it wasn't pretty. *"You need anything?"*

"No." It was fucking Saturday—couldn't they leave me the hell alone?

Silence.

"Tomorrow?" Matt asked.

"Not sure."

"Should we send someone?"

"No." I didn't want to see anyone, at least not anyone alive. The silence stretched on. I tried to say something, anything. Words wouldn't come.

Matt broke the silence. *"This isn't like you."*

"So?"

"All right. Answer a text tomorrow and let us know you're alive."

I disconnected and dragged the pillow back over my face, where I remained until the overwhelming darkness grew too much. I should have opened the shades, flipped on a light, ate. Instead I turned on the television, trying to register how the three screaming people were interrelated and who was cheating on whom. The captioning couldn't keep up with all the back and forth. And neither could I. My doorbell light flashed, distracting me from the screen. I watched the yellow light flicker on and off, on and off, until it stopped. Then I faced my television. Again, my doorbell light flashed. My attention shifted to the front door but I remained where I was, still in bed. After a minute the light came again; whoever was there wasn't taking the hint.

My front door opened and Dan entered, tossing a set of keys in the air, followed by Ben. The television flashed with a new brawl. I grew disgusted with myself and switched it off.

"Well," Ben signed when both my brothers crowded in my doorway. *"Look who's still in bed at one in the afternoon."* The furrow of his brows did not match the tease in his words.

I glanced at the clock. It really was one pm.

Dan sat on the end of the bed. *"Your friends are worried. Said something happened with Nica?"*

I jerked the sheets over my head. Dan yanked them back. *"Grandma's cancer diagnosis first came two years ago,"* I signed while on my back.

Dan and Ben exchanged a confused glance. *"We suspected as much,"* Ben said.

I sat up. *"What?"*

Ben shrugged. *"She had that cough, the same cough grandpa had."*

"Chemo was hell on Grandpa, I don't blame her for wanting to avoid it," Dan said. *"But she was ninety years old. She had a good long life. Still miss her."*

Ben waved. *"Remember when we played ball inside? I loved getting in trouble at Grandma's house. She couldn't hear us. Though she heard the window being smashed. I had no clue how. Even you couldn't hear it. Then she went easy on us. I thought we were in the clear, until she told Mom. Grandma sure knew how to punish us."*

Dan leaned back against my desk. *"She made up for Mom where it was needed. Motherly love? That was Grandma. We're in trouble? Throw that shit back to Mom."*

I struggled to keep my eyes dry. I didn't think anyone else understood. Should have known my brothers would. *"I never felt like an outcast as long as Grandma and Grandpa were around."*

"You're not. What's really bothering you?"

I couldn't say what I wanted to say. That Nica kept things from me. That her job was in trouble because of me. That we'd affected the care the Deaf elders received. I scrubbed my hands over my face, coarse stubble scraping at the pads.

Someone jabbed at my foot until I removed my hands from my face. *Pesky older brothers.*

"Come on. We're family. Family sticks together," Dan said.

"You're hearing."

"Not my fault my ears work."

"Give me a screwdriver," Ben began, *"I'll fix that."*

I glanced back and forth, from brother to brother. A small laugh rumbled in my chest.

Ben pointed at me. *"He looks funny when he smiles."*

I rolled my eyes.

"*What happened with Nica?*" Dan asked.

"*Besides telling me about Grandma's cancer diagnosis? She didn't tell me she lost her Deaf clients.*"

"*I'm getting the feeling she lost her clients because of you. So who should be upset with who?*"

I rolled my eyes again. "*Stop being a lawyer.*"

"*Stop needing me to be a lawyer. Sounds like she risked a lot to date you.*"

Ben waved for attention. "*Come on, out with the other part.*"

I shook my head, eyebrows drawn in confusion. My brothers raised their eyebrows in silent communication.

"*You think he's there?*" Dan asked Ben.

"*Damn straight he is.*"

I vocalized for attention. "*You two fuckers mind including me?*"

"*Bossy baby brother,*" Ben said.

I crossed my arms and waited. Dan copied me, leaving Ben to continue.

"*Nica won't turn you into Dad.*"

I blinked, mind scrambling. Dan continued. "*Mom likes control. Dad likes being controlled. None of us are like Dad. We're closer to Mom. So even though we don't want to be manipulated like Dad, we run the risk of being Mom in the relationship.*"

"*Point being, don't worry about it. Not when it sounds like Nica's trying to do everything she can for you. That's no game, that's love.*"

I closed my eyes. Maybe they were right. Maybe Nica did have reasons for holding herself back. Didn't make it hurt any less. Our union fulfilled my grandmother's last wish. In some small way it allowed Grandma to live on.

Or maybe it had nothing to do with Grandma. No matter what Nica threw at me I couldn't let go. She had my heart. Maybe I was whipped, or she had my balls. Grant would certainly tell me as much. My brothers were right—not like Dad, never like Dad. The real reason this hurt so much was because it was from Nica. Not the words that were said, but the person doing the damage.

No longer about grief but about heart.

Someone tapped my leg. Ben. *"Come on. Let's go eat."*

*****

Nica

"That was an impressively impressive Veronica, Veronica," Lexie said from across the bar table.

Understatement of the year. "I'm a horrible person. Horrible. I think even Cassie would want me to stay the hell away from her grandson now." Demonic little creatures chomped on my heart, ripping pieces out in a feeding frenzy.

"You've had three drinks and you're still wallowing?" Lexie polished off her glass.

My current future plans involved wallowing and more wallowing. Lexie better get used to it.

"I'd suggest you apologize, but that would be cruel."

"Cruel? To apologize?" I'd thought it, more than once. Even started a few text messages.

"Yes, cruel. Because then you'll be toying with that poor man's heart. Since we both know you'll just pull another Veronica."

"I was brutal to him. Brutal. Isn't an apology the least I can do?"

"Does brutal and apology belong in the same thought process?"

I eyed my glass. "After that many drinks I'm supposed to be lucid?"

"Touché." Lexie nudged the drink towards me. "Let him be. You notified Grant that you demolished his heart and then ran over it for safekeeping, he'll make sure he doesn't do anything stupid."

I sat up straight, images of Cam throwing himself off a bridge permeating my brain. "Now you're scaring me."

A crooked grin broke out on Lexie's face. "I suspect you didn't want the sabotage this time." She grabbed her phone and tapped at her screen.

"Is that Grant? Is Cam okay?" I reached across the table for her phone but she batted it away.

"Yes, that's Grant. I owe him twenty dollars now, thanks a lot."

I banged the table. "I don't give a fuck. I'll give you the money. How's Cam?"

Lexie held her phone closer to her. "You really didn't want this sabotage."

"Screw it." I collected my own phone, ready to ask Grant myself.

"He's drunk. Which you are."

I dropped my phone to the table, my heart breaking all over again.

"Great, now Grant's trying to start another bet for a pair of my underwear. Are you going to get back together with Cam or not? Because if you two are finished for good there's a bet I need to blow."

I stared off into the room, not seeing anything but blurred techno-colors. "I shouldn't, but I also shouldn't have in the first place."

Lexie came into my view. "Well, what do you want?"

I found my drink. "For Cam to not be Cassie's grandson."

*****

I still felt like crap on Monday morning but managed to get to work where I tapped my keyboard with a lack of enthusiasm, unable to register the words on the screen.

"Ooh, cookies," Rebecca said as she made her way into the office. She stood over the container I'd perched at the corner of my desk, care of my weekend baking spree. After selecting two she eyed me. "You look like shit."

"Thanks," I mumbled. "Lovely to see you as well."

"Still think you're a horrible person?" Rebecca turned on her laptop.

"Wouldn't you?"

"I'd like to be a supportive friend and say no, but yeah, yeah I would."

We both froze when Tess entered her office.

"She lives," Rebecca breathed.

My legs twitched, ready to move, but anxiety rooted me to the seat. "Best to let her get settled in first."

Rebecca clucked. I threw a balled up piece of paper at her.

Two home visits and a dozen phone calls later, I found the courage to enter. "Feeling better?" I asked from the doorway.

Tess nodded. "I lost my voice," she whispered hoarsely.

"Ouch," I said.

Tess smiled. "I should have learned ASL."

I scuffed one shoe against the doorframe. Tess gestured for me to enter. I shut the door and sat in the spare chair.

"Sharon talked with you?"

I swallowed and nodded.

"I'm sorry I wasn't here, I wouldn't have been able to say much." Tess laughed as a jeweled hand touched her throat.

"Rebecca and I already handled the switch, you should have received an e-mail with the new client assignments."

"I did."

I wrung my hands together, very much aware that my personal life was at the forefront of my supervisor's mind. "Do I have any recourse here? It's not fair to my clients to suddenly have a lack of communication."

Tess studied me. "Did Sharon explain why this had to happen?"

"No." A warning shimmied up my spine.

Tess tapped her desk with one finger. She plucked out a piece of paper from her cluttered desk and placed it on her lap, the jewels on her hands forming a barrier. "I don't know what exactly was going on, you never mentioned anything to me, certainly not that you had ever met the illustrious Cameron. Why don't we start there?"

I briefly recapped the meeting at Hospice.

"Oh, Nica." Tess rubbed her forehead. "Why didn't you say anything?"

"Probably because I knew it was wrong."

She tapped the paper. "Someone in his family made a complaint."

Well if that wasn't a sucker punch right to the gut. I threw my head against the wall. "Why didn't Sharon tell me?"

"Probably for the same reason I'm hesitant to show you the

letter." Tess's face etched with concern. The fine lines around her eyes and mouth were creased with stress.

I eyed the paper under Tess's hand. "Isn't there something we can do? For the best interest of my clients."

"There is already a formal hearing being set up, with all of senior staff. Maybe get Cameron to share his side."

I cringed. I doubted Cam would want to help me, not now. "I have to have a formal hearing on my personal life?"

"Sadly that's the price you pay for dating a former caregiver. Maybe Cameron needs to have a talk with his family?"

I felt sick to my stomach. "Let me guess, the letter was written by a Rhonda?"

Tess picked up her glasses and checked at the letter. She met my eyes. "Yes. How did you know?"

"That's Cam's mom."

Tess's mouth dropped open. "His mother wrote this?"

Why am I not surprised? I held out my hand for the letter. Tess hesitated but handed it over.

Dear Independent Senior Services,

My mother-in-law, Cassie Thompson, was a client of Independent Senior Services. After her death I became aware of a situation that had developed with her case manager, Veronica Anders. It appears that Veronica had been sleeping with Cassie's grandson.

It's not exactly appropriate behavior, considering Cameron was heavily involved in his grandmother's care. Although they claim nothing happened until a week before her death, I doubt this is really the case, making me wonder what type of preferential treatment Cassie received.

Veronica has stated she worked extra hard to get specific workers involved in Cassie's care. I fear that other clients suffered due to this preferential treatment. Veronica also complained about the high numbers of her caseload. This does not strike me as a good thing for a case manager to be doing.

Beyond this, Veronica found a way to get her hands on some of my mother-in-law's belongings. I fear that other elders have been taken advantage of in similar situations.

I should add that Cameron is deaf, much like his grandmother was. Veronica is taking advantage of someone with a disability. I've caught her signing things in a not so pleasant manner, bending the truth to suit her needs.

As an agency that deals with frail elders you should have better tabs on your employees. I expect you will take care of this and fix the situation.

Sincerely,

Rhonda Thompson

I handed the paper back. My hand trembled and my heart leapt into my throat. The vile words burned my retinas. The depth of Rhonda's hatred spanned farther than I could have even imagined.

"Who treats their own son this way?" I finally whispered.

Tess shook her head. "I don't know." She paused, clearly weighing her next words. "I have to ask, any truth in this letter?"

I forced myself to glance over the letter again. "I don't have the brooch. I know Cassie wanted to leave it to me though. I didn't alter ASL to suit any needs. I did mention to Cam's parents the high caseloads, to make them understand my job. Nothing else." I handed the letter back. "Sharon believes this?"

Tess sighed. "The complaints need to be investigated."

"But these are complaints related to a dead client."

"Nica, if you fight this you'll lose your license. We both know no one got hurt with you dating Cameron. But the fact remains: a social worker is not supposed to become involved with a client or family member."

I rubbed a hand over my mouth.

"I'll let you know when the meeting is scheduled. Cameron can prove he's not some invalid like the letter suggests. We'll fight this."

I blinked back the tears trying to escape. "And now I've lost my Deaf clients. Maybe I should hand in my resignation."

Tess placed a hand over mine. "Sharon didn't explain everything, did she?" Tess's voice was either soft due to her sickness or compassion.

"What am I missing here?"

Tess grasped her hands together. "Your Deaf clients were taken away immediately as a precaution. This meeting is not to get them back; it's to discuss your continued employment here."

My jaw fell open. "I'm going to be fired over this?"

"If the accusations in the letter are true, we'd be foolish to keep you on. But you and I both know the accusations are not true. We still have to research the claims."

"I really shouldn't have continued seeing Cam."

"Stop that. While I don't think dating Cameron was your best decision, you obviously care for him. We'll fight this letter."

I opened my mouth to tell Tess we'd broken up, but couldn't summon the words. What difference did it make now anyways? I stumbled to my desk, flanked by Rebecca before I could even sit down.

"What did you find out?"

I explained about the letter, the meeting, and my job being on the line.

"You better tell Cam."

"No, he doesn't need any further pain."

"You need a Deaf person to prove you weren't taking advantage of your clients," Rebecca whispered before returning to her desk.

I opened a text message to Cam and sat there. A million words needed to be shared, most of them beginning with "*I'm sorry.*" And yet I had to throw one more hurt at him: vile words from his mother.

Nica: I am so, so sorry for what I said. I had no right to hurt you like that, to betray your grandmother. I can't take it back. Please understand, it's why this is so complicated. I don't ever want to do that again. Yet I may have to. I found out what prompted my Deaf clients being taken away. A letter arrived here from someone in your family.

My thumb hovered over the send icon. I glanced up towards the heavens. What would Cassie want me to do?

I clicked send.

Chapter 20

Cam

I leaned back in my desk chair, hands behind my head, ankles crossed, as I eyed my phone on my desk. Nica's text message faded to black as the phone went into sleep mode.

"*She said she's sorry,*" Ashley signed.

"*She also told him about his grandmother's cancer diagnosis,*" Matt countered.

"*And then she contacted Grant to make sure he was OK. She's in love with him.*"

She'd verbalized as much and then denied and for the first time I understood, truly understood what she risked by being with me. Especially if someone in my family started this current downward spiral. But rather than trying to work things out together, she cut me off. "*If she's in love with me, it's causing her to run in the opposite direction.*" I sniffed my shirt. "*Do I smell? Is it my ears?*"

Ashley reached for a handful of pretzels. "*I suspect her issues are her own and don't have anything to do with you. Certainly not your deafness. But you might smell, that could be a problem.*"

"*Only one way to find out.*" I pushed forward and grabbed my phone, unsure exactly what to type. I needed to see her and I suspected if I asked nice she'd find an excuse to avoid me.

Cam: Tell me to my face.

I tossed my phone down, but not before Ashley read over my shoulder.

"*Sounds threatening*," Matt signed. "*Do we need to lock you in a cage?*"

No, I'd never hurt her. "*I liked it better when you were worried about me.*"

"*I still am, ignore him*," Ashley said.

I wasn't sure what my plan was. There was an overwhelming need to see her. She lost her Deaf clients because of me. The elders I grew up with would surely kick my ass if I didn't at least try to fix the situation.

"*He's going to go crawling back, I don't believe it*," Matt signed, putting his phone to his ear, which only meant one thing.

I swiped the phone. "*Leave Grant out of this.*" I'd get enough ribbing without Matt's help. It was going to appear like crawling back, I didn't care, not when it was the least I could do.

My desk vibrated with an incoming text.

Nica: I'm not sure that's a good idea.
Cam: I don't care.

"*Uh-oh, she's his new project*," Ashley said to Matt.
"*That's going to end badly.*" Matt shook his head at me.

Nica: OK.

A grin worked its way over my face. Yeah, I wasn't getting the hint about us. And I was making an idiot out of myself. I wiped my face clean and moved my phone to my pocket.

*****

Nica

I collected the plastic container of cookies from my car and stood up straight. The sun set behind the tall buildings, triggering the city streetlights to flicker on. I had no idea why I agreed to see Cam, never mind at his home. The peace offering in my hands was small and meager, but I had to do something.

Something that kept my hands off him didn't hurt.

I sucked in the smoggy city air before forcing my legs into action. This wasn't safe territory for my poor, crushed, broken, and bleeding heart. If he made a move towards me I'd be putty in his hands.

And now I wished he'd make a move. *Foolish woman, snap out of it. Handle the letter, tell him you're sorry, and go home.* Of course this didn't stop my heart from trying to jump ahead of me as I climbed the stairs.

I shifted the container and rang his doorbell. A minute later, footsteps echoed closer and my pulse kicked up another thousand notches. The door opened and for the first time in three days, I was face to face with Cam. The relief almost had me wrapping my arms around him. I gripped the cookie container tighter.

He stepped to the side and I entered the apartment. The next thing I knew my back was against the wall and he was kissing me. I dropped the cookies and flung my arms around him, letting his smooth lips vanquish all the hurt and pain of the last few days. One of his hands slipped under my shirt, rubbing against the bare skin of my waist. I really needed to put a stop to this, before we had sex against his front door.

Well…

No. I drew back. One gaze in his eyes and I almost kissed him again. Love shined there—he made no attempts at hiding his feelings. My heart cheered but my brain held firm to caution. The emotions were too much, and my eyes watered and spilled over.

"*I'm sorry*," I signed. I'd sign it a million times more if I had to.

A ghost of a smile crossed his face. "*I know. I'm sorry, too, I didn't mean for us to cause problems for you. A letter was written?*"

Oh God, could we go back to kissing? "*Yes.*" I bent and retrieved my container. "*Cookie?*"

"*How much did you bake over the weekend?*"

I cringed and moved the container into his kitchen. *"Half a freezer full."*

He laughed, a full and open laugh. I stopped, watching him. Somehow, with all the horrible things I said, he was truly doing better. I opened the container and handed him a cookie before taking one for myself.

"Double chocolate? Really bad weekend then."

I opted to check my shoes for scuff marks. He placed a finger under my chin and forced me to look at him.

"I'm sorry."

"We've established that." He leaned closer. *"How sorry?"*

I moaned when he kissed me. Only now the seduction of his mouth was mixed with chocolate, and I had no resistance for the deadly combination.

He broke the kiss. *"Tell me about the letter."*

I bit my lip and shook my head.

"Who wrote it? My mother?"

I was about to break through skin with my teeth. *"Yes."*

"My mother." Cam half laughed. *"My own mother. She leaves the brooch and then sabotages your job."*

He moved to pace but I grabbed his arm. *"She left the brooch?"* Rhonda wasn't just causing problems; she was setting me up.

"Yes. I was going to give it to you, but then June told me you lost them as clients. I should get it for you." He might have been able to move, if I didn't now have a death grip on his arm.

"No. I can't accept that."

"Grandma wanted you to have it."

"I'm under investigation for wrongful actions with my clients. I can't have personal artifacts given to me after her death. Especially from my..." I trailed off.

He raised an eyebrow. *"Boyfriend?"*

"We fought."

"And kissed." He stepped towards me.

I stepped back.

"I'm not family. I'm not permanent. I can't have it."

He froze, eyes flittering back and forth as if weighing his options. *"Your parents' divorce messed you up this much?"*

"No. My parents had the right idea. Friendship first, love second. When they split, life went on as normal and they were able to revert to friends. I've seen other relationships crumble, the children get hurt, the spouses get hurt. Over fifty percent of marriages end in divorce. If more people searched for the companionship there would be less heartache."

Cam shook his head, a slight back and forth motion, but one that clearly telegraphed he didn't agree. *"So, let me get this straight. Because fifty percent of marriages end in divorce there is no point in searching for love."*

I stared at him, unable to sign. I kept my hands busy grabbing another cookie.

"My grandparents loved each other beyond death. My parents, for all their flaws, are still married, as are my brothers, aunts, and cousins. Are that many of your clients divorced?"

I swallowed a chunk of cookie. *"No. But people our age…It doesn't last."*

"Unless you want it to."

My heart wanted me to listen, but my mind had unleashed the masking tape to keep me quiet.

"There is another way to look at this." Cam's lips turned upward as he inched towards me. *"If love scares you, and you're running, then you must love me."*

My heart jumped and struggled against the sticky confinement. *"I should go."* I turned to leave but he tugged me to him, my back to his front. His lips found the tender skin of my neck, kissing a path to my collarbone. Every nerve ending perked in anticipation of his touch. And judging by the bulge digging into my ass, I wasn't alone.

"I love you," his breath brushed my wet skin. "I never thought I would, not like this, but I do. I'll keep saying it until you finally admit it yourself. You have two choices: you can either admit your feelings, or work with me to fix the problem my mother created."

I turned. My heart ripped off the confining tape, but my mind clamped a firm hand to keep me still. *"How do you think we can fix the letter?"*

He smiled, but his eyes lost some of their spark. My heart cursed my mind. I was tired of hurting him. I stepped into him, placing one hand on his cheek. I kissed the corner of his mouth, caught the light come back into his eyes, then kissed the other corner before pairing my lips up with his.

He collected me in his arms. The earlier passion was gone though. This was serious. A confirmation that the desire to mess things up was so ingrained I'd sabotage without trying.

"*I'm sorry. I don't know how to do this.*"

"*Well, we kiss and then—*"

I shook my head, a revelation brewing. "*Relationships. I don't know how. I've only witnessed the kind that ends in divorce.*"

A loving smile broke out on his face. He held out one hand to me. "*My parents are messed up. I'm not so sure either. We trust each other to figure it out together.*"

Here was everything I could have wished for, and more. I put my hand in his. "*I trust you.*"

He yanked on our entwined hands until I stumbled into him, then he picked me up as he attacked my mouth. My heart nearly burst with victory, even as my mind pouted in the corner. I didn't care. No longer was this my client's caregiver. This was the man who had my heart, even if I couldn't tell him yet.

*****

Cam

"*Remind me again how discussing this while naked and eating cookies is a good idea?*" Nica lay in my bed, a thin bed sheet covered her body up to her armpits, the tub of cookies beside her.

I grinned as I bit into a cookie. "*Much more interesting this way.*"

Nica laughed. When her eyes met mine they spoke of intense emotions. In that moment I knew there was no way I was letting her go. This was real and mutual.

I put the cookie down and sat up. "*Is it just you dating me? Or was my mother trying to get you in serious trouble?"*

Nica shoved a cookie into her mouth. *"Trouble. I'm currently under investigation and a meeting is being set up to decide if I lose my job."*

I bit my lip instead of the cookie. *"What? You might lose your job?"* I had to work hard to keep my hands in check and not let my anger leak out. Dan was right. I was more of a risk to Nica than anything she'd said.

She nodded, eyes watery. *"I thought it was bad enough that I lost my Deaf clients, but that's nothing compared to losing all my clients."*

"We're not hurting anyone. Grandma's neighbors enjoy us dating. How does this hurt them or any of your other clients?"

Nica fell back against a pillow. *"Have you forgotten what I said the other day? That hurt you. That compromised a promise I made to your grandmother."*

"That's me, not your clients." I kissed her shoulder, determined to fix this situation for her. I put my head down next to hers, waiting for her to peek at me. *"And you've apologized."*

Any and all heat from my statement died as liquid filled in her eyes. She was about to sign when I kissed her.

"I'm not letting you get away. But I'm not letting you lose your job either."

"What are you thinking?"

"I'm putting my creative team to a different sort of task."

Chapter 21

Nica

The following evening I lounged in Cam's living room. Chinese takeout boxes covered the coffee table but I barely had a stomach for food. Cam's friend Matt had a pad of paper in front of him, ready to write down any ideas to solve the complex situation. His girlfriend Ashley sat nearby, twirling noodles with chopsticks. Lexie had a fork in the sesame chicken container. The communication was a mix of English and ASL, everyone but Lexie using both as we talked.

The doorbell light flashed, and Cam stood and let the final invitee in, Grant. "Solve the problem yet?" Grant asked in both languages, taking in the table. "Ohh, Chinese. *Perfect.*"

"Not yet, we're still compiling ideas," Ashley said.

Grant nodded, though he was busy checking out the food. "Where's the chicken?"

Lexie paused with the fork in her mouth. She swallowed as she held out the container and the fork. "Want some?"

One side of Grant's mouth quirked and he reached over, taking the container and the fork from her.

Matt whacked the table with his pad of paper, making a loud sound. "Do we have any idea what was in the letter?"

My stomach plummeted. I locked eyes with Cam. Should I tell him? No, I'd already hurt him enough. "The letter challenged my communication abilities and claimed I was taking advantage of my Deaf elders."

"You sign fine, shouldn't they know that by now?" Ashley asked.

"They know I can sign, the question is if I'm purposely miscommunicating."

Lexie scoffed. "That's the same for all of us. We're out there on our own. I could mess up a ton of shit. The letter must have been bad."

I glared at Lexie, mentally willing her to shut up. "Which is why my entire job is in question here, not just my Deaf clients. A meeting is being scheduled with upper management. We'll see what our options are. I'm not looking forward to discussing my personal life with all my superiors." I shuddered at the thought.

Grant dug his fork into the bottom of the sesame chicken container. "Who wrote it?"

Cam ran a hand through his hair. Tension seeped back into his shoulders. "My mother," his voice came out cold and deep and his fingers dripped with scorn.

"Rhonda's reached a new level of being a fucking bitch."

"You just like swearing about her," Lexie said.

Grant leaned forward. "Damn straight I do, especially when she deserves it."

I ignored them and the serious vibes passing between to keep an eye on Cam. He hadn't said much about his mother's hand in all this, but an unerring edge came over him each time it was mentioned. I fought the urge to cry at the bleakness of the situation. "This is hopeless."

Cam squeezed my leg. "It's not hopeless. We just haven't come up with the right solution yet."

I faced him. "And if we don't?" I held his stare, reading all the emotions swimming around in the different shades of green and beige.

Matt stomped on the floor to get our attention. "Cam doesn't take no for an answer. It might take him until the day before the meeting, but he'll come up with something."

"What right does that old bitch have threatening you like this?" Grant grabbed the last pot sticker and waggled it in Cam's direction.

"You gonna let her get away with this? If she knew anything about you, or Cassie, she'd find a way to attack Nica that didn't affect her Deaf clients."

I sighed. "It's complicated."

"No, it's not complicated. It's simple. Rhonda's being a bitch and continuing to pull the poor little invalid deaf crap."

"Back off, Peterson," Ashley seethed loudly through clenched lips and no signing.

"No, I won't back off," Grant said and signed. "If he's going to fight this letter, then he has to be willing to stick up for Nica to his mother." He turned to Cam. "So, what's it gonna be?"

"You're right." Cam stood, angry energy radiating off his shoulders, and yanked his phone out of his pocket.

"Cam?" I asked, waving for his attention.

"I'm calling her." He glanced at Matt and Grant. "You two are helping."

"Yes, let's fry the bitch," Grant exclaimed.

I jumped up and grabbed Cam's arm. "Have you even contacted her since that dinner with all four of us?"

He shook his head.

"Then do you really want to talk to her with guns blazing?"

His eyes were full of stone. "Yes." He tapped his phone and handed it to Matt.

"This isn't good," I said without signing.

"Nope, but it's about time. As much as I hate admitting Grant's right, Rhonda's had this coming for years," Ashley said. "Heck, each time I've caught her bad mouthing him I was willing to bitch her out myself."

Bad mouthing, like calling her Deaf son disabled and making him into an invalid? "In what way?"

"Oh, what hasn't she tried? Yelling at him? Done that more often than I can count. Stating he wasn't smart enough, when it's obvious to the rest of us he's damn near brilliant? My favorite is still the time she bitched him out for his speech, the man is Deaf and had a cold. Some mother."

"But he's never talked back to her?"

Ashley shook her head. "Nope. Well, he's signed some nasty things behind her back. She never caught him. They seem to have that trait in common. She's not going to like anything he's about to say."

"There goes a good relationship with the in-laws," Lexie muttered.

I glared. "I think that went out the window when Rhonda threatened my job."

*****

Cam

I paced the full length of my living room, thankful the room was large and spacious. I clenched my fists and wished for a punching bag.

"If you need something to punch." Grant held his hands out by his side.

I shook my head. I'd only punch Grant if Grant deserved it.

Matt handed the phone to Grant and signed the line was ringing.

Nica waved for my attention. *"You don't have to do this."*

"Yes, I have to."

Matt signed the line was answered. *"Hello, C-A-M-E-R-O-N,"* he interpreted.

"Hello, Rhonda," Grant spoke and signed. *"Grant Peterson here. Cameron wanted to talk to you so Matt and I are helping."*

"Grant." Matt rolled his eyes, indicating the type of tone Mom used. Not that I gave two shits right about now.

"What did you write?" I signed, eyes on Grant to verify he said the correct words.

"What are you talking about?"

Coldhearted bitch. *"You wrote a letter of complaint to Nica's work."* I fisted my free hand into a ball until my knuckles numbed.

"C-A-M, it's hardly professional."

I prayed for patience. *"Does it affect you?"*

"That's not the point, C-A-M-E-R-O-N."

191

How many times did she have to say my damn name? *"Does. It. Affect. You?"* I wondered if I should ask Grant to shout, then realized he probably was anyways.

"Yes, my son is being taken for a ride by a social worker with ulterior motives."

I glanced at Nica, her hand over her mouth, eyes large. I turned back to Grant. *"How do you know? What do you know about Nica? What do you know about the work she did for Grandma? Nothing. You know nothing. All you know is that Grandma was her client."*

"And you two are screwing around."

I laughed and wondered if she could hear. *"For the thousandth time, we met at a bar, the next day we found out who each other was."*

"And she wouldn't have recognized you from all the pictures at Grandma's place?"

"Nica would have been talking with Grandma, not studying her pictures. Besides which, the most recent picture was my graduation."

"You look the same."

"I look the same as my four-by-six graduation photo from eight years ago?"

"She should have recognized you."

"But she didn't." I should have left the room with Matt and Grant and not had Nica present. *"What. Did. You. Write?"*

"I pointed out that it wasn't appropriate. That it seemed a little too convenient that you two met right when Grandma was being moved to Hospice. How Nica got her hands on an old woman's belongings. And I scolded the agency for not stopping this earlier."

I collapsed to the arm of the couch. The threat to Nica's job became painfully clear. *"You have no idea what you're talking about. Nica and I never met before that bar. Do you have any idea that she lost her Deaf clients over this and may lose her job?"*

Matt hesitated. *"Good."*

My mother's words knocked the wind out of me. I never knew her to be this coldhearted. The last remaining fibers of family connection disintegrated. She was a woman who had messed with my life for the last time. *"Listen to me carefully, Mother. I never want to talk to you again. Here I am trying to save the job of the woman I love, the woman I will marry one day, and I have to fight against a stupid letter you wrote? Have a nice life.*"

I grabbed the phone and disconnected the call. It rang two seconds later. My mother's name popped up on the screen. Matt reached for it but I clicked ignore. A minute later it rang again. Her number. I powered the phone off. Hands fisted in my hair, I faced the wall. My mother started this mess. The woman who was supposed to be there for me no matter what, who was supposed to always have my back. Who was supposed to love me.

No, there was a different woman who had claimed and proved she was there for me. I closed my eyes. *Grandma, what are we going to do?*

My words came back to haunt me, wrong thing to sign in mixed company. A familiar hand grasped mine. I turned. Nica. Her eyes were large with that same fear she often displayed at the intensity of our relationship. She tugged me into her arms. I clung to her, planting a kiss on the top of her head before releasing her.

"*I guess it's my turn to say you didn't see that,*" I said, unable to stop the corners of my mouth from turning.

She managed a slight smile. "*I guess you're right.*"

I gazed into her eyes, knowing she was worth the fight, seeing all that warmth coming from her, in contrast to the cold woman who gave birth to me. I kissed her temple.

"*Just when I thought Rhonda couldn't get any worse,*" Ashley spoke and signed.

"*I think this surpasses her bitchiest moments to date,*" I said.

"*I don't want to come between you and your family.*" Nica brushed my hair off my face.

"*You're not. She is. You did nothing wrong.*"

"*We need to brainstorm a list of options to save Nica's job,*" Matt said.

"*Number one, hire a hitman from Jersey directed at Rhonda,*" I said.

"*Finally,*" Grant dramatized.

Matt collected the paper and pen and wrote it down.

Ashley tapped a finger to her lips. "*So it took one letter to get Nica in trouble. We need a way to counteract that letter.*"

"*… bonfire,*" Lexie said.

Grant eyed Lexie up and down, a wolf on the prowl. "*You're definitely my kind of woman."*

"Careful… throw you… fire."

Grant's smile grew.

I let my eyes travel around the room as I contemplated the different ways to make Mom's letter have less of an impact. I leaned forward and Nica rubbed my back.

"What will it take to knock down that letter? I will certainly state, in writing or in person, that you kept things professional in face of the situation." The wheels turned, a thought clicked into place. *"That's what we need. More letters. I'll talk with my family, find out who's on our side. If they are, they will write in support."*

I turned to Nica. *"We know your Deaf clients approve and love you. Have them write letters. What about your other clients?"*

Nica turned white. *"I keep my private life private."* She glanced around the room. *"Normally. That's why I'm V-E-R-O-N-I-C-A at work when no one in my personal life calls me V-E-R-O-N-I-C-A."*

"Veronica, don't… silly," Lexie teased.

Nica rolled her eyes.

I refused to back down. *"This could save your job. I know how much Grandma loved you. And I know her neighbors will come to your rescue. I'm talking to my family. It's a large enough family, I should be able to get some support."* I hoped.

"And if it doesn't work?"

"Then you're not seeing them again professionally anyways."

Nica rubbed her knees. *"I'm liking the hitman from Jersey idea more and more."*

I laughed and brushed her curls back. I would save her job. My mother had manipulated my life for the last time.

Chapter 22

Cam

I tapped my fingers on my work desk—attempting to dispel the nervous energy coursing through me—while I waited for Dan to appear on my cell screen. I glanced to the whiteboard now hanging between my desk and Matt's. A chart had been set up, with the names of my family members down one side. Two columns waited to be filled in, either in support or against. A minute later Dan appeared.

"What's up?"

"Mom's on the warpath again. Do you have any problems with Nica?"

Matt turned around from his desk to watch. He grabbed the filled popcorn bowl, leaned back, crossed his ankles, and settled in to watch the show.

Dan grinned. *"Is this a trick question? Or have you wised up and decided you were wrong to be so upset? Or…wait. Mom?"*

I nodded.

"Mom hasn't had anything to obsess over in a while. Ben and I were taking bets on what the next crisis was going to be. Figured the funeral would give her some ammo. Then you show up with a new girlfriend, walked right into that one, brother. I don't have a problem with Nica. What did Mom do?"

"Nica lost her Deaf clients and may lose her job because Mom wrote a letter complaining about our relationship."

Dan blinked. *"Did not see that coming. That's low, even for Mom. Wow."*

"I need your help, will you write a letter in our support?"

"Yes, sure. Tell me what to write."

195

"Whatever you think about Nica dating me in regards to Grandma."

"You want me to write I feel bad for Nica being swept up with you?"

I rolled my eyes. *"In regards to Grandma, you got a problem with that?"*

"No. Just picking on you."

"Write a letter and send it my way."

"Will do."

I disconnected. Matt wiped his hands on his beige dress pants, then placed the popcorn back on my desk, and marked a check in the positive column of the whiteboard. *"That's one. How many family members do you think you'll be able to collect?"*

I set down my phone. *"I'm hoping on most. I'll settle for half. I'm about to find out what they really think of the sole remaining Deaf family member."* Ten children were born between my grandparents and me. All hearing. Twelve born after me, also hearing. I was the black sheep. The mistake. At least according to my mother. How many others agreed with her?

"You sure this girl's worth all this trouble?" Matt asked, his back to the rest of the office.

"Yes." I glanced over at Ashley on the phone. *"You going to get your ass in gear soon with Ashley?"*

Matt leaned back and grinned. *"You racing?"*

"Nica won't even admit she loves me." I knew she did, I felt it. How was it possible to feel another person's emotions? Not that my own behavior wasn't anything short of obvious.

A wistful expression crossed Matt's face. *"Ahh, the indifference stage, I miss that."*

I came back from my own wayward thoughts and eyed my friend. Matt sat with the same nonchalance he always did.

"You're not answering me now."

Matt turned around, which was all but admittance in itself. I was going to need to bump up production schedules. The last office engagement set us back half a week.

I grabbed a handful of popcorn and threw it at Matt. *"Warn me before the interoffice scream fest starts."*

Matt didn't respond, and I tapped my phone, connecting to my other brother.

"*What's wrong?*" Leave it to Ben to jump straight to the point. He never wasted time with formalities.

"*Mom's on the warpath. What do you think of Nica?*"

"*Damn, I owe Dan fifty bucks. Next time let me know about the new girl first.*"

There wasn't going to be a next time, but I didn't dare mention that. Ben could be as single-minded as our mother. And what was with people betting on my love life? "*You can argue with Dan later, focus. Nica, what do you think?*"

"*Oh, I'll be arguing with him later.*"

"*Focus.*"

"*On what?*"

"*Nica.*"

"*Nica? We like her. You kiss and make up?*"

I ignored the last comment. "*Any problem with her being Grandma's social worker?*"

"*Why would there be a problem?*"

I paused, giving Ben a minute. I knew it wouldn't take long.

"*What did Mom do?*" And my brother didn't disappoint.

"*She wrote a letter complaining about our relationship, Nica might lose her job.*"

"*Shit. Zoey knew there must be a reason Mom was being nice to her. Mom's all sweet, we were worried she was sick.*"

"*Not sick, lost one son.*" My jaw tightened to an uncomfortable degree.

"*That bad? Wow. She'll come around.*"

"*I won't.*"

Ben opened his mouth to respond, then caught my expression and nodded. "*I'd say never say never, but she's not giving you many options here.*"

I was willing to stake my life on it, but now wasn't the time. "*Will you write a letter supporting Nica?*"

"*Of course.*"

I fielded a few more remarks and disconnected. Matt put a second mark in the positive column.

"*Looking good.*"

"*I still need to go up a generation.*" I pushed my cell aside. Break time was over.

*****

Nica

I stopped by Tess's office after a client visit and was waved in. With the door closed behind me, Tess removed her glasses.

"How are you holding up?"

I shrugged, stuffing my turmoil inside. "I'm keeping busy."

Tess frowned. "We have a meeting set up for next Wednesday. You'll get an e-mail about it. Let me know how Cameron wants to participate."

The internal turmoil morphed into a dull ache. I didn't want this meeting to become a reality. The stress would eat me up, but what was social work without a little stress? I could handle the stress if this situation went nowhere. Cam being involved in a meeting that put my job on the line was a chilly reminder of my dabble with mixing personal and professional. "This is not my idea of a fun meeting."

Tess gave me a sympathetic smile. Of all the people to lend me support, I wasn't sure I deserved it from my supervisor. "We'll get through this."

I accepted the comfort, for a brief moment, and forced myself back to work. I shuffled to my desk, trying to hold my head high. Instead of wallowing in pity I contemplated what to bake when I arrived home. Thankfully the stress had killed most of my appetite, so I wasn't in danger of gaining too much weight.

Rebecca waved me over before I could reach my desk. "Hey," she began in a low voice, "tell me what you think of this."

Rebecca moved her laptop to show me an e-mail, from June, stating that she "Need see case manager. Important emergency."

I laughed. "Not an emergency. See if she'll respond to you via e-mail."

"I did, she insisted I come visit. Said you could interpret."

I sighed and leaned on Rebecca's desk. "I doubt Sharon would like that. You can always see her and find out what she wants, the building isn't too far away."

Rebecca began typing. "You better get your clients back, they're a hassle."

"Tell Sharon. They are more work than hearing clients. I have to do all my phone calls in person."

"Want me to mention the letter-writing campaign?"

I tapped a finger to the desk. "Want? No. Should you? Probably."

Rebecca handed me a piece of paper and a pen. "Write me a note in ASL grammar. I'll play secret messenger."

*****

I was all set to go to the grocery store on my way home, but the stress had me drained. The gooey, chocolaty warmth couldn't compete with the need to curl up in bed. After snuggling with Oreo for ten minutes I forced myself up. The enthusiasm to bake left me before I could crack open my first egg.

I would wait for Cam. His presence would surely get me into baking mode. Or at least, batter-creating mode. Which, my girly parts admitted, was better than eating cookies. And top notch for stress relief. So I waited. Curled up with my romance novel, the words couldn't hold my attention. Every paragraph I glanced up and checked the time. Not even the heart-pounding climatic scenes could help when the time trickled past Cam's promised arrival time.

Late nights, limited time off. That was Cam.

I set the book on the couch and scratched a happy Oreo. Cam's work needed him; he was probably still catching up from the time he took off for the funeral. And who was I to make demands, we'd barely dated. I resumed reading and stopped checking the clock when Cam buzzed from the lobby. He had one foot into the apartment before I said, "*You're late.*"

He kissed me. "*I know, I'm sorry. I spent a decent amount of time calling family and felt I needed to catch up on some work. The good news is both my brothers and my Aunt Kat are writing letters so far."*

I wanted to call him on not telling me he'd be late, but thought better of it. All I wanted was to curl up with him and forget everything. I leaned into his sturdy frame, aching for comfort.

"Your grandma's neighbors have been harassing Rebecca. They want to help save my job, but I can't have any further involvement with them. You'll have to handle it."

He wrapped an arm around me. *"I'll do that."*

"Thanks." I snuggled in, not feeling as content as I should.

"What can I do to make you feel better?" He rubbed a hand up and down my arm, a slow, soothing motion that still caused goose bumps.

Text me when you're running late, I thought but decided against it. Instead I shrugged. Emotions bubbled up inside me, pushing against my throat like bile. Yet no words would come.

I turned my head and gazed into his eyes. I saw love there. I saw the concern. But for a moment I wondered if he was worth risking everything for. Then he leaned down, his firm lips kissing me with all the passion he had. And I forgot my jumbled emotions, forgot my concerns, forgot even my name in his embrace.

At two in the morning I was wide awake, Cam and Oreo sleeping peacefully beside me. All my torments back in full force. How was I going to survive another week waiting to find out if I'd lost my job? I listened to Cam's soft breathing. I didn't know, I just didn't know.

*****

Cam

Hands behind my neck, feet propped on my desk, I stared at the letters-of-support chart. My guilty conscience had me pushing my job aside to work on saving Nica's. There was nothing I could do about missing dinner the previous night except make it up to her. The empty squares on the board mocked me. I hadn't had the balls to contact anyone else. I wasn't so sure I wanted to find out what my non-signing family really thought of me.

Coward.

Instead I moved my feet to the floor and checked my personal e-mail. I scrolled down the list and found letters of support from both my brothers and my aunt. I printed them, and set them up in a folder. About to shut down I noticed an e-mail from my cousin, Grace.

Hi Cam,

Mom told me what your mother did. I am so sorry. Grandma always had nice things to say about Veronica. To the point that, well, let's just say it's bittersweet to see the two of you together now. She'd wanted that for years. We knew the two of you were making sure Grandma got the services she deserved. Maybe that was our mistake, never asking you to make sure that was the truth. If so, I'm sorry. I can't change that if I'm wrong, but I can help make sure Veronica doesn't lose her job over whatever your mother wrote.

I'm attaching a letter of support. If you need me to mail it to Veronica's work please let me know. And let us know how it goes. Keeping my fingers and toes crossed.

Love,

Grace.

I rubbed my eyes, blinked several times and reread the letter. I hadn't realized Grandma spoke about Nica and me to anyone else. I thought it was just me who had to listen to the pleas. I downloaded Grace's letter and printed it out as well.

Back in my inbox I noticed two more letters from my family, both with positive words of support. Even my conservative cousin who never spoke to me was on my side. My family was talking. Support was coming in without me making any calls. Support for Nica. Support for me. Maybe I wasn't the black sheep I thought.

I made three more checks in the support column and stepped back. A sense of familial pride welled within, a sense of connection to a family where I was now the only Deaf person. I'd need to find out who my brothers and aunt had contacted. Time to man up and contact the rest.

Ashley waved for my attention. *"Three more checks?"*

I smiled. *"Yes."*

"Good job."

I laughed and explained it wasn't my doing.

"Still. That's wonderful. What about you?"

"We're still figuring out the details. Not enough time to get an interpreter. It might be best for me to write my own letter. I worry it won't be enough."

Ashley turned to her boyfriend. *"See, Matt, he'll do anything for Nica."*

"Young love, it won't last."

Ashley shook her head and left the area. Matt watched her the whole way. My interest was piqued. This wasn't normal Matt behavior. Then again the fake appointment he had earlier that morning wasn't normal either. When Ashley was gone Matt reached into his pocket and dropped a small black box on my desk.

"For me? Really? You shouldn't have."

Matt leaned over the partial wall. *"Scream fest coming soon, you've been warned."*

I opened up the box to see three diamonds nestled together on a white gold band. The light hit the ring and I was almost blinded.

"How did I do?"

"I'm predicting screams I might hear." I gave the ring back to Matt. *"Congrats. When does the screaming start?"*

"Still working on the final details. Assuming she hasn't taken to searching my drawers and pockets."

Matt returned to work, and I pondered if Nica would want a three stone ring or a solitaire. *Getting ahead of yourself, Thompson. Give her time.*

*****

Nica

My overbooked appointments caused my pulse to race. For the next four days I'd scheduled myself four to five visits. Each day. On a normal day three visits pushed the limit of what I was able to accomplish. I could squeeze in a few more, but I'd never find the time to complete the paperwork. As it was I had no clue where I was going to find the time to finish what I already scheduled. "Well, that's it, I can't book anymore." I pushed myself back. Wednesday was open for paperwork, the day of the meeting. After that, nothing.

Rebecca came over and tapped Thursday on my calendar. "Schedule the appointments, you aren't going anywhere."

I glanced at the never-ending list of clients I needed to visit. "Are you so sure?" Dread raced through my veins, an icy cold front that made me want to shiver. Part of me wished the meeting was that day so I could get it over with. The other part wished it was further away so I could accomplish more work. Mostly I wished this was never an issue in the first place.

"Still regret dating him?"

I glanced up at my friend, letting her words sink in and the giddy sensation lessen all my worries. "No." Despite the turmoil of stress I didn't regret Cam.

"Whoa, Nica's letting her guard down? It must be love."

"Shut up," I grumbled, struggling to keep my lips from turning upwards, and picked up the top case from the mountainous pile that needed to be written up. Rebecca tapped the calendar again. "Keep scheduling. It won't be your issue if the visits have to be cancelled."

I focused on my computer. Safer territory.

Chapter 23

Cam

I stared at the building through my rearview mirror. How many times had I parked in this very spot? Too many to count. On a normal visit I didn't stop to look at the building. No, on a normal visit I would grab the groceries from my trunk and head in to see Grandma.

This wasn't a normal visit.

I couldn't fight the sensation I was forgetting something. I always stopped at the food store first, called Grandma's videophone, and watched her figure out her food list. Usually compiled with some complaining about her diet and a few requests I would "forget" to pick up. She scolded me good for my selective memory but I never budged. If I could shop for her one more time, I'd get her whatever the fuck she wanted.

The urge to leave was strong but I hunkered down. Grandma would want me to be here, would want me to get as much support as possible for Nica.

In the building, the security door was propped open and a crowd already in the meeting room. Excited energy bounced around as the group chatted. Smells of home cooking lingered in the air.

June hobbled towards me, leaning on her cane. She hugged me before signing, *"Where's Veronica?"*

"She's not allowed any further contact. You'll have to deal with me instead."

"You better save her job."

"That's why I'm here."

I gestured June into the room. No sooner had we arrived than I was engulfed in one conversation after the other. Hands flew in eager signs, some overlapping, interrupting each other to talk to me. Did I know Grandma had a collection of dirty playing cards? (Yes.) Did I know what happened to those cards? (No, and I didn't want to think which family member claimed them.)

A half hour after I arrived, I moved to an edge of the room and waved for everyone's attention. Since many of the elders were still confused why Nica wasn't there I explained all that had happened with her job, including the letter my mother wrote. The snippets of angry signs from the crowd made the admission enjoyable. If only Mom could see them now.

I settled down at a table to assist anyone who needed help. Most of these elders were raised orally. Unlike me their schooling may have been oral as well, whereas I had teachers and peers who signed. Some had me write the full letter, others needed help with some word choices and spelling. A few didn't need my help at all.

Of course, my help with the letters was only a small fraction of what the elders wanted to talk about. Quite a few of them felt the urge to play up Nica, as if I hadn't already fallen in love.

Before I could start to plan my escape, June caught my attention. *"I told you I had something for you, good thing you came back."* She gestured towards another elder, who grabbed a cloth shopping bag. The bag was curved from whatever was inside, and a piece of blue tissue paper covered the top.

I collected the bag and removed the paper to find a knitted afghan in thick bands of color, starting in a light blue then getting deeper before switching over to shades of purple.

The floor vibrated and I glanced up at June. *"Your grandmother was working on this when she died. The last time I saw her she gave it to me, asked me to finish it for her. This isn't for you, it's for you and Veronica. Both of you, together. The light blue was done by your grandmother, she wanted to use blues and purples, your favorite color and Veronica's. The rest of us knitters each took one shade to help finish her last task and give it to the new couple."*

I thumbed the light blue stitching, the weakest of the bunch, a clear indication of Grandma's failing health. Each of the women who helped let me which know color she did. They also told me how happy they were to see Nica and me together.

My heart ached. This was something I never thought I'd get: a new gift from the woman who raised me.

"Thank you," I told the crowd of women. *"I will cherish this, always."* I gave them each a hug.

"Make sure you share that with Veronica," June admonished.

I tucked the afghan and letters into the bag and kissed her cheek. *"I will."*

*****

Nica

I opened the door to a grinning Cam. He leaned into me and gave me a kiss hello that had me hoping we would move things to my bedroom. Or the floor—I wasn't picky.

A few minutes later he released me and brought a bag into the living room. Feet rooted in place, I tried to get my breathing under control. Cam displayed no signs of being affected by our embrace, except for the telltale bulge in his pants. He spread papers out, eyebrows furrowed in concentration. Oreo walked into the room, stretched, and ignored me to hop up next to Cam. She put one paw on Cam's thigh, another reaching for his chest. Head still buried into the papers he removed one hand and scratched her.

My heart swelled at the sight of this man.

He caught me staring, a dangerous grin curving his lips. *"What?"*

I sat down next to him and gathered the cat into my arms. *"Nothing. How did it go?"*

He rummaged through the papers for a minute before responding. *"I collected ten letters today, but a few said they weren't your clients. I have eight letters from my family."* He faced at me. *"Are you sure we can't get more clients on board?"*

My eyes grew wide. *"More? We have eighteen letters, plus you. That's nineteen to one."*

"We don't know how bad the one is."

My gut knotted at that small detail. I still hadn't told Cam about the letter. Not that I'd read it and not what was in it. I couldn't tell him what his mother wrote in regards to her son. Those vile words would not pass my hands. *"True."* Liar. *White lie, but still.* Liar.

"We should have kept the hitman idea."

"She's still your mother." I needed to remind myself of that fact. Vile words or not, Rhonda was his flesh and blood.

He shook his head. *"No, my mother is the woman that raised me. She's dead."* My heart tore for him, but before I could do anything about it he reached for the bag. *"My grandmother had one more surprise, and your conniving clients helped."*

I didn't know what to say about that and froze when Cam displayed an afghan in shades of blues and purples.

"Grandma was working on this when she died. June and a few others helped finish it."

I brushed my fingers over the fibers. *"That was really sweet of them to do for you."*

Cam shook his head, a smile on his face I didn't trust. *"Not for me, for both of us."*

I dropped the afghan back to the couch. *"Us?"* I choked out as my chest constricted.

"Yes, us. Your favorite color and mine. Dying woman's last wish."

No, Cassie's last wish was the two of us to stay together. She didn't realize what she was wishing for. *"I can't accept anything else from my clients, not while under investigation. You'll have to keep it."* I pushed it back towards him, remembering a very similar game of hot potato I played with Cassie.

He tucked the afghan back in the bag. *"For now."*

The lobby buzzer rang, and I nearly leaped up, grateful for the reprieve. "Hello?" I asked as I signed to Cam.

"I'm coming up, buzz me in," came Lexie's voice. I glanced back at Cam, not wanting to push him off. But Lexie didn't stop by for foolish reasons. I buzzed her in.

"Lexie's coming up, sorry."

Lexie stormed in a few minutes later. She threw her bag and jacket toward the kitchen table. She missed. Both items fell to the floor. Lexie paid this no attention, strode over to my liquor cabinet, and poured herself a tall drink. She downed half the glass before facing me.

"I guess you're not going anywhere soon?" I asked in both languages.

"Bite me."

I apologized to Cam and interpreted.

Lexie brought her bad attitude over to the couch, shooed the cat away, and fell backwards with her drink. I sat across from her.

"What happened?"

Cam stayed to the side, wide eyed.

"Hi Cam." Lexie waved with her free hand and turned to me. "Tell him thanks for the proof not all men suck."

Cam held up two hands and inched farther away. Either Lexie was scaring him, which I couldn't blame him for, or he was angling himself to better lip-read.

"What. Happened?" I asked.

"My date for the last week? Total jerk."

"I gathered as much. Details or I take the drink away."

Lexie inhaled, followed by a deep drink. "Tanner was normal and nice. Too normal and nice—" She shot Cam a look "Sorry."

"I'm normal?" he asked.

Lexie rolled her eyes. "I was warming up to the normal and nice idea. Tanner made it seem fun and sexy, when I tuned him out. Last night—" she took another gulp "—he called me a goddess while we were in bed."

"Never listen to a man in bed. Wait until you're dressed for him to say it again," Cam said.

I eyed him and waited for him to meet my gaze. *"Then I have a few questions for you later."*

A twinkle shone in Cam's eyes. *"The answers are the same."*

"Enough lovey-dovey, Mr. and Mrs. Complicated."

My heart skipped a beat. "We're not married," I stated, refusing to meet Cam's eyes.

"Yeah, yeah." Lexie brushed me off. "Then this morning he calls me up and tells me he's getting back together with his ex. I was a fling, a freaking fling!" Lexie threw her head back against the couch.

I rose and sat down next to her. "You love your flings."

Lexie raised her head. "I want more. Where's my complicated good guy?"

I faced Cam. "Got any single friends?"

Lexie scoffed. "Grant won't be any better."

"I'm not talking about Grant."

An hour later Lexie had finished her second drink, and Cam had left to handle a relay call in the bedroom. "Do you two spend any time apart?" Lexie teased.

"Occasionally."

"You make falling in love look so easy."

My heart squeezed tight, desperate to latch on. "Stop using that word. And what's easy? I'm about to lose my job over him."

"And yet he's still here."

"But I'm risking everything for a man I've known three weeks."

"He came highly recommended from your client."

I groaned. I'd stayed clear of that recommendation for a reason, and now I was paying the price.

Lexie fiddled with her empty glass. "I want that. Someone that looks at me the way Cam looks at you."

"And how's that?"

"Like you're the only thing in this world that matters. And you look at him the same way."

I bit my fingernail. The emotional chaos inside refused to be denied. "I do?"

Lexie nodded.

"I'm afraid I'll mess this up."

"So don't."

It sounded so simple, so easy. So terrifying. And deep down

inside: exactly what I wanted.

*****

Cam

I paced Nica's room. Why had I even answered Dad's call? I held my cell phone, a female interpreter on screen, my other hand free to talk. The interpreter wore black, wearing a headset, and both her hands free to sign.

"*You haven't contacted your mother again*," the interpreter signed.

Stating the obvious, Dad. "*I don't plan to.*"

"*She's your mother.*"

Theme of the day. I tried to keep the ball of rage in my chest. "*She sabotaged N-I-C-A's career. She had no right to do that.*" Fury seethed from my words. I wished I could apologize to the interpreter.

"*C-A-M, come on.*"

"*Do you even know what life was like for Grandma these past few years? How much time I put in to help her out? How much work N-I-C-A did to keep Grandma home and safe?*" I made sure to spell out Nica's name, as the interpreter wouldn't know her sign name. Come to think of it, neither would my father.

"*How does this relate to your mother?*"

"*What services did elder services provide? What was Hospice doing before she moved? What did Grandma even think of N-I-C-A? Can you answer a single one of these questions?*"

"*Isn't this a little ridiculous?*"

At one point I might have agreed. That was before I knew other family members could answer these questions. "*No, it's not. Grandma would have been lost without N-I-C-A's help. She's the only one at her agency that knows ASL. The services wouldn't have been the same without her there. But Mom has a bug up her ass about who I'm dating and had to take it out on N-I-C-A. Why couldn't she have taken it out on me like normal?*"

"*You have to admit that dating Grandma's case manager is awkward.*"

"*No, I don't. Because we dealt with that in the beginning. Grandma helped with that in the beginning. Not three weeks later."*

"Mom didn't want to hurt you."

I laughed. If I was too loud Nica could let me know later. I wondered if I finally mastered a maniacal laugh. "*And what about you?*" I shook my head, no use asking this question. "*Too late. If she feels bad she can retract that letter. But as far as I'm concerned things will never be the same again.*"

"You're fighting too hard for a girl you hardly know."

"I know her. She's going to be around for a long time."

Dad continued a losing battle. I was used to being treated like a child, even at thirty. Whether the treatment was due to my hearing loss or birth order I didn't know. Or rather, I didn't care. I was done. I wasn't backing down.

"*What will it take to make amends?*"

"*Besides retracting that letter? I don't know. Right now I can't think of anything.*"

Chapter 24

Nica

Monday morning a sense of dread consumed me, and increased exponentially the closer the meeting putting my personal and professional life on the line came.

I shoved my hands into my hair, staying under my covers. The longer I stayed, the more I could avoid the inevitable.

Besides, the bed was cozy and I had a cat sleeping at my side.

The bathroom door opened and Cam entered wearing jogging pants and a T-shirt. He moved to my bed, covering one of my hair-tangled hands with his own. *"It'll be over soon,"* he said.

"What? My career?" I rolled over. Oreo stretched at the disturbance as Cam's arms circled around me.

He kissed the back of my head before turning me to face him. *"Two more days and you'll be able to put this behind you. I'm here for you."* He drew my body closer.

I breathed in and absorbed his tropical scent, wishing it would take me someplace exotic and away from my personal hell. I willed myself to behave normally as I sat up and smiled. *"Get going or you'll miss time at the gym."*

He kissed me hard, lingered with his lips pressed against mine. The warmth of him traveled straight through me. *"Everything's going to be OK."*

I nodded and walked him to the door. Before he left, he turned around and handed me a set of keys. *"I have a late meeting tonight. I'm not sure when I'll get out. Let yourself into my apartment if I'm late."*

I stared at the keys.

"Relax, it's my spare set, in case I'm not there when you arrive."

I swallowed my nerves and accepted the keys. After he left I allowed myself a few pity tears. Forget losing my job, I was losing myself. The threads unwound one by one. Add a precocious cat and I'd be stripped bare in no time.

*****

Cam

I tapped my foot and shifted my arm to check my watch, again. By all accounts the meeting was going well, just long. Had any meeting ever ran as long as this?

The answer seeped into my veins, and I kept my eyes on the interpreter, though I no longer paid attention. Yes, plenty of meetings had dragged on this long, sometimes longer. Reason one why my interpreter was not flipping out and why we had two, "just in case" it went over the allotted time one could handle.

If the meeting length was normal, then the only thing different was me. I'd never been a time watcher before, always going with the flow. I also never had anyone waiting for me. Any dates were casual at best, or casual enough that they never invaded my work mindset.

Nica did.

Since we met, nothing had been the same. And sitting here, tapping one finger in an increasingly exponential speed, nothing would ever be the same again.

I searched for the remorse—my job had been my first love—and found nothing. This job still my career, my ambition, and no one could pry it from me. But these hours, it no longer worked. Not for Matt and not for me.

Delegation. Business was good, we could offer a few promotions, take the weight off our backs. But promotions and delegations meant letting go. Could I do it?

My phone vibrated in my pocket, and I had the urge to reach for it in case it was Nica. Not work. Ashley was right. Nica changed everything and for the first time, I felt okay with the change. Better than okay. I felt full. When this meeting ended I had some place to be, someone to see. Not an empty apartment and more paperwork to fill the void.

Fill the void. That's what I'd been doing. My childhood, outside of my brothers and grandparents, had been missing that key element. Communication and acceptance. My job required me to work harder, longer, to prove myself. I did so willingly but now I had a different outlet for that void, a soother and balm to the internal struggle. And it all resided in one beautiful soul.

This meeting was proof I'd succeeded in my career. Nica was proof it wasn't all I needed. Love. Her. The package deal. As soon as I ended this godforsaken long-ass meeting, I'd get to see her. I'd be complete.

When the meeting finally finished I skipped dinner, grabbed dessert, and raced home. Nica was in the living room, reading a book when I arrived.

She belonged here. The location didn't matter, nor did the furniture or the book or the weather outside. Her. She mattered. The stress and frustration wanted to melt away, but her shoulders were stiff. I had to take care of her.

"*Sorry I'm so late,*" I said as I walked over and kissed her. Her lips were warm but not inviting.

"*Is this normal?*" she asked.

I sensed the wariness in her. *Tread carefully, Thompson, she's a mess with the upcoming meeting.*

"*Usually not. I had a feeling, that's why I gave you the keys.*" I tugged her close. She resisted at first but soon relaxed into my embrace. Plans to delegate or not, long meetings would happen again. Best to not make any promises I couldn't keep. "*You're like me with food and stress, so I got dessert instead.*"

"*Dessert?*" she asked, a small smile breaking the downward turn of her mouth.

"*Yes. I wasn't sure what mood you were in, so I got a dozen cupcakes. You can share the leftovers with your coworkers.*"

Nica jumped up and investigated the box of goodies.

"*Glad to know I did something right,*" I said.

She placed a hand on my cheek. "*You do plenty right. We're still learning each other, while being thrown into one stressful debacle after another.*"

"*Good to know. Now eat. Although I could wear the food if it helps.*"

She picked up a dark chocolate cupcake with purple frosting. With her pointer finger she swiped some frosting off the cupcake and traced my lips. "*Interesting idea, we haven't tried it that way yet.*" She licked the frosting off. Her tongue on my lips was enough to have me dragging her to the floor for more.

*****

Nica

I placed the cupcake box on the corner of my desk, displaying it prominently to anyone nearby, and collapsed on my chair. My scheduled was overbooked. My too-large pile of paperwork impossible to complete. I wanted to cry. There was no way I was getting all this done by Wednesday, especially with the lack of comprehension I currently possessed. The good news was that today was Tuesday. The last day I had anything booked. I would have all of Wednesday to catch up, if I could focus on anything other than the doomed meeting.

I grabbed a pink highlighter and drew a large question mark on Thursday.

"Cupcakes, yummy," Rebecca said as she glanced over the goodies upon her arrival.

"Cam bought them for me last night. I could only stomach two." *And one of those ended up more on Cam than my stomach.* I turned on my computer and forced myself to buckle down.

"Only two?" Rebecca leaned forward and felt my forehead.

"Yes, two. My blood pressure is through the roof, I don't need any more sugar."

Rebecca skirted around the desk and rubbed my shoulders. "It's going to be all right."

"It's not, but thanks for the vote of confidence."

"We're not going to be down a case manager based on one letter."

I froze. We might be. Care of one exceptionally bad letter. The accusations put more than my dating choices into question. I worked, and each time reality seeped in I forced it aside to continue working. I handled the pitying actions of my coworkers. I pretended everything was normal while visiting my clients. I finished off more paperwork than I would have thought possible.

An hour after I was supposed to leave I realized I hadn't even eaten lunch.

*****

Cam

I tweaked the spreadsheet. I moved columns, cleaned up borders. Ensured the most important points were up top. I glanced back through my papers to be sure I got every last detail represented.

Six tiles fell to my desk: GO HOME.

I glanced up to see Ashley and Matt. *"What? No scramble?"*

"It's the blunt edition," Matt said.

I moved the tiles off my papers. *"As soon as this is ready I'm leaving."*

Ashley gripped the partial partition and leaned forward. *"The meeting is tomorrow. Nica needs you. This can wait."*

"No, it can't."

Ashley threw up her hands. *"Men, they never learn. Your grandmother's going to haunt you until the day you die."* Ashley whacked my head. *"Dumbass."*

She turned and left in a huff. I rubbed my sore head.

Matt glared. *"Thanks, man, you're messing up my evening plans."*

After they were gone I checked my e-mail and found the one I'd been waiting for.

Dear Cameron,

Sorry for the late e-mail. I agree that having you at the meeting might be too complicated. I did want to present you with specific questions to answer. I've struggled with the initial letter. Nica's seen it, so I'm sure you are aware of what was written. In order for you to know what you are up against, you deserve to see the words as the rest of us are seeing them.

Therefore I've also attached the original e-mail from your mother. I'm sorry I have to share this with you. From everything we've discussed, I'm hopeful we can ensure no ramifications to Nica and her job.

Sincerely,

Tess

I reread Tess's e-mail, a hollow sensation in the pit of my stomach. Nica had seen Mom's letter. She'd said nothing to me, even confirming she didn't know how bad the letter was. I asked her to trust me. Instead she went right on withholding information, not giving herself fully to me, to our relationship. My head throbbed. She lied.

I opened up the e-mail. Time to see for myself what my mother was capable of, without having to lip-read.

*****

Nica

I walked the length of my apartment. A rumble in my stomach reminded me that I was overdue for a meal, any meal. Of course, the mere thought of food had my stomach holding up a huge "hell no" sign. No food—I'd wait for Cam. I checked my phone, still no text from him. *This is ridiculous, relax.* Maybe the television would hold my attention. I flipped the channels and found every commercial. I turned the television off and resumed pacing my apartment.

My world crumbled around me. Had been from the minute I met Cam. One month ago. A month prior my life had been so simple. My job was as secure as a government funded non-profit could be. Sure, I was lonely. But lonely never threatened my job.

If Cassie hadn't moved to Hospice that night, Cam and I would have never met. Rhonda would never have written that letter. I wouldn't be—I glanced at the clock—seventeen hours away from losing my job.

I put my career on the line for Cam, who was supposed to be there to comfort me. Who was working. *His one true love*, I thought glumly. *His job.* I scoffed and hopped on my elliptical machine. A typical male, his job came first. His job was secure yet he continued to work long hours. All the while I waited around as mine faded away.

A small voice inside told me I was stressed and therefore sabotaging. Again. My aggression beat that voice into a bloody pulp. I couldn't think straight, could only feel. The rest of me was numb from the hell of the past month. Only rage left.

I bumped up my speed, trying to burn off my anger. Legs moved fast, lungs breathed deep. The bloody, pleading voice whimpered that it was too little, too late.

*****

Cam

I printed my mother's e-mail. The paper weighed heavy in my hands, a paper filled with hate. My mother. My own mother wrote this. And Nica shielded it from me. Did she find some truth in me being a disabled invalid? Was I just a child that needed to be taken care of?

I grabbed a highlighter, pink was the closest to red I could find, and highlighted the abrasive words in Mom's letter. When I was finished the entire letter was pink, far too cheerful for the words on the page. I ripped the paper into tiny strips, recycled it, and printed a new one. This time I skipped the highlighter and left the office.

The drive didn't calm me, only set my anger to simmer. I was ready to have it out with Nica the minute I opened her door. Instead I became rooted to the spot. She didn't sign a word to me. Her plump mouth almost thin in the tight line she held it. Her brown eyes cold. Even her curls seemed to curl away from me. I stepped towards her and she stepped back.

I had never seen Nica angry before. I had seen her happy, sad, stressed. She had always kept a collected front. Now she was bare. Not the way I wanted to witness her exposed.

Well, I was bare, too. For as angry as I was, she still caught my heart.

Oreo glided into the room, glanced at her mistress, and promptly walked out. *Smart cat.* I wondered if it would be best for me to do the same. Take my anger with me. Let her deal with hers. No. I needed to get this off my chest. And whatever was eating her needed the same. The thought of the letter burning a hole in my back pocket was fuel enough to be the first to talk.

"*You read the letter.*"

Her eyes softened a degree. "*What letter?*"

"*Don't treat me like I'm stupid or someone to be controlled. My mother's letter. Tess mentioned you had seen her e-mail.*"

I read the swear word on her lips as she turned her head to the floor. She breathed in deep and faced me. "*Yes. I read the letter.*"

"*You didn't tell me.*"

"*No, I didn't.*" The distance between us was larger than the length of her kitchen, where we stood at opposite ends.

"*Why? You pitying the poor Deaf man? Wanted to control me with puppet strings?*" It didn't matter how much I felt for Nica, I would never let someone do that to me.

"*What?*" She stumbled forward. "*You think this was pity or control? I'm not your mother. You really wanted me to tell you what she said? To tell you that your own mother thinks you're deaf and dumb? I didn't want to repeat those horrible, horrible words.*"

"*Y-E-S. You should have let me know. Then I could have yelled at her with the full knowledge of what she did.*" My chest ached as I breathed hard.

Nica rubbed a palm over her eye. "*No.*"

"*I don't need to be protected.*"

"*Your grandmother had just died… You didn't need any more hurt.*"

Something shifted. I could almost sense the cosmic beating my grandmother was giving me. At a loss I stood my ground, unsure where to go from here.

Her eyes watered but didn't spill over. "*You know, it's better this way. We hit this blockage now, stop the conflict, and you can go back to your first love.*"

That hit me upside the head. I was sure it wasn't just the words. "*What first love?*"

"*Your job.*"

Even though no one moved, the distance between us grew. In a few more minutes the Grand Canyon would be able to fit in-between.

"*I don't love my job like I love you.*" Once the words were out I winced. I mentally slapped myself, no cosmic grandmother needed.

"*Oh really?*"

"*That didn't come out right.*"

"*Actually, I think it did.*" Her eyes flashed, freezing me with cold. Her pupils shrank and she stepped back, hugging herself. "*I'm guilty of trusting with everything but my heart. My heart I hold back, keeping it safe. You caught me at a weak point, you exploited my heart.*" A tear fell down her cheek. I wanted to brush it away but her glare immobilized me.

"*I was there for you when you needed it most. I didn't know you, but I trusted. And somehow my heart got out, making this mess even more complicated. I could never stay away, even when I knew that's exactly what needed to be done. Now I'm paying the price. Alone. I was there for you and where are you? You're working. Late. Again. Your job is secure, what the fuck are you working so hard for?*"

I moved my hands to sign but she rambled over me.

"*You have to choose, either your job comes first, or I do. But it's only been a month. Who are we even kidding here? We don't know each other. Not yet. You've chosen your job, like I should have. That first night was innocent. The second was not. I should have never seen you again in person.*"

"*Wait—*"

"*No.*" Her sharp hand motion cut me off. "*I can't do this. I know I can't save my job, but I can save my heart. I need someone who chooses me first. And that's not you.*" She marched to her bedroom and closed the door hard enough a picture vibrated nearby.

I ran my hands through my hair. I inched towards her door. *Get a grip, Thompson, fix this.* Only I didn't know which way to go. Part of me still wanted to shake her for keeping the letter from me and feared what else she'd do. The other part wanted to barge in there and kiss her. And a final part wondered if that's how Dad lost his balls.

I ground my teeth, the internal warzone shooting rockets and grenades, sides refusing to surrender. I raised a hand to pound a fist through the door. But let it fall to my side. She could shut me out, but she couldn't cut me off. I grabbed the marker for her wipe board and erased her partial shopping list with my sleeve before adding a message of my own.

When you're ready to stop keeping things from me, to stop holding back, to be in this 100%, you know where to find me.

She wanted the distance, she got it. I capped the marker and left.

Chapter 25

Nica

"Sabotage complete. Are we celebrating with dessert or booze?" Lexie asked, her head in my freezer an hour after Cam left. "Lord knows you have plenty of desserts in here. I'm surprised they haven't defrosted from the angry words on your board."

"Don't remind me, erase them already," I muttered. My mother reached over and soothed my hair. Lexie had gathered the small group after forcing me to confess to leaving Cam.

Lexie wrenched a filled cookie bag out of the freezer. "Nope, the words were directed at you. Your job."

"You need to eat, sweetie." Mom placed a hand on my shaky arm. I shook my head.

"Food. Veronica. Pick something or we do," Lexie said.

"What happened to booze?"

Lexie's hands went to her hips, freezer bag hitting her thigh, ready to take action. "Do you want to still be drunk tomorrow?"

"Why not? I'm losing my job anyways."

Mom stood up. "Pizza, it might still be open at this hour." She grabbed the phone and placed the order.

I jerked upright. The few tears I had allowed myself to shed had long since dried up, leaving behind a gaping wound in my chest. I rubbed the inflicted spot. "It's not supposed to hurt this much."

Lexie rubbed my shoulder. "It is when you love him and are being stupid."

222

"Not stupid. The first smart thing I've done since I saw him at the bar."

"Nonsense," Mom said, rejoining us at the table. "Meeting Cam was smart, being with him smart. Now you're scared."

"You want to harass me—" I gestured "—there's the door."

Mom turned to Lexie. "Should I blame myself for Nica's unrealistic view on love?"

"No, that's a Nica specialty."

"But she had to learn it somewhere."

"Why would it be your fault?" I asked.

Mom leaned back. "Your father and I divorced when you were still young, neither one of us remarried. We weren't exactly the poster couple for love and marriage."

"You were the poster couple for how to have an amicable divorce."

"We were the poster couple for how to stay detached. Which you've done right up until Cam."

His name made my heart crack further, so I straightened my spine, determined to get through this. "I'm not detached."

"Hey, Pinocchio," Lexie said. "Your nose is growing."

"Okay, I'm a little detached," I admitted. "I still say my parents had the right idea."

Mom pressed her lips into a tight line. "We didn't always succeed."

I blinked at my mother. "I was never aware of any problems."

"It wasn't always easy."

Mom's words plucked a nerve I couldn't identify. "I grew up knowing I had two parents who loved and cared for me. You never talked badly about each other. You just didn't stay in love forever." I'd always respected my parents. They'd taught me love didn't always work out, but it didn't mean the end of any sort of connection.

"Oh, Veronica. In trying to shelter you from the divorce we sheltered you from the truth. I still love your father, and last I checked he still loves me. We couldn't live together."

My heart turned, absorbing this new information. "What? But... What?"

Mom let out a sigh. "Oh, we are the most incompatible couple ever. He likes to go out, travel, constantly socialize. I like to stay home, read a book, watch a movie. Where I'm neat he's messy, he saves I spend." She laughed a humorless laugh. "But we loved each other, we loved you. We knew we needed to stay a team for you. And, to be honest, we needed to stay in each other's lives."

"You're still in love with Dad?"

"I loved him when I married him, I loved him when we had you, and I love him to this day. There's a reason neither one of us remarried, sweetie."

Lexie leaned into me. "I think your mother is still porking your father."

I shuddered and ignored her comment as I continued to try to process my mother's bombshell. "But, but... You were friends first, you focused on friendship?"

Mom laughed, this time with humor. "Oh, the lies we tell ourselves. Your father and I did meet as friends. We both fell while friends, both of us too chicken to change anything until your aunt had enough and played matchmaker. We loved each other long before we found out we weren't compatible. Don't you see? You've been searching for compatibility, the one thing your father and I didn't have."

"So," Lexie began, "I guess the question is: are you compatible with Cam? We know you love him, even if you continue to deny it. Are you compatible? Can you live with the way he does things for the rest of your life?"

"Shouldn't you be trying to win, or lose, a bet with Grant?"

Lexie waved a hand, as though brushing the notion aside. "Bets off. Hook ups off. You two are cannon. Now, can you live with him?"

"I can't live with his work hours."

"True love is knocking her on her ass, and she's still hung up over this work thing." Lexie tsked.

My mouth turned to sandpaper. "Because this is fucking terrifying, all right?" I stood and got a drink of water.

Mom shook her head. "You're as flustered as your father made me."

"I'm not flustered," I exclaimed, flailing my arms and spilling some water on the floor. I forced myself together with a shaky breath, sat down, and rested my head on the table.

"She's flustered," Lexie agreed. "But that could be in part due to the stress."

I whimpered. Why couldn't they support me and stop analyzing my latest sabotage? The sabotage protocol was dessert and drinks, laughter, and moving on. Never had it gone like this.

Mom wrapped her arms around me. "I know you won't admit this to us, but consider it for yourself. You love this boy, and from everything you've told me, he feels the same for you. That's rare. That's special. Freak out if you have to, it's normal. Just don't forget to follow your heart once the scare passes."

I remained still, listening to my mother. I no longer knew which was scarier—admitting my feelings or losing Cam.

*****

Cam

I stomped into Grant's gym, found Grant, and pointed to one of the walls. Grant crossed his arms, eyed me up and down, and shook his head.

"*W-H-A-T?*" I was not in the mood and Grant better figure it out, fast.

"*Fancy clothes for rock climbing.*"

I studied my dress shirt and pants. I undid the top two buttons and yanked the shirt off. "*Better?*"

"*It's a start. Change your shoes.*"

I wanted to be up a fucking wall, not changing my shoes and following rules. I swore all the way over to the shoe rental and all the way back, while Grant laughed his ass off.

"*You're loud when you swear, I love it.*"

I turned off my vocal cords and yanked my shoes on. Grant handed me a harness, and I stepped into it before making my way up the wall. My concentration shifted from my mother, the letter, and Nica, and to the climb. I figured out which hand holding to reach for, where to place my feet, as I pushed and pulled my way up the course.

Mind blank, I stilled. Grant stood at the base, holding the other ends of the ropes, watching me.

"*What bit your ass?*"

I wrenched the letter out of my back pocket and let it float down.

Grant caught it. With one hand he managed to smooth out the letter and read. "*Fucking shit. You sure this is your biological mother?*"

"*Nica knew about the letter.*"

"*So?*"

"*She didn't tell me.*"

"*I wouldn't tell you either if I were in her shoes. Rhonda makes it sound like Nica was manipulating you. When I'm pretty sure it was the other way around.*"

I shook my head.

"*Why are you here? Aren't you supposed to be home saving her job? Because with this letter you have your work cut out for you.*"

"*You think I can't override this letter?*"

"*Not if you're climbing my walls after fighting with your girl.*"

I kicked off the wall and brought myself back to the ground. "*How did you know we fought?*"

Grant crossed his arms and said nothing.

"*All right, fine. But we're finished this time.*"

"*One, you're not finished. You're roped up in her so much you've handed over your balls. Two, it's because of you and your mother she might lose her job tomorrow. Go home. Be super C-A-M-E-R-O-N and save her job. Then you can decide what to do about her.*"

"*I don't hand over my balls. Not like my father.*"

"*Like your father? No. No way would you subject yourself to your mother's bullshit. But like Matt, like your brothers? Yeah, you have. And if I have to tell*" *you that Nica is nothing like your mother, then you really need to have you head examined."*

My shoulders heaved as I absorbed Grant's words. For all his goofing around he got it right more often than not. I grabbed the letter.

*****

By the first streaks of the dawn light I was willing to accept that Nica was right. We didn't know each other. Not well enough. Not yet. Not if I needed Grant to show me she wouldn't undermine me like my mother. Not if I didn't know how to fix the situation, how to get her back into my arms, how to make her feel better.

Distracted by my pathetic state, I stumbled into the kitchen in desperate need of coffee. On the table sat the folder with the letters of support, held down by the box with the brooch. Fitting now that I knew my mother had used it as leverage. I needed to take a picture, to prove that Nica didn't have it. I popped the lid and a folded piece of paper tumbled out.

The letter my grandmother wrote for Nica.

Shit. I never gave it to Nica as I should have. The final letter, the most important one. Regardless of my mother or me or my family or the other Deaf elders, this was the reason for the whole mess—my grandmother's care. And nothing supported her happiness with Nica's work more than this letter.

I smoothed it out, and knew I needed to get it to Nica, whether she gave me the cold glare of death or not. But, first, this letter would help save her job.

I glanced up to the heavens, where I could all but see Grandma with her arms crossed and foot tapping, waiting on me to get my head on straight. *"I will fix this,"* I signed. I had to. For my grandmother. For Nica. To prove to my mother once and for all she had no control over my life.

*****

Nica

I fought the sense of dread as I willed myself into the office. My feet felt like lead, my heart pounded, and my head screamed from the drinks Lexie allowed me.

A small crowd waited for me. "I appreciate the solidarity, but let me work," I grumbled as I made my way to my desk, pushing past Rebecca and Tess.

"It's going to be all right," Tess said.

I ignored her and turned on my computer. "I have a ton of work to finish."

"You can do that tomorrow—there's bagels," Rebecca said.

"I'm not hungry." Quite the opposite in fact; my stomach didn't want to eat anything, ever again.

"Lover boy make you breakfast?"

My empty stomach lurched. "No. We broke up."

"What?" the two women exclaimed.

I pressed a hand against my temple. "I didn't tell him about the letter, he keeps putting his work before me, it wouldn't work." At least, that's what my drunken-self decided at midnight.

"At the end of the day you might want to revisit this," Tess said.

I already wanted to. "I have five hours of torture until the meeting. Can we not talk about anything related to why I'm losing my job?"

They reluctantly agreed, and as a gesture of good faith I ate half a bagel when prompted.

*****

Cam

My computer monitor displayed the forty-nine unread work messages I'd accrued since yesterday, and I had begun clicking down the list when something hard whacked me against the back of my head. I let out a swear word and turned, rubbing the spot, and half expected to see my grandmother with a brick in her hands. Instead I saw Ashley holding her pocketbook, appearing rather pleased with herself. Matt stood two steps behind, hands in his pockets.

"*What the hell is wrong with you?*" I signed.

"*With me? You're the one who didn't listen to me and leave work on time.*"

I caught the fire in Ashley's eyes. "*Have you spoken to Nica?*"

"*Text. Don't behave stupid. Didn't your grandmother teach you anything? Stop working and spend time with her.*"

I picked up a folder and flung it at Ashley. She caught it before it scattered all over the floor. "*I was working on this.*"

Ashley opened it up. Her mouth dropped as I noticed a shiny ring on her hand. She showed the folder to Matt, who gave me a glance with eyebrows raised high. I copied his expression and he nodded. We'd talk later. "*Wow.*" Then she closed the folder and hit me. "*Stupid, you should have told her about this.*"

"*Before or after I yelled at her for not telling me she read my mother's letter?*"

"*Get out of here,*" Matt said.

"*And do what?*" I ran my hands through my hair, feeling helpless, useless, and tension deep in my bones.

"*Be there for her. You love her, right?*" Ashley asked, sitting on my desk.

"*More than I would have thought possible.*"

"*Show her. Make a grand gesture. Or are you really going to tell me you don't know enough about her to do something big?*"

"*Like flowers?*" Matt asked. Ashley stared at him, long and hard, and then rolled her eyes.

The words were enough to slap me across the face. I did know her. I knew exactly what needed to be done. The only question was if there was enough time to do it.

"*Not flowers. A giant cookie. With writing.*" I walked over to Ashley and kissed her on the cheek. "*And what would you like to celebrate?*" I smiled at her surprised expression. "*It's blinding. Congrats.*" I clasped hands with Matt.

"Whatever you think, oh mighty director." Ashley smirked. *"As long as you get Nica back."*

Chapter 26

Nica

I sat at the large table in the center of the conference room. A lump in my throat threatened to cut off oxygen. My hands shook so I folded them in my lap. Around me, Tess, Sharon, the executive director, and two other members of the senior staff chatted. Business as usual for them; meanwhile it was another day in hell for me. Even an hour ahead in time was such a question mark I didn't know what to make of it.

The last member of the senior staff joined us at the table. Sharon organized the papers in front of her, tapping them into a neat pile, and began the meeting. "Thank you all for coming today. I appreciate everyone's understanding about this sensitive topic. I'm sorry that we have to follow through on these claims." Sharon passed around papers to the other staff. "Two weeks ago we received a letter from a family member of Cassandra Thompson, one of Nica's clients, expressing some...unusual concerns."

The full body cringe was involuntary. I wished for an invisible cloak and the ability to leave and let them talk without me present.

Tess continued. "Nica had started dating Cameron Thompson, not realizing he was grandson and caregiver to Cassie. Cassie had moved to Hospice House at that point and was on suspend in our system."

Sharon picked up her glasses from the table. "All right, let's get to the point—a letter was written by Rhonda Thompson, who I've been informed is Cameron's mother. This letter raises some bleak points. Tess has been in contact with Cameron, and he has presented an outline that counteracts each point. We still need to discuss them."

Outline? What Outline? I glanced at Tess. She slid a blue folder across the table to me. Inside were several fancy spreadsheets. The first one was titled: *Incorrect Claims Made by Rhonda Thompson.*

"Before we address the specific concerns, it is my understanding that we have twenty-one letters written in support of Nica against any claims made by Rhonda. Is this correct?" asked Sharon.

"That is correct," Tess said. "Eleven letters are from members of Cameron's family. Ten are from elders that lived in the same building as Cassie. Most of them were also Nica's clients, but not all. We also have a letter written by Cassie herself, prior to her death."

My eyes shot up from the stain at the center of the table I'd been focused on. Tess slid a wrinkled letter over to me and I grabbed it.

Tess held up another pile. "These are all the letters, including a photo copy of the one addressed to Nica that I just passed to her." She handed the pile to her left.

I knew of many of these letters, but seeing them all together, all for me, gave much needed comfort.

I unfolded the letter, finding Cassie's shaky handwriting giving me permission to date Cam. I swallowed a laugh. She had to write that letter, didn't she! My finger brushed her words, wishing I could give her one more hug.

Sharon resumed. "Cameron's spreadsheet pinpoints the accusations put forth in Rhonda's letter. The first of which is the appropriateness of Nica and Cameron dating. I don't care who Nica does or does not date. I do care if this particular situation crossed any lines.

"The second accusation is that the two were dating for longer than claimed. A factor to be considered as it changes the dynamics of what we are discussing here."

I held my breath. If I stopped breathing this meeting would be over in a matter of minutes. Tempting.

"Tess and I have looked over Nica's notes on Cassandra's case. There were quite a few that involved Cameron."

Sharon reached for a thick stack of papers. I forced myself to keep breathing. I had no idea if any of my notes could be misinterpreted. If so, how could I prove we never met prior to the bar?

"Some of the notes do suggest a high level of compatibility. Tess and I have been arguing over them." Sharon handed the papers around as I continued to rack my brain for anything problematic.

Tess plucked out a piece of paper and slid it across the table. I grabbed it and noticed three of my notes from the system were on the page, the first from two years ago, when Cassie's health took that first big decline. Highlighted in yellow on the page: *Case manager comforted grandson and assured him that elder services would be able to provide additional support when client returns home.* I wanted to shout. This was an e-mail. I was doing my job.

The second note was from six months prior, when Hospice first stepped in. Highlighted in that section: *Grandson, Cameron, e-mailed to report Hospice is now involved and services need to be adjusted. Case manager assured him she would get in contact with Hospice and handle any arrangements. Betty Harper identified as Hospice social worker. Cameron proceeded to discuss situation with case manager for several e-mails, expressing concerns over lack of support from the rest of the family.*

A growing dread filled my stomach. I checked the last section. It was from two weeks prior to Cassie moving. Two weeks prior to Cam and my meeting: *Had long e-mail conversation with Cameron Thompson, client's grandson, regarding continued decline in health and plans for the future. Other programs discussed, as well as possible nursing facility placement. Case Manager to research availability at facility for Deaf elders.* The following section was highlighted in pink. *Cameron expresses interest in a face-to-face meeting to continue discussion.*

Shit. I had completely forgotten about that e-mail. He'd also wanted to have other family members present for the meeting. I kicked myself, why hadn't I mentioned that in the note?

I glanced up at Tess, a great deal more worried about the outcome of the meeting. I listened to the group going back and forth on whether or not it was an issue when Cam and I started dating.

"Let us review the notes after Nica leaves." Sharon put down the papers and moved them to the center of the table. "Moving on: preferential treatment. This is another reason Cassandra's notes were analyzed. It does not appear that any preferential treatment was given prior to when Nica and Cameron claim to have met, and I don't see how she could have received preferential treatment while at Hospice. Furthermore there are several letters from Nica's clients who appear to be just as happy with her work as Cassie was.

"Next is a claim that Nica had received an expensive item of Cassie's. Rhonda felt that Nica was taking advantage of her elders."

I willed my voice not to shake. "I don't have the brooch. Cassie did request I have it in a will-type letter she wrote with Cam years ago. I was completely surprised by it and never expected or wanted anything like this. The last time I saw it was on Cassie."

I shuffled through the other papers in the folder. Along with spreadsheets there were graphs, all chronicling the support points made in all the letters. The last was a large chart from Cam himself, divided into sections of different points: me working hard to keep Cassie at home, supporting Cam when the rest of his family wasn't, and the last section claiming I didn't deserve to lose my job over family issues.

I gripped the edges so tight the page creased. This was what Cam did, what made him good at his job, the reason why he would always put his job first. Yet a small part of me began to wonder, and a flicker of hope kindled.

I refocused on the meeting and Tess speaking. "After seeing the concerns raised by senior staff, and the letter, Cameron e-mailed me a video this morning and requested it be played during the meeting."

Tess grabbed her laptop and set it up at the end of the table. After a few minutes of technical problem-solving, the video loaded. Cam appeared on-screen, his living room in the background.

"Good morning," he spoke while he signed. I fought the urge to close my eyes. He shouldn't be forced to do this. "My name is Cameron Thompson. I want to apologize to Independent Senior

Services for the letter my mother, Rhonda Thompson, wrote.

"I want to make a few things clear, and felt it was best to do this with my own voice. The only reason I speak the way I do is because my parents forced me to. Spoken language is not easy for a Deaf person to learn. I spent my entire childhood in speech therapy. Both in school, out of school, and at home.

"My mother doesn't sign. Not one word in ASL. So my mother has no idea how Nica communicates in ASL. My mother disapproves of the language.

"Nica is fluent in ASL. Something my grandmother appreciated. Something I appreciated as her caregiver. Grandma wasn't able to communicate with many people involved in her case, except her case manager." A small smile crossed his otherwise somber face. "Part of the reason she was so intent on playing matchmaker.

"My mother had in-laws that were Deaf and a son that is Deaf. Yet she knows nothing about the Deaf Community. She sees me, her youngest son, as impaired. Disabled. Less. She's never seen my accomplishments. She thinks I need to be taken care of."

He held out his hands. "I don't. I cared for my grandmother out of love, out of respect. My grandmother gave me my language, my culture. Love. I know the care she received would have been different without Nica. My own interactions with Independent Senior Services would have been different. Nica and I communicated only through e-mail until we met in person, but she understood the importance of e-mail for me. She gave me respect and treated me like I was any other grandson caring for a grandmother.

"Beyond that she made accommodations for my grandmother's communication needs. Ensuring she received the same quality of service as a hearing client would. Not every professional does that. Not everyone does that. Case in point, my mother. You don't need the full story of my family. But you need to understand this letter—" he held up a wrinkled paper with yellow highlighting throughout "— is another instance in my life, in my grandmother's life, of my mother disrespecting us because we can't hear."

He reached to the side and collected a small box, opening it to reveal the brooch. "My mother claimed Nica had gotten her hands on a personal item of my grandmother's. She means this brooch. The brooch never made it to Nica, although that was my grandmother's wish. My mother left the brooch for me, and followed that up by e-mailing Independent Senior Services.

"My mother's game is personal, related to me and not to Nica. Yet Nica is the one being harmed. Nica's other Deaf clients are being harmed. Communication is vital, precious, and rare. Nica was able to provide all of this. If my mother wins, those clients lose.

"I understand you need to take her complaints seriously. As a co-director myself I truly understand. But please weigh her words against mine, against my family's, against Nica's other Deaf clients, against my own grandmother's letter. My mother is just one person. No one else in my family stands with her."

The video stopped, Cam's image paused on screen. I blinked back tears. My heart clenched. He filmed this video after we fought. I shut the door on him and he still did this for me.

Tess put the laptop away as Sharon spoke. "Nica, I know this has not been fun for you. The way that you have continued to handle yourself professionally speaks volumes to your work ethics, regardless of this situation."

I stood, doing my best to keep my legs from shaking. I nodded to the senior staff and left the conference room. Outside the closed door I leaned back against the wall and collected myself. Only there was no collecting myself, not while they still held all the cards. I pushed off the wall and made the journey back to my desk. My mind spun left and right, up and down, going over everything that had happened during the meeting. Too much, it was all too much. I could no longer handle it. Time to turn off my mind. I'd done too much thinking in my life; maybe it was time to be peacefully ignorant.

At my pod, I moved to the window and sat down in the chair in-between my desk and Rebecca's. "How bad was it?" Rebecca asked.

I swallowed a shaky breath. "Bad."

"And the outcome?"

"They're debating it right now."

Rebecca was kind enough to chat about other topics and help keep my mind off of my pending doom. The seconds still crept by. My entire future had a huge question mark over it. But the worst was over. Or so I hoped.

What felt like ages later Tess appeared at the entrance of the pod. "We're ready for you, Nica."

I hauled myself up and stood to follow Tess, wondering if this was how a prisoner felt on the way to a sentence.

Or a guillotine.

When we reached the door, Tess placed a hand on my arm. "It's going to be all right," she said softly, giving me a smile.

We entered the room, tension thick in the air. I returned to my seat while Tess closed the door and rejoined the group. My heart raced. I held my sweaty hands tightly together as one foot tapped.

Sharon spoke. "Nica. First of all let us all say we're sorry you had to go through this. It has been a very unusual situation, and one that has not been fair to you, nor your fault. There has been some debate over the accusations and how the situation should have been handled." Sharon glared directly at me, her eyes anything but warm. "I still feel you should have never pursued this relationship after learning who Cameron was. That being said, we don't find any wrongdoings on your part in relation to how Cassandra's case was handled, or how any other cases might have been affected."

Relief wanted to flood, but I couldn't let it, not yet. "What about my Deaf clients?" I was surprised my voice didn't croak.

"They will be transferred back to your care."

I hadn't realized I was holding my breath until I let it out. "Thank you." I tried not to smile in front of Sharon's still-scowling face.

"For the duration of your employment here, I don't want to ever hear about this situation or another one like it again."

My smile faded. I still had my job, but I had lost some respect from my director. Not a win-win. I reminded myself that it could have been worse. Much worse.

I also needed to thank Cam. I had no doubt my continued employment was due in part to his help. I didn't know if I'd manage to thank him without throwing myself at him, but perhaps that wouldn't be such a bad thing.

*****

Cam

I tapped a pen to my keyboard, watching the impromptu office party. As predicted, no one was getting any work done. Not that I cared. Matt was part of the celebration, so that took his mind off work. And I had Nica to worry about.

Ashley wrapped her arms around me from behind, giving a squeeze, before moving into my line of sight. *"Chocolate-covered popcorn balls, genius. Did someone flip the switch and get your brain working again?*

I smiled, hard not to with the beaming bride-to-be bouncing in front of me. *"Guess so."*

She glanced at my phone. *"Any word yet?"*

I shook my head and slipped my phone in my back pocket. *"No. I'm expecting an e-mail from her supervisor with an update."* And the length of time passing made me worried about the outcome.

"She'll come around."

Ashley didn't wait for a response; she turned around to show someone else her ring. I could only hope she was right.

*****

Nica

I breathed in deep as I made my way back to my pod. The office air filled my lungs. I had the urge to stop, close my eyes, and breathe. Instead I continued moving forward, each step lighter than it had been in weeks. Rebecca waited for me.

"And?" she asked.

I could have danced in the aisle. "I'm still employed and I get my clients back."

Rebecca cheered and gave me a hug. "Now we can celebrate."

"With more bagels?" I moaned. My stomach still wasn't buying into the whole food concept. Though sweets would be requested in the not so distant future.

"Nope, better than bagels, check your desk."

I walked over and found a small pink pizza-sized box on my desk. I was about to ask about it when I noticed the logo on the top— from the bakery Cam frequented.

My stomach did a little cheer even as my heart fumbled with its beats.

"What?" I asked in a whisper. I ran my fingers along the edge of the box, disbelieving he would do this after everything I'd done.

"Open it," exclaimed Rebecca.

I moved my hands over the sides and stopped. My heart kicked into gear, pounding against my rib cage. I knew what would be on the inside. I also knew that the moment I saw it I would be gone. It would be only Cam for me, forever.

An image of him flashed to mind, and I was ready to jump on it. He helped save my job. The least I could do was be honest about my feelings, for both of us.

I lifted the lid. Inside the box was a giant chocolate chip cookie. White frosting on top spelled out: *I CHOOSE YOU*. My hand covered my mouth and I was powerless to stop the tears from falling.

Tess approached. "He dropped this off earlier."

I glanced back and forth between my friends. "He did?"

"How else did we get the original letters from your clients? Or his spreadsheets?"

I blinked. Why didn't I put two and two together? "Is he still here?"

"No, he said you might not be too happy to see him."

Now or never. If I wanted this, and I did, I needed to go to him. "I know I almost lost my job and—"

"Go," Tess said. "You've done plenty of work the past week anyways. Another point in your favor that did not go overlooked."

"Thank you," I whispered before drawing Tess into a hug. I

grabbed my belongings, and the cookie, and headed out into the cool October air.

At his building I studied the reds and browns from the bricks and the way the sun reflected off the windows. Somewhere inside was the man my heart chose. Was the man I hoped would be my future.

If this went bad I was eating the entire cookie by myself. Tonight.

I entered the building and found his office. Inside sounds of talking and laughter greeted me. I was about to talk to the receptionist, when a voice behind me halted the action.

"Well, well, well." Grant put an arm around my shoulders. "Look what the cat dragged in."

I cringed. "I'm here to see Cam," I said and signed.

"A little on the nose with that one, don't you think?" Grant signed as he spoke, one handed, the other still holding me firm. "Come on, I'm joining the party. Matt and Ashley got engaged. You'll distract them from my bellyaching."

Not letting go of my shoulder, he led me around a corner, where the noise level intensified. The atmosphere was very much a party with people standing instead of sitting at desks. I found Cam by a neat and tidy desk I guessed was his. His smile faded as his eyes met mine.

"Look what I found." Grant let go of me and went to hug Ashley.

I stared at Cam. Those same eyes could call to me from across any room. Only this time I knew the color wasn't brown, I knew the green and tan specks that circled the insides. I knew exactly whom I was walking towards.

He leaned against his desk. *"I have no idea how the meeting went."*

I dared a small smile. *"I still have a job."*

"And your Deaf clients?"

"Transferred back to me."

He sighed in relief and shifted towards me before he stopped. *"Why are you here?"*

"You saved my job."

"Yes."

"And sent me a cookie."

He rubbed the back of his head. *"I'm sorry I wasn't there for you last night. I was working on the spreadsheets for today. I kept thinking if I made it better it would somehow ensure your job would be saved. I haven't gone back to my long hours."* He spreads his hands over his tidy desk. *"See, nothing out. I've been working long hours on you."*

A tear escaped and rolled down my cheek. Cam closed the gap between us and wiped the tear away. The feel of his skin against mine had me wanting to jump into his arms.

"I'm sorry I didn't tell you about the letter. I'm not used to sharing everything with one person. I was trying to prevent causing you any more pain, but I guess I failed."

I couldn't hold the tears in. They fell down my cheeks in a slow rhythm. I watched him watching me, his face full of concern. This man had my heart, and we had proven to be more than compatible. I wanted to be the irrational one. After a month of knowing each other I was ready to jump in with both feet. Forever.

"I've never said this to a man before. When I do, I'll mean it. One hundred percent. I can't promise it will be easy, because I know it won't be. But I won't be able to handle it if this ends." I breathed in deep. *"I love you."*

He tugged on my hand, knocking me off balance. I stumbled forward until my body became flush with his. He brushed my hair back before lowering his head and kissing me. A chorus of cheers and catcalls erupted but I ignored every sound.

"No more complications?"

I laughed. *"I'm not sure I can promise anything."*

"How about we continue to spend as much time together as possible and see what happens?"

"I think we can give that a try."

Chapter 27

One Year Later

Cam

I woke up in my own bed, soft light filtering through the shades. Nica, as always, rubbed her head into the pillow, the golden tones of her curls shimmering in the morning light. I smiled, my heart full at the familiarity to our morning routine. Not wanting to wake her, I carefully moved to her, kissed the back of her head, and slipped out of bed.

I needed a few moments to readjust, the boxes lying everywhere a stark reminder: slightly different morning routine. After stepping over several of them, I noticed Oreo curled up on my grandmother's final blanket. I scratched the feline, causing her to jerk awake in surprise. She stretched, pushed her head into my hand, and then curled back up when I moved away. The first floor had a few lingering boxes, but I paid them no mind, continuing downstairs to the workout room. Not quite like Grant's gym, but it saved me from more complaining from Nica if I were to wake up even earlier.

The only piece of relationship advice my brothers agreed on: keep her happy.

The weights and treadmill helped me wake up, and I had to admit, the solitude and scenery did me good first thing in the morning. I pushed myself a little harder, working off the extra adrenalin. By the time I made it upstairs, Nica's side of the bed was empty, covers disheveled. I headed into the kitchen before finding her, dressed and eating cereal. Yeah, this could work, this could work very well. The grin came strong and fast.

"Nice seeing you on our turf, instead of yours or mine."

She rolled her eyes and dropped her spoon into the bowl; a few droplets of milk splattered the table. She wasn't that awake yet, or she would have cleaned the spots up right away. *"We've been here almost a week."*

I grabbed a napkin and dabbed at the spots. *"Not on a normal work day."*

"True. You better be worth this new longer commute I'm dealing with."

I kissed her. *"I am."*

A half hour later I left for work. Or at least, that's what I let Nica think.

*****

Nica

After Cam left I finished my coffee, my mind finally waking up and adjusting to the early start. I went over to the refrigerator. On one side we had ASL alphabet magnets, used to play word scrambles. A habit we'd started at Cam's condo.

I moved the hand shape letters into what I wanted to say: WELCOME HOME, then scrambled them up to say: MELOCEW EOMH, before leaving for work.

The longer commute meant new traffic patterns, and I had no idea what to expect. Arriving on time meant I'd call the first day a success. It was certainly better than commuting from Boston. As I removed my coat at my desk, I studied the two pictures on my small shelf. One was of Oreo, the other of Cam and me in front of our new house. I tried not to grin goofily at it. I failed.

"Look who made it in. How's the new house?" Rebecca asked.

I draped my coat over the back of my chair. "Still a mess. I thought taking a week off to move would mean everything was done. Not quite. Cam has far too much stuff."

"Complaining doesn't work when you're smiling," Rebecca said.

I loaded up my client listing and settled into work. A few minutes later Lexie arrived, having taken over a recent job opening. Lexie pointed to my shirt. "Is that Cassie's brooch?"

I gazed down at the diamond-shaped object of sentiment. "Yup. One year ago I met Cam, figured it was fitting."

"I liked you better when you were fighting your feelings."

Rebecca leaned on her desk, her chin nestled in hand. "Still struggling to find an exciting normal?"

Lexie blew a strand of hair out of her face. "Yes."

"We need to go clubbing or bar hopping or something."

"Just check for complications before heading home," I teased.

"Like you're complaining," Lexie said.

A few hours later I was still catching up from my week of vacation. Lexie stopped by my desk and placed down a clear vase filled with a dozen chocolates in the shape of roses, each decorated with a single letter.

"What is this?" I asked, turning the vase to get a good look at the goodies.

Lexie shrugged. "It was delivered. I was walking by when the receptionist was about to call you."

I eyed my friend and wanted to call her bull but was too drawn to the gift. "Why would Cam send this here when he can bring it home?"

"More romantic this way?" suggested Rebecca.

I shook my head and focused on the letters. In order they read: E R M A N A C I N Y R M?

"That makes no sense, did the shop mess up?" Rebecca asked.

"Nope," I said. "Cam and his friends love to do word scrambles, he's gotten me into it, but they usually aren't this hard."

I laid out the chocolates on my desk to rearrange them, and placed the question mark at the end, since that was easy. The rest left me stumped.

RACE MANY RIM?

The small crowd around my desk laughed. *Nope, that's not it.* I rearranged them a few more times and saw my name appear so I moved those letters aside. I was left with MAY RE RM.

"My rare M Nica?" asked Rebecca.

I laughed and shook my head. "Not likely."

I rearranged them again and stopped cold.

MERRY MA NICA?

"That makes no sense either," Rebecca said.

My heart tried to leap into my throat. Was this really happening? "Change the E and A," I whispered.

Rebecca gasped, and Lexie moved the two chocolates in question. I stepped back, staring at my desk.

MARRY ME NICA?

I knew this was coming, Cam had mentioned it nearly a year ago at the beginning of our relationship. Buying a house together had been a big step. Still, I didn't expect him to take the next one so soon. I gawked at Lexie. "He didn't go to work, did he?"

Lexie grinned. "Nope."

I laughed, heart close to bursting. "That bastard."

"Well, where is he?" asked Rebecca.

Lexie angled her head towards the door. "Outside."

I began to head out. Then an idea popped into my head. I came back, grabbed one chocolate rose, and went to find Cam.

*****

Cam

I waited in the parking lot by my car, keeping one eye on the entrance doors. My hand trembled as I clutched the small box in my pocket. I should have delivered the damn flowers myself, then I wouldn't be stuck outside wondering at her reaction and what expressions I could elicit on her face. Either way it was too late now.

I contemplated texting Lexie for an update, but Nica rushed through the doors and scanned the parking lot once before settling on me. The sides of her mouth turned upward enough to let me know she was trying to keep it all inside. She got it under control by the time she reached me.

"*You said you were going to work,*" she said.

"*I stopped in for a minute.*" I was at the bakery anyways, and Ashley had demanded to see the arrangement.

She rocked on her heels. "*You gave me a chocolate word scramble?*"

I caught the glint in her eyes. She had to have figured it out. In her hand she twirled one of the roses, and I caught that it was the letter Y. My nerves dissipated. I grinned and stepped closer to her.

"*Yes, a dozen chocolate roses.*"

"*Mixing the traditional flowers with food?*"

"*You solved the scramble, making me work for it?*"

She nodded.

"*Well I see the letter you happened to grab.*"

She moved the chocolate behind her, but finally let herself smile. "*Are you going to say it with words or only in chocolate?*"

I dropped down to one knee and wrenched the small box out of my pocket. "*Marry me.*"

"*I believe the scramble had one more word.*"

"*I needed a dozen.*"

"*Sure.*"

I gazed up at her, still on my knee, and wanted to laugh. "*You going to answer me?*"

She smoothed down a piece of my hair, the answer to my question clear in her eyes. "*Yes, I will marry you.*"

I stood and scooped her into my arms, pressing my lips to hers. She made me complete, whole. Now and forever. I broke the kiss to give Nica her ring.

"*It's not chocolate,*" I said as she slid it on.

She laughed and placed one hand on my cheek. "*Why would I need chocolate when I have you?*"

THE END

In Loving Memory

The cat in this book, Oreo, is based off of a real life trouble maker of mine. When I first drafted the novel I made the fictional Oreo older than the real Oreo, worried about the real Oreo being around when the book came out. Sadly, real Oreo passed away as a spunky ten-year-old. She kept me company while I wrote this book, even deleting paragraphs she deemed unworthy. Like her fictional counterpart she was deaf and had no desire to learn any form of communication beyond "scratch me" "love me" and "let me eat the food you have cooling." She loved my son from the moment he came home from the hospital and would have enjoyed using the corner of this book to scratch her head. RIP Oreo, and may you live on through your fictional counterpart.

Acknowledgments

Some novels have a short path from creation to publication, others take a long and windy road. This is part of the latter.

I first wrote *A Perfect Mistake* back in 2013 as part of NaNoWriMo (National Novel Writing Month, highly recommend checking it out for anyone who wants to write a novel), the first—and only—time I participated and "won" (by writing 50,000 words in a month). This was the third book I ever wrote, my first attempt at a contemporary romance.

Since I wrote this so early in my career, I really honed my skills on this novel. I've had so many eyes on it, met so many wonderful critique partners. I entered it in contests, got feedback, revised, and revised, and revised again. In the first draft the only Deaf character was Cassie, during revisions I had that lightbulb moment and realized Cam was Deaf as well, and always meant to be.

A huge thanks to all the writers who helped me with this novel, some of you dealt with some pretty rough words! I fear I'm going to forget someone! In no particular order: Josie Leigh, Adrienne Proctor, Vanessa Carnevale, Brittany Cherry, Heather DiAngelis, Karen Mahara, Laura Heffernan, Paris Wynters, and anyone who read a chapter, pitch, or blurb, or simply helped provide support along the way. And my mother, for braving her daughter's sex scenes and providing us both the uncomfortableness of editing them together.

I'd like to thank Emma Wicker and Kate Foster for believing in this novel and holding my hand through those final changes to get it ready for publication. Along with the rest of the Lakewater Press team, it's been an honor to be a part of this family!

To my husband and son: I know writing takes up a good chunk of my time. Thank you for always believing in me and supporting me. And letting me be attached to my keyboard.

A special thank you to all the social workers out there. I worked as a one myself for a decade, spending most of that time in elder services. My clients taught me so much about life and gave me a more positive outlook on aging than most twenty-somethings tend to have. I got to work with some wonderful elders, both hearing and Deaf. I know it's not an easy job, but a rewarding one. And a necessary one.

And no, I have never gotten involved with a client's family member.

About the Author

Laura Brown lives in Massachusetts with her quirky abnormal family. Her husband has put up with her since high school, her young son keeps her on her toes, and her two cats think they deserve more scratches. Hearing loss is a big part of who she is, from her own Hard of Hearing ears, to the characters she creates.

You can follow Laura on Twitter.
or visit her website at laurabrownauthor.com

And, if you loved this book,
please consider leaving a review on Goodreads!